STONES FROM THE RIVER
The autobiography of a Christian

STONES FROM THE RIVER
The autobiography of a Christian

Christopher J Sharp

ATHENA PRESS
LONDON

STONES FROM THE RIVER
The autobiography of a Christian
Copyright © Christopher J Sharp 2007

All Rights Reserved

No part of this book may be reproduced in any form
by photocopying or by any electronic or mechanical means,
including information storage or retrieval systems,
without permission in writing from both the copyright
owner and the publisher of this book.

ISBN 10-digit: 1 84748 048 9
ISBN 13-digit: 978 1 84748 048 4

First Published 2007 by
ATHENA PRESS
Queen's House, 2 Holly Road
Twickenham TW1 4EG
United Kingdom

Printed for Athena Press

To Alex and Matt

Become ... Children of God ... in a crooked and depraved generation, in which you shine like stars in the universe...

Philippians 2:15

Contents

Introduction	11
Early Recollections	15
School days	26
Making Decisions	37
Change for the Better	46
More Decisions	55
A Home of Our Own	67
Crusades	77
Baptised in the Holy Spirit	86
Into the Seventies	95
The Northolt Fellowship	108
Full-time Elder	127
A Whole New Ballgame	143
'Westlife' and Poetry	153
Family Matters	170
Into Europe	178
Time Marching On	189
A New Millennium	200
Marion	215
Looking Back, Looking Forward	219

Introduction

> ... As for the twelve stones that had been taken out of the River Jordan, Joshua set them up at Gilgal. Then he said to the Israelites, 'When your children in days to come ask their fathers "What is the meaning of these stones?" tell them this, "You see the Jordan. Israel crossed over it dry-shod, because the Lord your God dried up the waters of the Jordan in front of you until you had crossed ... so that all the peoples of the earth may recognise how mighty the hand of the Lord is, and that you yourselves may always stand in awe of the Lord your God."'
>
> Joshua 4:20–24

I never really knew my grandparents. They were all born in the Victorian era when the popular maxim that children should be seen and not heard held sway. Both sets lived only a few miles away and along with my parents and my sister, I visited them fairly regularly. On such occasions conversation took place almost exclusively amongst the grown-ups and concerned adult subjects. I was merely a bored spectator and listener. For me, the best part of such visits was the ride on the train and bus and the possibility of bedtime being delayed because we were late arriving home.

Consequently, I never had any real relationship with them. Anything I knew about them was gleaned from what I overheard or from asking questions at home. Even so, my knowledge was minimal. My mother's father used to work on the railways. My father's father was a very serious man, a lay preacher in the Strict Baptist denomination and rarely talked of anything except his church and the people in it, or so it seemed to me. Both men were very stern and I certainly felt intimidated by them if not actually afraid of them. The grandmothers were much softer and kinder but were no more than acquaintances to me.

Happily, times have changed. It has been a great pleasure to spend time with my grandchildren as they have grown up, playing games, taking them out, teaching them new ideas and generally being good friends. But of course I had already reached the age of fifty before they were born so there is a whole half-century of my life about which they know very little. Am I being vain in thinking that those years were of such importance that they should be interested? Certainly, they were different from those of many of my contemporaries. Also, life has changed so much in the last fifty years that some of my recollections will come as quite a surprise to today's young people brought up in a post modern, high-tech age. I think it's a story worth telling, and so the idea for this book was born. I wanted my grandchildren to know the history which may have helped to shape what they are and what they are going to be. It is dedicated to them but I hope that others will find it absorbing and maybe even challenging.

In recent years, we have become obsessed with celebrities. We see them on television and in magazines and newspapers full of pictures and gossip about the rich and the beautiful, whether they are in sport, showbusiness or, in some cases, totally devoid of any talent. Young people are being brainwashed into imagining that this is the life and that anything else is going to be drab and boring. I want to show that this is just not true. I am an ordinary man with no great claims to fame. I am not rich and have such crooked teeth that I could never claim to be beautiful. But life has been extraordinary, full of incident and satisfying, partly because I believe that I may have had an impact for good on other people's lives. The Bible says 'It is more blessed to give than to receive.' I would endorse that statement and add that in giving, one actually receives a great deal of happiness.

But one of the biggest changes to have taken place in my lifetime has been the demise of Christianity in Britain. In today's multicultural society, many young people are growing up with little or no knowledge of God, the Bible, or of who Jesus Christ is. Christianity has been relegated to the dustbin of history and deemed to be irrelevant in the twenty-first century. In the biblical story quoted above, a memorial was set up using stones taken from the bed of the Jordan to act as a reminder to future generations of a great miracle: proof that God was real, powerful and active. In the same way, I hope this record of my life will be a landmark to show that God is still very much alive and can make a huge difference to life when He is taken into the reckoning.

A last word about my grandparents before starting the story proper. Whatever else they may have been, I do know that they all had a strong Christian faith, which they passed on to their children – including my parents – and this has had a huge impact on my life. It is also possible that whilst we never really talked, they may well have prayed for me and I may never know what a difference that has made. So our history does matter. It is not just genetic material that is passed on from generation to generation but lifestyles, ideas and faith as well. I am so grateful for all the influences which have helped to make me the person I am today and I would like to think that this record of my history will contribute something very positive to the next generation.

Early Recollections

I was born on 15 March 1939 at a private nursing home in Ruislip less than half a mile from the house where I was to spend the first twenty-three years of my life. My parents had purchased it when they got married in 1934 for the sum of £900. It still stands today and allowing for the fact that it has probably undergone some modernisation, would now fetch in excess of £300,000. Incredible!

The timing of my entry into the world was not ideal since before I was six months old, World War II had commenced and was to last until after my sixth birthday. Of course at such a young age one has very little understanding of what is going on, of the horrors of modern warfare or the deaths of millions of soldiers. I suppose I grew up with a general awareness that war was something very bad and that everybody was very worried about what might happen, but I have no clear recollections of any incidents until the latter months of the war when the V2 rockets were used. They were commonly known as 'doodlebugs' and I remember hearing them flying over the house, their engines droning. The engines would suddenly cut out and we would wait for the explosion as they fell to the ground, hoping against hope that it would not be anywhere near us. My other memory is of VE Day when victory over the Germans was announced on the radio. I had no idea what difference it was going to make but I certainly felt happy about it and was aware of the relief obviously felt by my parents.

Most of my early memories were of our house and the ordinary things that made up our days and weeks. The house was much the same as many other semidetached houses: two reception rooms, one at the back and one at the front, and a kitchen, all leading off a long narrow hall. Upstairs were three bedrooms, a bathroom and separate toilet. Outside were a prefabricated garage, a coal shed and quite extensive gardens. There were, however, some major differences from what we are used to today.

The front room, as we always called it, was our main living room, a combined lounge, dining room and playroom. We had a large radio but no television or gramophone. (TV was in its infancy in the 1940s and although gramophone records were available, no one had thought of stereo records let alone CDs.) It was heated by a coal fire which had to be cleared out and re-lit every morning during the winter months. In later years we replaced it with a gas fire. The back room was reserved during the war years for our 'Anderson' shelter. This was a very large table-like structure made of very solid cast iron and big enough to house a double mattress underneath it. Whenever we heard the air-raid sirens sounding, day or night, we would all go and snuggle up on this mattress until the raid was over. I assumed that the tabletop was sufficiently strong to protect us from falling masonry should the house suffer a direct hit from a bomb, but fortunately, we never received an answer to this hypothesis. After the war, the shelter disappeared and in due course, a piano and a three-piece suite took its place. This room became the best room and we rarely used it except perhaps on Sundays for some strange reason, or when entertaining special guests. All the bedrooms had their own built-in gas fires – as a substitute for central heating – but otherwise were much as today. The big difference was in the kitchen.

Our food was all kept in a larder. This was a cupboard big enough to walk inside, lined with white ceramic tiles with shelving stretching from floor to ceiling. There were ventilation holes at the back and somehow these helped to keep it very cool, except in hot summer weather. At such times, Mum would take the bottles of milk out of the larder and put them in a bucket of cold water which she changed every few hours. Of course, a larder could never hope to be as efficient as a modern refrigerator for keeping perishable foods fresh. Along with the absence of a freezer, it was necessary to shop more frequently for such things as eggs, meat and cheese.

The second oddity was the table. The tabletop was hinged and could be turned to a vertical position to reveal a mangle underneath. This was a machine consisting of two cylindrical wooden rollers mounted adjacent to each other on a cogged wheel system so that by turning a handle, the rollers would revolve in opposite directions. Wet washing was passed between the rollers, the handle turned and the excess water was thus squeezed out and ran down a series of channels into a bucket suitably placed under the mangle – all very necessary in the days before automatic washing machines and spin dryers.

The third commodity was also associated with washdays. This was a 'copper'. I am not at all sure why it was called this because I suspect, looking back, that it was actually made of galvanised iron. Nevertheless, it was always known as the 'copper'. It was a large cylindrical tub, about a metre tall and about eighty centimetres in diameter. Underneath was a gas burner. The vessel was filled with water, heated by the gas burner, and the dirty clothes and soap powder then added. The gas would be turned down low and the whole lot kept simmering away for some time to get the clothes clean with occasional stirring from a long wooden rod. There was a spout at the side through which the dirty water could be emptied. After putting the clothes through the mangle to remove the soapy water, they would be returned to the copper which would be filled by a hose connected to the tap with fresh cold water for the purpose of rinsing the clothes, before again putting them through the mangle. What a business! As well as this, certain items – sheets and pillowcases and some of Dad's shirts – had a further treatment in the copper with a solution of starch which left them feeling stiff and less prone to creasing.

One last feature of the kitchen was the boiler – not a compact gas boiler mounted on the wall, but a coke-burning stove with a chimney going up to the ceiling. This provided our hot water and was therefore kept going all through the year. Every morning and evening, it would be necessary to rake out the ashes from the stove and refill it with coke from the supply in the coal shed.

Outside, the front garden consisted of lawn and flowerbeds plus the drive leading to the garage. The back garden was extensive, with a long lawn at the end of which was an area containing two plum trees, four apple trees and a pear tree. There was a vegetable garden near the coal shed and then another area given over to soft fruit bushes – blackcurrants, redcurrants, gooseberries and worcesterberries. (The last were a cross species –

gooseberry in shape but with the colour and taste of blackcurrants. Curiously, I haven't seen or heard of them for over forty years. Can some horticulturalist tell me what happened to the humble worcesterberry?) To complete the picture, there were patches of raspberry canes, strawberry plants and rhubarb, a rockery and more flowerbeds.

Mum, like most housewives of the time, was industrious and well organised. Each day and each week had a routine which was rarely broken. Monday was washday and as can be seen from what I've already said, this was no easy task. Imagine having to boil up all the bed linen and a week's worth of dirty clothes from each member of the family, rinse them and finally put each item through the mangle by hand. It took the whole morning. Even if it was raining, Monday remained washday and the damp clothes would then have to be dried indoors hanging over a rail in the kitchen which was lowered and raised by a rope and pulley. It meant that the kitchen felt damp and clammy and I hated wet washdays.

Shopping was obviously a major task. Not only did we need to shop more frequently than today because of the absence of freezers but Mum had no car to drive. It was a fifteen- to twenty-minute walk to the shops in Ruislip High Street and everything had to be carried back by hand in baskets or bags – a serious limitation on what could be bought on any one trip. The two main destinations on each shopping expedition were to Howard Roberts and Sainsbury's. The former was a grocer where we bought tinned goods of all kinds, and anything in jars or packets – jams, Bovril, sugar, tea and so on. Sainsbury's was the place for meat, eggs, bacon, cheese, flour, butter and margarine. But it bore no resemblance to the Sainsbury's superstores of today. It was just a large shop with tiles covering the walls and floor to give an incredibly clean appearance. The counters selling different commodities were placed around the edge of the store with a large clear area in the centre. Cheese did not come in ready-cut and packaged slabs. Huge cheeses could be selected and a piece of a size to suit the customer cut from it using a fine wire and then individually wrapped. Similarly, carcases of bacon could be selected according to their relative leanness and rashers sliced off to the customer's requirements using a machine. Butter was taken from a huge slab and patted to shape and size using wooden implements called butter-patters before being placed on grease-proof paper and wrapped by hand. One might have to queue at each separate counter and the items bought had to be paid for there and then before moving on to the next one. So shopping could be quite a time-consuming business. An additional complication was the use of coupons. These were not 'money off' coupons such as one might have today but ration coupons supplied by the government. Throughout the war years, food was in short supply because the German submarines torpedoed and sank many ships bringing imported food to Great Britain. It was also necessary for every effort to be made to manufacture armaments for the war and so farming and food-processing factories were somewhat neglected, again resulting in food shortages. Every person was therefore issued with a ration book containing dated coupons which entitled one to buy so much of each foodstuff in any one week, and these coupons had to be surrendered at the time of purchase. Once gone, there was no way you could buy any more of that particular food until the next set of coupons became valid.

Here are some examples of ration allowances during the war years:

Bacon or ham: four ounces per person per week

Sugar: eight ounces

Cheese: one ounce

Butter: two ounces

Jam: two ounces

How Mum ever managed is beyond me. Almost certainly she and Dad went without some things so that my sister and I could have at least enough to keep us healthy. Once the war had ended things gradually improved and weekly rations steadily increased until the end of rationing for good in 1954. But all this meant that I grew up with a mentality that nothing should ever be wasted and certainly this was exemplified by the way in which Mum managed our weekly menu.

Another important part of Mum's weekly schedule was cleaning. For many years we had a home help who came on Tuesday and Friday mornings. Mrs Porton was a very large lady who, it seemed to me, always smelt of polish. But she was a very kindly person and very conscientious in her work. She would dust and polish the furniture, hoover the floors, clean the bath, the toilet and the hand basin and anything else that needed doing. On other days of the week, Mum would do some of these things as well, so that the house always appeared spotlessly clean and tidy. Probably that is where I developed my love of tidiness. 'A place for everything and everything in its place' has always seemed a good motto to me.

During the week, when Dad was at work, Mum would do all the cooking. At weekends, Dad would lend a hand but Mum was definitely in charge. I was too young to remember clearly our eating habits during the war years when food was so scarce, but as the situation started to improve, we had a very regular pattern. On Sunday, we would have a joint of meat – beef, lamb or pork, usually in rotation. This was accompanied by Yorkshire pudding, potatoes and vegetables. This would be followed by a fruit pie with custard, the fruit having come from the garden. Monday being washday, there was no time to cook and so we had cold meat carved from the remains of the joint together with various pickles, whilst the potatoes and vegetables left over from Sunday would be fried up and referred to as 'bubble and squeak'. Tuesday, there would still be some of the joint left over and this would be sliced up, heated in gravy and served with fresh vegetables. I used to find this rather dull but Tuesday's speciality was a treacle tart for 'afters' – my favourite! Wednesday would see the last of the joint minced up mixed with onion and mashed potato and fried as rissoles. I was very fond of these, especially with a liberal helping of tomato ketchup. With luck there would also be a piece of treacle tart left over for me while Mum would have something I didn't care for. Thursday we would nearly always go to the shops for fresh meat – perhaps a chop, liver or sausages and perhaps there would be chips to go with it, while Friday was fish and chips day. (Catholics, of course, always used to eat fish on Fridays. We were not Catholics but still followed this pattern almost religiously.) Sometimes Mum would also make a sponge pudding on which we could have golden syrup or jam and custard; a great treat as far as I was concerned. (You will probably gather that I was far more interested in puddings than in main courses.) Only Saturday was unpredictable because there was more time and Dad was at home to help. Sometimes we might have a casserole, or a meat pie. Then it was Sunday once more and the whole sequence would start over again.

It might seem that Mum's life was all work, but because she was so well organised she would normally be able to sit down by mid-afternoon and listen to the radio or read a book, or the newspaper, or one of the women's magazines which were delivered each week by the paper-boy. Then at about 4.30 she would start to prepare tea for me and my sister. Bread and butter and jam and cakes were our staple diet but we probably hardly noticed what we were eating because we were so caught up in listening to the radio. Five o'clock was the time for *Children's Hour*. For many years this was the programme that every child listened to. It was usually hosted by Derek McCullough, who was always referred to as 'Uncle Mac' and was as well known then as David Beckham is today. He was also greatly loved and every child felt as if he really was their own personal uncle. For almost an hour, we were treated to short stories, plays, music and talks about subjects that were both interesting and educational. We had our heroes who appeared in series of plays – boys or girls who got involved in exciting adventures or who solved crimes single-handed like real detectives. We learnt a great deal about the countryside and in particular I remember a regular item by Helen Henshell who trained our young ears to appreciate and enjoy classical music. There was other music on the show, often requested by listeners, but it was *not* pop music, which had not really caught on in the 1940s. Instead it was humorous songs by singers like Danny Kaye or popular classics probably first introduced to us by Miss Henshell. What a difference from today's TV shows for children! I deeply regret the passing of *Children's Hour*. I am saddened when I realise that many children in the twenty-first century are growing up with scarcely any knowledge of classical music or natural history and usually think of these things as 'boring'. To me, they were and still are some of the really special things in life. *Children's Hour* encouraged children to be children, encouraging them in childhood pursuits and protecting their childhood innocence; whereas it seems to me that today's children are treated as young adults much too soon and therefore miss out on many of the delights of being a child.

As the programme drew to a close, Dad would come home from work, usually bringing a loaf of bread. He always insisted that the bakery in Ealing near to the place where he worked made the best bread for miles around. He would eat his tea while talking to Mum about the day's events and then at 6.45 it was time for another radio show before bedtime. This was *Dick Barton, Special Agent*, a fifteen-minute radio soap broadcast each weekday with an omnibus edition on Saturday mornings. I always listened to both and so got my thrills twice over. Dick Barton was like the forerunner of James Bond. With his sidekicks Snowy White and Jock Anderson, he would get into all kinds of dangerous scrapes and each episode would usually end with a situation from which it seemed impossible for them to escape. But escape they always did and the next day they would go on to still more daring adventures, saving the country from the most evil crooks, spies, gangsters and mad scientists. If ever I was naughty, I would be threatened with being sent to bed early, which meant missing Dick Barton. To me that was the worst possible punishment!

From an early age, Mum would always say a prayer with me at bedtime before turning out the light, so I grew up with the notion that God was there. As I grew older, it was me who said a simple prayer instead of Mum. Around the age of six, I started having recurring nightmares and from that time onward I would always include the words, 'Please God, don't let me have any bad dreams,' and my prayers were answered.

Apart from being an efficient housewife and a caring mother who was always there when I needed her, Mum was also the family organiser. She was the one who wrote the Christmas cards, and who wrote letters and made phone calls all year round to keep in touch with all her relatives. Both her parents had been members of huge families – each with ten or twelve children – so that Mum had about twenty aunts or uncles, most of whom I never knew although I often heard their names mentioned. There were, of course, lots of cousins too and I could never hope to fathom what the family tree looked like although I believe my sister has tried to do just this in recent years. In today's world, where small families are the norm, it is hard to imagine keeping in touch with so many relations. We visited some of them, and some came to see us and always it was Mum who made the arrangements. If it hadn't been for Mum, we would never have booked any holidays (more about those in a later chapter) or an annual visit to the theatre, which was very much for her benefit, as we always watched serious plays and never went to a pantomime. The only pantomime I have ever attended was at the age of about sixty. Personally, I don't think I missed much, but I might have felt differently at the age of six.

Dad could not have been more different. He had been diagnosed with a weak heart when in his twenties and so, understandably, Mum made sure that he 'didn't overdo it'. This suited him well, because he was a quiet and retiring man and preferred a quiet life. Perhaps this was the result of being brought up in the small country village of Aston Clinton near Tring in Hertfordshire. He had obtained a degree in chemistry and spent the whole of his working life with one company – The Autotype Company Ltd in West Ealing – finishing up as a director. They manufactured and supplied materials for colour printing – something we take for granted today – but Dad was actually a pioneer in discovering and developing the process known as photogravure printing. It was based on gelatine and I remember, on the odd occasion when he took me with him to work on a Saturday morning, seeing huge sheets of gelatine as high as a house hanging up to dry in the factory. It was probably because of this that Dad never ate jelly, which of course is made primarily from gelatine! He was very conscientious in his work and would often bring home technical magazines connected with his business and read them during the evening. He loved reading, and his real delight was murder mystery stories. Every Friday he would go to the library in Acton Vale and bring home three such books and always read them during the following seven days. In later life, this figure was reduced to two a week, but I think this was because he had read most of the contents of the library already. Because of his heart, he rarely did any heavy work. He helped with the cooking, did some of the gardening, and in particular made jam, and bottled fruit from the garden in Kilner jars. It was this fruit that provided us with our Sunday pies throughout the winter. (Summer fruit could not be bought all year round as it is today, and remember there were no freezers.) He would tackle simple decorating jobs (I learnt how to paper a wall by watching him) but that was about his limit. Because he was not really a DIY man, I grew up with very little idea of how mechanical things worked or how to use tools – a situation which remains unchanged to this day.

But if that was a disadvantage, there was one thing I did learn from my father and that was a love of nature. After the war was over and petrol rationing was less severe, we obtained a small Ford car and sometimes on summer Saturdays, Dad would take us out to the countryside he knew so well – Tring Woods. As we walked, he would see and point out things which otherwise would have gone unnoticed. Birds, flowers, fungi, insects – nothing escaped his sharp eyes and he could also tell us the names of each and every one. I would like to think that over the years I have developed a similar gift. Certainly I share his love of the countryside and all of God's creation that is there to be marvelled at by those with eyes to see.

There are three more things which remain uppermost in my memory from those early years and curiously, they are all related in some way to Sunday mornings. If the weather was fine, our whole family would go to Ruislip Woods, only about twenty minutes' walk from our home. We could see the woods over the rooftops from the back bedroom and in May and June we could often hear the unforgettable call of the cuckoo, probably residing in the woods. Another sound on Sunday mornings was that of the church bells being rung at St Martin's parish church, almost a mile away, and occasionally there would be a repeat performance one weekday evening, presumably when the ringers were practising. And then on other Sunday mornings there would be the sound of a bugle band; the Boys Brigade marching through the streets on their way to church parade at the local Baptist church which I was later to attend. Why should these sounds be so evocative? Perhaps because they are all noticeably absent from suburban life today.

School days

So far I've said very little about my sister, Barbara. It is time to remedy that because she was a very important part of my early life and a big influence on me.

Unlike many siblings who tend to fight and argue for much of the time, we were always good friends. Not surprisingly, Barbara took the lead in most of our games because she was three years older than me but the age difference was no great barrier and we played together a great deal of the time. In those days, the concept of vaccination was relatively new and so it was quite common for children to suffer from measles, mumps, chickenpox, scarlet fever and other so-called children's ailments. Because they were highly infectious diseases, it was inevitable that they spread rapidly around the classroom. So it was no surprise when, shortly after she started school, Barbara had time off at home with measles, mumps and chickenpox in quick succession. During these weeks, she and I continued to play together as if nothing had happened. Every time our doctor called to see us – Dr McCarthy was a large Irishman with a very red nose – he insisted that I would succumb to the disease before his next visit. To his amazement and unbelief, I never did and maybe this was an early indication that I had a strong immune system. Certainly I have had excellent health throughout my life, for which I am very grateful to God.

It wasn't long after this that we started to play schools. Barbara and her best friend Dorothy were the teachers and I was the pupil. The result of this was that I learnt, at home, to read, to write and do simple arithmetic so that when I started proper school at five and a half years of age, I found everything too easy almost to the point of being boring. But of course, it also meant that I was able to make rapid progress. I had a good brain and because I did not mess around like some of the kids, I learnt quickly and throughout all of my junior school life I was usually the boy with the highest marks. Unfortunately, this didn't mean I was top of the class. There were two girls who usually pipped me for that distinction. Daphne Bate was a plain and rather plump girl who lived across the road from me (and who eventually went to Cambridge University if I remember correctly). Marion Dobb, on the other hand was a real beauty with strikingly big brown eyes and long lashes. I often sat next to her and had I been more interested in girls, she might have been my first girlfriend. I sometimes wonder what happened to her and how many hearts she broke in later life.

The fact is, however, that I was interested in neither boys nor girls. I was very shy and was usually a loner. Maybe it was because I was never very interested in food, or maybe it was just something to do with my metabolism, but I was a very thin child. Some adults used to refer to me as 'skinny', which I hated. Strangely, I don't recall ever being bullied or teased about it by other kids. Nevertheless, I was very self-conscious about it. It may not have been true, but I imagined that because I looked so puny, I must also be weak and so would not be able to run as fast as other kids or be strong enough to fight them or do many of the things they did. So I never got involved in fights or the games they played and tended to keep myself to myself. I probably preferred female company (such as the lovely Marion Dobb), if only because girls were less threatening.

One incident exemplifies my attitude only too clearly. I was invited to a birthday party of a boy who lived just down the road. Martin Asprey was about my age and had an older sister who was one of Barbara's school friends. Out of politeness, Mum bought me a present to take along, but I merely went to the house, handed in the present and came away again without any explanation. I simply didn't want to be with all those other children. Who knows what awful games I might have been expected to play or what horrible food I might have had to eat? It was only in the last few weeks of junior school, when I was eleven, that I actually accepted a birthday invitation from a boy in my class who lived on the northern fringe of Ruislip. About ten of us spent a long summer afternoon and evening, running and hiding and playing some kind of 'wide game' in the fields and woods adjacent to his house. It was a new experience and I really enjoyed it. Perhaps I was starting to grow up!

But I am rushing ahead. As I made my way up through junior school, I did make one special friend – Peter Briggs. He was a clever lad like me and preferred the more academic kind of pursuits rather than the physical kind. We got on really well, and we often spent time together playing board games or cards. He and his older brother knew many different types of card games and I was eager to learn from them. Although we both had a strong competitive spirit, we were evenly matched at most things and so we never fell out with each other. Amongst the many games we played was chess, something my father had taught me. The practise I got playing regularly with Peter and his brother paid dividends in later life when I was to play at quite a high level for my college and university teams.

At age eleven, Peter and I moved on to different secondary schools, but we remained good friends and continued to meet up for regular games sessions for another seven years, until we moved on to different universities and lost touch.

Apart from Peter, I never played with other children from junior school and in this I was obviously unusual. But I did many other things that a normal boy would do, except that I played alone. I had model cars and trains; I built things with Meccano; I did jigsaw puzzles; read books; listened to the radio and collected things. Cigarette cards were popular, and the craze at school was to 'play' for them. Two or more players would flick the cards – held between the first and second fingers – against a wall. As soon as a card fell in such a way as to partly cover another card, all the cards on the ground were won. It was a bit like gambling but with practise it was possible to develop a level of skill so that you won more times than you lost. I was quite good at it, I seem to remember. In autumn, conkers were another popular pastime. A hole would be made through the chestnut with a skewer so that it could be hung on a string. We then did battle to try to smash each other's conkers by striking them against each other. There were always a lot of disputes because some boys were accused of cooking the chestnuts to make them extra hard – which of course was cheating!

I collected stamps. Dad's company did business with many countries of the world and he would take the postage stamps off all the correspondence and bring them home for me. As time went by and I built up quite a sizeable collection, I became more and more interested until eventually one Christmas, I became the proud owner of a *Stanley Gibbons World Stamp Catalogue*. This listed every stamp that had ever been issued up to that time, for every country of the world. It showed that stamps belonged to sets issued at different times and with different themes for designs. They also showed how much the stamps were worth either as used or mint (unused) items. For weeks, I spent every available moment browsing through my *Stanley Gibbons* in conjunction with my collection. I was worse than my father when he had his head in a book!

Another of my particular hobbies was the keeping of scrapbooks. At some point in my childhood, a baby polar bear named Brumas was born at London Zoo and for weeks, if not months afterwards, the papers and magazines were full of pictures of Brumas. I kept every cutting I could find to make my own record of the event. On the last page of one of Mum's weekly women's magazines there was always a picture of some scene of a town or village from around Britain. These were cut out and went into another scrapbook. This was probably the beginning of a life-long affection for the country I love. Over the years, I have bought many books which feature pictures of Britain, both town and country, and in particular I am fascinated to see the changes that have taken place over the last hundred years, especially since the coming of the motorcar.

And then there was the cricket scrapbook! 1947 was a very historic year for cricket lovers in England. It was dominated by two batsmen, Dennis Compton and Bill Edrich, who broke nearly every record in the book during that summer. If you want to know the details you must look them up in the *Guinness Book of Records* or find a *Wisden Almanac* for 1948. Dennis Compton was more than just a cricketer: he was the first post-war sportsman to really take on celebrity status. He was as talked about and admired as David Beckham is today. Moreover, both Compton and Edrich played for Middlesex and so not surprisingly, Middlesex were the county champions that year. As an eight-year-old who lived in Middlesex, what better incentive could there be to become a cricket fanatic and a Middlesex supporter too?

Twice a week throughout the cricket seasons, our daily newspaper – the *News Chronicle*, which sadly no longer exists – would publish the current county championship table and once a week the current batting and bowling averages for the season. These tables were religiously cut out and entered into my scrapbook each year along with articles dealing with internationals and other important matches and of course anything about my Middlesex heroes, like for instance when Compton was hit on the head during a test match against Australia in 1948. He retired hurt, had stitches to repair the wound and then returned to score a century. He was Batman and Super-Man all rolled into one!

I soon discovered that Peter's elder brother Robert was also a cricket fanatic. The Briggses had a big house and a very large walled and lawned garden and occasionally in the summer, the three of us would play cricket. I soon got the taste for it. As I got older, I was invited to go with Robert and Peter to Lords, the headquarters of cricket, to watch my favourite team, Middlesex. This was in 1950 and having once sampled the delights of watching first-class cricket there was no stopping me. I went four or five more times that season, often on my own. I still remember most of the Middlesex team during those early years of the fifties. Compton and Edrich were there of course and so were Jack Robertson, Sid Brown, Jack Young, Alan Moss, Leslie Compton (Dennis's elder brother who was the wicketkeeper) and in particular I found a new hero in a seventeen-year-old slow bowler by the name of Fred Titmus. I suppose it was because he was only five or six years older than me that I felt a strong affinity with him. Maybe it also had something to do with the fact that he was quite small. I soon aspired to becoming a slow bowler and modelled my action on Fred Titmus, who of course played many times for England in later years.

Because of my shyness and reticence to mix with other children, it was difficult to play proper cricket. But I was imaginative and resourceful if nothing else. On one side of our garden at home was a brick wall, the side of an air-raid shelter erected during the war. The house next door to ours had been converted into a small private school by the owner and the shelter was now used by the school as storage space. For me it was just what I needed to practise my cricket. During the long summers, which seemed to go on for ever and always be sunny, I would spend many hours throwing a tennis ball at the wall and when it came back, I would defend a real set of stumps with my trusty bat playing off-drives, on-drives, square cuts, leg glances and every other stroke in the book. I would try to 'bowl' fast, slow, off-breaks and leg-breaks and sometimes would pretend it was a match between my favourite teams and count runs and wickets accordingly – four if I hit the house, one for the nearest fence, two to the rockery and so on. Imagination was a long way short of the real thing, but I always enjoyed myself.

When I went to secondary school, we played proper cricket in the summer. But as probably happens in many schools even today, teams were selected by captains who were popular sporty types who in turn picked their friends. If you were a shy loner like me, you got left until the very end to play with the 'no-gooders'. There was an under-13s team, under-14s, the 'colts', the third, the second and finally the first eleven. In general it was the same boys who made up these teams as they progressed up through the school. Although I believed in my own ability, I was never once even considered for any of these teams until my final year at school, aged eighteen. When it was announced that there would be an optional net practise during the Easter holidays for anyone interested, I took the plunge and went along. Suddenly, the games master, Mr Terry, realised that I could bowl very tidily and was no mug with the bat either. To my amazement (and everyone else's too) I went straight into the first eleven for the opening match of the season. I took a wicket, held a good catch and batting at No. 11 held out for nearly half an hour to save the game for the school. The next week, I was promoted in the batting order to No. 8 and took a couple more wickets. But by now A-level exams were looming. When asked about my availability for the next match, I decided that with an exam on the following Monday, I needed the weekend to do my final revision. This seemed perfectly reasonable to me, but not to Mr Terry. To him sport was everything and in his view, playing for the school had to take priority over any exams, even though the outcome might affect the rest of the student's life. I was not picked again and that was the end of my school cricket career. Shame!

But cricket remained and still remains one of the great loves of my life. In my teens, I thought how wonderful it would be to play first-class cricket full-time as a professional and actually get paid for doing what I most enjoyed. Of course I knew this was only a dream but I continued to play for various clubs until beyond my fiftieth birthday. But I am rushing ahead once again. Suffice to say that there were some very memorable times in my early love-affair with cricket. In 1953, we won the Ashes back from the Australians amidst great excitement and I shall never forget the famous test match in 1956 when another slow bowler, Jim Laker, took all ten wickets in an innings and nineteen in the match, also against the Australians.

I was never very good at other sports throughout my school days. Perhaps it was the same problem over again of never playing with the good guys and so never developing any latent skills I might have had. One memory does stick out, however, and it is not a happy one.

When I was about seven, Mum took Barbara to the swimming pool as she was teaching her to swim. I went along as well because I was too young to be left on my own and sat on the edge of the pool watching. I don't know what happened but suddenly I slipped into the water and the next thing I knew I was standing on the bottom with my head well below the surface of the water. Fortunately I had the presence of mind (or maybe it was just a panic reaction) to reach for the metal Tube that went round the edge of the baths and haul myself out. Mum and Barbara hadn't even noticed my temporary disappearance, but I had been very frightened.

Soon after this, my class at school started to make regular compulsory visits to the pool with the good intention of teaching every child to swim. I hated it! It was bad enough having to undress and parade my skinny little body in front of the other children, but I found that within seconds of being in the water, I was shivering with cold, my muscles were therefore tensed and I could no more float than fly, let alone swim. Every visit was the same: I made absolutely no progress whatsoever; no one made any attempt to help and each visit was like purgatory to me. Nothing has changed. Maybe it is because of an absence of fatty tissue on my body or maybe I have heavy bones but the fact is that I don't float. Put me in water and I sink. Consequently, panic sets in because when your head is going under water you are afraid you might drown. So you are fighting desperately against the water and to relax (which everyone says is what you should do) is quite impossible. I know I am not unique and others do suffer similar problems but it does seem to be a rather rare phenomenon and others are quite unable to understand. But there it is. I don't float and I can't swim. If I go into water above my knees, I start to shiver and generally feel very uncomfortable. So it will not surprise you to know that I have lived for the last thirty years within five minutes walk of a large modern swimming pool, but have *never* once entered it!

I cannot talk about school days without including Sunday school. From about the age of six, my sister and I were sent to Sunday school at the local Baptist church for an hour at three o'clock every Sunday afternoon. We sang hymns and choruses, said prayers, learnt Bible stories and sometimes heard about missionaries in foreign countries. I tended to treat this very much the same as day-school. Unlike some of the other boys in my class who talked and messed around, I listened and tried to learn. I remember there was once a competition to win a beautifully illustrated Children's Bible. Each class put forward their best pupil who then went before a committee of very scary adults to try to answer some very hard Bible questions. I represented my class but only finished with a consolation prize. And the winner of the whole contest was ... Barbara! I didn't mind. She deserved it. Not only did she know her Bible really well, but she was kind, thoughtful and as perfect a sister as I could ever imagine.

Because I did so well at Sunday school, I felt that I was a 'good boy' and rather looked down on some of my fellow pupils at school who I assumed never went to Sunday school or church. I was soon to be disillusioned. I omitted to mention that my junior school was a church school and about twice a year we all marched down the road to the parish church for a service. It was taken from the prayer book, and contained responses, sung psalms and involved standing, kneeling or sitting at various times. I was completely at sea with no idea what was going on and felt very small and uncomfortable as a result. I decided then and there that the Church of England had got it all wrong and was *definitely* not for me!

The end of the war meant it was easier to travel, and so in 1946, I had my first real experience of a family holiday at Swanage in Dorset. Few families had cars in those days, and even if they did, petrol was still in such short supply that most long journeys had to be made by train. Waterloo Station on summer Saturdays was horrendous; a seething mass of humanity, pushing and shoving and hauling huge suitcases as the queues filled the station concourse and spilled down the steps into the road outside. As a very small boy, all I wanted to do was hold my mother's hand very tightly for fear of being lost for ever in that crowd. But unlike what I was used to when travelling on London Underground, the trains were really exciting – my first encounter with steam engines. I do not understand how anyone can fail to find these machines truly awesome – especially when seen in action with steam hissing from various orifices and smoke belching from the chimney. As for the coaches, they had corridors down one side from which sliding doors opened into separate compartments, each seating about eight travellers. One always hoped to find an empty compartment, but rarely did. I am pleased that a few of these old carriages are still in existence and in use along with preserved steam engines at a number of restored railways around the country. But for how long, I wonder? The nostalgia for them may die out with those who travelled on them.

Swanage was wonderful, a delightful seaside town sheltering at the foot of the Purbeck Hills. The beach was sandy and clean; there was an attractive harbour, good cliff walks and many places of interest like Corfe Castle and the Blue Pool all close at hand. But what really excited me were the hills. I had never seen real hills before and now all I wanted to do was to climb them; over the top to Studland village, along the ridge to Corfe Castle, or the other way to the Old Harry Rocks. I made it clear to my mother that in future wherever we went on holiday, there had to be hills!

She was very cooperative and after returning to Swanage the

following year, we stayed at Minehead and Lynton in 1948 and 1949, exploring the hills of Exmoor and the Quantocks. But the greatest treat was yet to come. In August 1950 we went to the Lake District for a fortnight.

Before I tell you about that, I ought to mention that on this occasion, my father was allowed to borrow one of his firm's company cars and for the first time ever, we went to our holiday destination by car rather than by train. This is worthy of note because of the way Britain has changed in the last half-century. At that time there were no motorways. The country was still recovering from the war and many of the city bypasses that exist today had not been built either. Getting from Ruislip to Ambleside was a major feat of navigation made possible by the Automobile Association which *did* exist by then and which supplied routes for any prospective journey just as they still do today. I remember many of the places we passed through on that journey and it is intriguing to look at an up-to-date map and see the convoluted route which we took. One of the reasons I remember those place names is that in order to overcome boredom on the journey, I started to collect the names of public houses and noted their locations (so as not to confuse one 'Red Lion' pub in one town for about twenty different others). I suppose I was being hopelessly optimistic if I thought I could ever list every pub in the land, but this was another of my 'collecting' hobbies and was a source of fascination for quite a few years. Even today, it is interesting and instructive to see the Railway Arms in a town where the railway was abandoned and dismantled many years ago.

Everyone had said how wonderful the Lake District would be, but I was a bit concerned. Lakes might be very pretty but what about hills? I needn't have worried. We stayed in a guesthouse run by two old ladies at Waterhead near Ambleside, overlooking Lake Windermere and with exquisite views of mountains and hills across the lake. On our first day, a Sunday, the sun shone and we walked over the fells to Troutbeck. I was captivated by everything I saw: here were real mountains towering into the sky, and challenging me to climb them at the earliest opportunity. I couldn't wait. But on Monday morning, it started to rain. The mountains disappeared into the mist and everything looked very drab and grey. It rained for the rest of the day ... and all day Tuesday ... and finally stopped around lunchtime on Wednesday. We continued to have some rain every day for the rest of the holiday but even that could not dampen my enthusiasm. I was hooked and knew that I was going to spend many of my future holidays in this magical place.

I have one other vivid memory of this holiday. Staying at our guesthouse was a Mr Halliwell, a charming gentleman who was the principal of the Leeds College of Music. During some of the wet days, we spent much time talking with him and his wife and it became obvious that he liked young people. There was a piano in the lounge and he encouraged me (and Barbara) to play it and showed real interest in our musical prowess. He talked about orchestras and instruments and classical music and ignited a desire in me to make music. I had only recently started piano lessons so it was a real boost to my musical education. This was a case of the right person coming along at the right time. I didn't realise it then, but God was already on my case.

Making Decisions

In 1950, it was customary for every child at the age of eleven to take an examination known as the Eleven Plus. This determined what kind of secondary education the child would enjoy or endure. Those who passed would be offered a place at a grammar school, although not necessarily the one of their choice unless they obtained really high marks. Those who failed were sent to a secondary modern school, usually the one nearest their home. The difference between the standard of education in these two types of establishment was very considerable.

Debates about the fairness of the system have been going on for over fifty years and there are points on both sides of the argument. However, because I was a bright lad and passed the exam with flying colours, it worked well for me. At the time, Britain had still not recovered from the war and the school-building programme was behind schedule. Consequently there were no outstanding grammar schools near to Ruislip. My choice was therefore to go to Latymer Upper School in Hammersmith, a 45-minute journey on the Underground.

I was not good at getting up in the morning and it was therefore fortunate that school did not start until 9.25, but I confess to arriving at the very last minute on a great many occasions.

A new school meant more decisions. The extracurricular activity at the school with the highest profile was the Guild. Basically, this was an amateur dramatic society and everyone was encouraged to join, presumably so that shows with large casts could easily be accommodated. I had never acted and the idea of drawing attention to myself on the stage was unthinkable. I declined to join. There was also the Combined Cadet Corps, which I saw as nothing more than boys being trained to be soldiers. I hated war, weapons and even uniforms, which in my mind were associated with war, and so once again I resisted the pressure to join and said a firm 'no'. There were other organisations representing various sports or hobbies but the only one I ever joined was the chess club.

However, I was not as much of a loner as in my junior school days. I did make some friends. On my very first day at Latymer, I had the unpleasant experience of tasting my first school dinner. In the past, I had always eaten lunch at home but of course that was no longer possible. The food was probably not that bad, but I found it hard to stomach and so was still struggling to clear my plate long after the other boys had left the canteen – with one exception. This was a very small boy from my class who obviously had the same problem as I did. John Croft was his name and he lived in Belmont near Harrow. He was extraordinarily tiny but, as I discovered later, he was very gifted at woodwork. He had his own set of tools at home and it was his hobby. We couldn't have been more different, in that I was the world's worst at practical things. Nevertheless, our experience in the canteen brought us together in such a way that we remained friends for the next few years. Travelling back and forth on the Tube also meant that there were times to chat with fellow pupils and although I was still basically very shy, things were improving.

As at most schools, there were some interesting characters on the staff. Our school chaplain – Rev Cann (or was it McCann?) was a small man with a very round face, accentuated by his bald head, his dog-collar and a perpetual grin. He was as unlike an Anglican vicar as I could have imagined. He was always telling jokes and spent much of our religious studies classes trying to disprove or find rational explanations for the miracles described in both the Old and New Testaments of the Bible. With my Sunday school background this was quite disconcerting. Nevertheless, he was outspoken about the rest of his faith. I remember his words on one occasion to those who had expressed doubt concerning the existence of a life after death: 'If you are right and I'm wrong, at least I've enjoyed my life. But if I'm right and you're wrong, you're going to be in big trouble!'

We had a history master, Mr Sopwith, who was known as 'Beery' for the simple reason that he always stank of alcohol. He was a miserable man who never smiled and frequently scowled, so maybe he had some personal secret which had driven him to drink. Mr Tuttell, our geography teacher, was another serious man who rarely smiled but who surprised us all on one occasion with an unexpected note of humour. Speaking about rivers with muddy bottoms winding across their flood plains, he suddenly came to an abrupt halt and then, after a moment's pause, enquired of the class, 'Have you got a muddy bottom?' Another of his statements is firmly imprinted in my memory: 'If a thing is worth doing, it's worth doing well.' That made good sense to me and has become a life principle ever since – but with mixed consequences, as will become apparent.

More decisions followed in the coming years as I had to choose which subjects to specialise in and which subjects to give up. I had a natural gift for mathematics and I was fascinated by chemistry, probably because of my father's work. On the other hand, I found languages very difficult (with the exception of Latin which was so beautifully logical) and history was just plain boring (although my mind was changed in later life when I started to read a great deal about certain periods of history). I therefore gradually moved in the direction of maths, physics and chemistry. I also determined to study music and managed to fit this into my timetable. I have mentioned that we had acquired a piano at home after the war years and at the age of about eleven, Barbara started to have lessons with a lady who lived down our road. I used to listen to her practising and was convinced that I could make much better music, so I started to sit at the piano and improvise and when I was ten, I too commenced weekly lessons, taking regular exams both in piano playing and also in the theory of music. I found this latter subject particularly of interest as I often attempted to write my own compositions. It was thus a natural progression to study music at school. It became obvious from the start that I had an exceptional gift and so taking up the piano proved to be a very important decision in future years.

In general, I believe that Latymer School gave me an excellent education in most subjects, with the possible exception of English literature. From the age of twelve we commenced reading Shakespeare plays, something I have always felt was a serious mistake. I don't think I was unusual in having read little more than children's books such as Enid Blyton stories up to this time and to suddenly be plunged into Shakespeare has always seemed to me on a par with a mathematics student being asked to jump from multiplication tables to calculus overnight. I was totally out of my depth and finished up hating Shakespeare and indeed much of the other literature we were forced to read. No doubt it was the method of teaching which was at fault, but the outcome was that I was so turned off that it was some years before I rediscovered books and reading, and I was still left with a residual aversion to Shakespeare. Since my school days, I have never watched one of his plays and have no desire to do so, in spite of the protestations of many of my educated friends. Perhaps one day I will feel differently.

Before long, I was into my teenage years. Being a teenager in the 1950s was very much simpler than it is today. For the majority, there was no peer pressure to wear any particular style of clothing, take drugs or indulge in particular activities. We had respect for our parents, our teachers, the police and indeed for most adults and we had none of the luxury goods that today's teenagers have, simply because there was not much money around. But one thing that is characteristic of teenagers that never seems to change is that they are selfish. It is part of growing up and trying to assert one's individuality; wanting to be a person in one's own right and not dependent or reliant on parents any more. The result is usually manifested in disobedience, arguments, rows and general non-cooperation: and in these respects I was no exception. I can't remember what the issues were, but I do know that I became moody, irritable, always wanted my own way and could not have been very nice to live with. But things were going to change.

There had already been some changes in our household. Barbara had grown up and unlike me, was even nicer than ever. She was head girl at her school, and she now went regularly to church and also to the youth meetings and was usually helpful and kind at home. I didn't understand at the time what a Christian was, but looking back, it seems to me that she was a pretty good example. I also attended church occasionally, mainly because Mum and Dad expected me to, but it seemed like a waste of my time and I was always looking for any excuse not to go. In 1952, we had holidayed at Barmouth in North Wales and met the Firth family from Stoke d'Abernon in the stockbroker belt of Surrey. Their only son was the same age as me and we had got on well. He was at a boarding school near Reading and as we became pen pals I would often insist that my Sunday evenings must be spent at home writing to Charles Firth.

However, as time went by, there was something else that attracted me to church – girls!

It was in the summer of 1953 on holiday that I had first become aware of my sexuality. We stayed in Tresaith, a tiny Welsh village on the coast of Cardigan Bay which seemed still to be living in the nineteenth century. There was no electricity in much of the village (our guesthouse had its own generator in the garden). I also remember watching two wizened old women dressed in long black dresses who swept up the litter from the beach every evening and burnt it on a bonfire at the mouth of a cave. If I had been younger I would surely have been convinced they were witches with flying broomsticks. But the beach was sandy and safe and while Mum and Barbara spent long hours swimming and Dad sat in a deckchair reading his library book, I had nothing to do but wander up and down admiring the waves breaking on the rocks, having an occasional paddle and desperately wishing that some members of the fair sex whom I had observed sitting and playing nearby would come and join me. But of course they didn't.

By this time, I had progressed from Sunday school into a boys' Bible class which met in a separate hall a hundred yards from the church, but on anniversaries and other special occasions we would join with everyone else, including the girls' Bible class, and I couldn't help but notice some very attractive young ladies there. However, I was much too shy to approach any of them, let alone actually talk to them.

Back home, there was a girl a bit younger than me who used to come past our house, walking her dog to the park about five minutes away. I started to offer to take our dog (a black cocker spaniel called Lady who smelt anything but ladylike!) for walks and by a bit of detective work, even found out the house where this girl lived. We would sometimes pass each other in the street, but she never looked in my direction and I never even discovered her name. I was not having much success.

And then a major event occurred which set my thoughts on a different path: Dr Billy Graham came to London! Graham was a young American preacher who had been holding huge city-wide evangelistic crusades across the USA with amazing results. Men and women and young people were becoming Christians in their thousands and in just a few years, Billy Graham had become a household name there. Now he was coming to England, at the invitation of a number of national church leaders. Inevitably there were those who were opposed to his visit. They imagined that he was some kind of super-salesman using underhand techniques to persuade people to commit their lives to Christ. Others assumed that he must be making a lot of money out of his crusades. In fact neither was true. Billy's preaching was simply and straightforwardly based on the Bible and as the years have passed, most observers have put his incredible success down to just two factors – prayer and the power of the Holy Spirit.

Anyway, Haringay Arena in North London was booked for the crusade in March 1954 and right from the start it was packed out with 12,500 people every night so that the crusade was extended to three months, ending with a huge rally in Wembley Stadium in June. I was vaguely intrigued by what I heard about the crusade and Barbara was very anxious that I should go along. But I was worried about the possible consequences. As I have already mentioned, it had been apparent for some time that something had happened to Barbara – she had a peace and serenity about her that I could not fathom and her lifestyle seemed to me to be above reproach. I assumed that this was something to do with the fact that she was often at the church and now frequently at the crusade meetings. Supposing I ended up like that – I would be so embarrassed! But eventually, I gave in. I think maybe there was some kind of bribe involved. I can't remember exactly, but I know that one cold wet March evening, I found myself at Haringay listening to Billy Graham.

It was amazing. What he said was so clear: 'I was a sinner in God's sight.' I didn't need persuading about that; I knew I was thoroughly selfish. 'God loved me' – I'd never realised that before; I'd always believed God was there but that he could actually love *me*... well! Also that 'Jesus died on the cross to take the punishment for my sins and by trusting in Jesus as *my* saviour, I could be forgiven and have eternal life.' Fantastic! Boy, did I want to be forgiven! And who wouldn't want eternal life? But there was a cost involved. Jesus wanted me to hand over my life, so that I would be living for Him, seeking to please Him in everything I did. That meant a radical change in lifestyle for me. Everyone would notice. People would talk about me. It would be so embarrassing! But then again... The time came when Billy invited those who wanted to receive Christ into their lives to come forward and stand in front of the platform. I am not exaggerating – I literally had to hang on to the seat in front of me to stop my legs from marching forward. Talk about a battle! I was fighting God for all I was worth. I knew what I should do, but I still wanted to do my thing – to continue in my selfishness – for a bit longer.

The statistics tell us that during those three months of the Greater London Crusade, nearly two million people attended meetings addressed by Dr Graham and 38,400 people made decisions to become Christians. I was not one of them.

But *something* had happened: I couldn't get these things out of my mind. I started to go to church every Sunday (the Baptist church where I had been brought up and attended Sunday school) and discovered to my amazement that essentially the same message was being preached every week in one form or another. Presumably, this had been true before my Haringay experience, so how come I had never grasped it before? I hadn't any explanation but it was clear that somehow my mind and heart had been opened up to the truth and it was now up to me to decide what to do with it. I could no longer say that I didn't know.

The battle went on throughout the summer, hearing the message most Sundays and continually saying no. But towards the end of the year, I started to weaken (although my attraction to the girls may have had something to do with it). I had noticed a very pretty young lady called Vivienne and it seemed that the only way of ever meeting her would be to attend the young people's get-together which happened after the Sunday evening service. That was a start, and then there was a social evening on a Saturday once a month, which was called a 'squash' (I've no idea why!) where the same group of young people played games, enjoyed refreshments and finished up with a short talk. I never got anywhere with Vivienne but at the December squash I made the most important decision of my entire life.

The speaker pointed out how much time we spend in eating and drinking to keep our bodies healthy; how much time we spend in education to equip and train our minds; and then asked the question, 'How much time do we spend on our eternal souls?' Good question! I realised in a flash what a fool I had been. Surely the most important thing in this life was to be prepared for eternity rather than to be preoccupied with what passes away so rapidly with time. That night, I invited Jesus into my life. I asked Him to forgive all my past sins, to make me the person He wanted me to be and to give me the eternal life He had promised. I went home a new person! It was 18 December 1954.

One week later on Christmas morning, I took our dog for a short walk. Christmas was going to be a bit strange because an aunt was very ill and so the usual get-together of all the relatives had been cancelled and we would have a quiet day, just me, my parents and my sister. As I walked, I suddenly felt an amazing sense of peace and joy come upon me. I just *knew* my sins had been forgiven and that Jesus had come into my life. I hadn't told anyone yet, but I had absolutely no doubt that I was now a Christian and that all that I had been told was for real. Things would never be the same again!

The first thing to happen after the Christmas holidays was the 'mock' O level examinations (O levels were the forerunners of the GCSE). Because Latymer was a grammar school, most of the boys were pretty intelligent and although I had always had good reports, it had not been the same as at junior school. But suddenly things changed. As I entered each exam, I prayed that God would help me to remember what I had revised and to express myself clearly without making silly mistakes. When the results were revealed, my performance turned out to be my best ever and for the first time ever, the best in my whole class. I was encouraged!

In March, a party of young people from the church went one

Saturday to a meeting at the Royal Albert Hall hosted by a man called Tom Rees. At the end of his talk, he invited anyone who had become a Christian during the previous three months to wave a hand in the air. The lights were dimmed so I did not feel too conspicuous. I waved my hand. The secret was out: I was a Christian and I was happy to be so. Six months later, I was baptised by immersion as a way of declaring what had happened to me.

These were vital decisions which helped me to start to overcome my shyness. My past didn't matter any more because I was a new person. Also, because God had accepted me, I felt that other people might now accept me. It was only a beginning and it would be many years before I would truly overcome my feelings of self-consciousness and inadequacy, but it was a start and from now on things would be constantly changing.

Change for the Better

Before becoming a Christian, life had revolved around school and homework. Suddenly, and for the very first time, I found myself with a social life. There were three events each week which clamoured for my time and attention.

The first was after church on Sunday evenings. This had been the starting point of my Christian journey. It was an informal time when about thirty young people – teens and early twenties – got together for a chat over light refreshments usually followed by a time of singing hymns and choruses. The usual accompanist was a very gifted pianist who played with such gusto and skill that we felt stirred to sing our hearts out. But eventually it happened that Bill was absent one Sunday. Word had got around that I could play the piano and so my services were commandeered for the evening. Just as I had once been convinced that I could play better than my sister, in a similar way I felt that given a little time, I could learn to accompany with as much aplomb as the masterful Bill. It was not really pride or arrogance but a curious aspect of my character at that time since it amounted to confidence in my own ability whereas I appeared to lack this in so many other areas. Anyway, this was something that God used to help me overcome my shyness. For a year or so, I was only the reserve pianist but my talents were clearly recognised and appreciated and that helped to give me a sense of identity.

The second meeting was on Tuesday evenings – the Young People's Fellowship. This was a much more formal occasion, not dissimilar to a Sunday service except that everything was geared to young people's likes and dislikes. I learnt a lot about the Bible and am thankful even today for the grounding that those meetings gave me in understanding the basics of my faith.

The third meeting was on a Friday night where an older group – mainly folk in their early twenties – met at the home of a lovely couple called Bob and Kathy Payne. This was not an official church meeting but simply a group of friends who wanted to spend time together and grow in their faith. It was Barbara who first suggested that I go along and I am so glad she did. We used to sit around – mainly on the floor – and for an hour or more would study the Bible in depth. Then we would spend time sharing about each others' lives, including any particular areas of difficulty or crisis, before embarking upon a long session of prayer. Of course we did pray and we did study the Bible on Tuesdays but somehow this was different. Maybe it was the warm atmosphere of being in a home or maybe it was the intensity and deep desire of each person present to really mean business with God, but from my very first visit I was hooked. I couldn't wait for Friday evenings to come round and I knew that God was really at work in my life through these times at the Paynes'. However, there was a problem.

I was one of only two teenagers among the group, and because the rest were that much older, they were past the student phase of life, past the parental control stage and therefore prone to keep very late hours. Sometimes, a few of the group would return to another house for coffee and a chat and I couldn't resist going with them with the result that I started to arrive home at midnight or even later. Mum and Dad were *not* happy and I was in a dilemma. I was thrilled to have found a group of real friends who were helping me to grow in my faith but at the same time I was being disobedient to my parents – hardly appropriate for a Christian. We eventually found a compromise but it was a difficult period.

Following the Billy Graham Crusade, many young people had been added to the church and in particular, one or two Teddy Boys. These were youths who went about in gangs, dressed in Edwardian-style clothes and generally caused trouble. One of these converted Teddy Boys, Malcolm, who became my sister's boyfriend (and eventually her husband) was keen that others should hear the gospel of what Jesus had done. But the crusade had long been over so another way had to be found. As a result, the Friday night group with some help from some of the Sunday group started up what came to be known as 'Tea for Teds' at the local Girl Guide hut. This was a building just a hundred metres from Ruislip High Street which we paid to hire for a couple of hours each Sunday evening. We provided refreshments as well and effectively transferred the church get-together to this new venue, except that we invited the gangs of youths to come in off the High Street and then preached the gospel to them. It was far from easy. Those who went out on the High Street were known as 'fishers' and always went in twos for their own safety. There were sufficient church young people to carry off the singing without too much difficulty but the preaching was always punctuated by heckling and the occasional crude remark or blasphemy. These meetings went on for more than a year and it was here that I first tried my hand at preaching. Talk about being thrown in at the deep end! But I survived the ordeal and soon realised that I wanted to do more.

Opportunities soon appeared. One of the young men in the church (it could have been Malcolm again, I don't remember) made the discovery that many small country Baptist churches had no full-time minister and because the congregations were small, they struggled to find people willing to conduct their services. It was suggested that the young people at Ruislip should form a 'Witness Team' to help meet this need. Teams were usually four or five strong; someone would be responsible for planning and leading the service acting as a sort of master of ceremonies; someone would read from the Bible; someone would lead in prayer; someone would share a personal testimony about their experience of becoming and living as a Christian and someone would have the onerous task of preaching the sermon. Occasionally, we would take along someone with a really good voice who would sing a solo and that usually meant a pianist to act as accompanist. So there was plenty of scope for everyone, including me. It was a great training ground and it helped me to forget my self-consciousness and get used to public speaking, and of course, playing the piano in public too.

Yet another initiative within the young people's work at the Baptist church was the introduction of an annual house party. The group had grown significantly in the few years following the Billy Graham Crusade and someone thought it would be a good idea to go away together for a long weekend, involving a balance of meetings and of free time in which to relax. The first of these was duly arranged at a lovely conference centre called Rosehill near Reading from 7 to 9 March 1956.

It was an amazing time. One does not expect summer weather in early March, but the sun shone all weekend and it was unseasonably warm. We spent some wonderful hours walking in the beautiful grounds of Rosehill and on an organised ramble in the adjoining Berkshire countryside. Even better were the meetings addressed by a retired missionary from Fiji called Bob Stokes. After so many years, I cannot possibly remember what he said, but I know that God said something to me through Bob Stokes. I felt challenged to give my life wholly to God for whatever purpose He might want. The idea of going to Fiji was very attractive but at this stage there was nothing specific.

There were many other good things happening among our group. We sometimes met for coffee on a Saturday morning at a small restaurant in Ruislip High Street. During the summer months we would play tennis, a sport at which I proved to be quite adept. John, one of my particular friends, was mad keen on classical music and he revived my own interest. We used to sit at his house and listen to records and a group of us would attend the promenade concerts at the Royal Albert Hall several times during the season. These occasions were great fun and any young person with a love of classical music should make such a visit an essential part of their education. If you have ever watched the *Last Night of the Proms* on TV, you will have some idea of the fun and games that accompany every performance to a greater or lesser extent.

Now, it happened that one of our close neighbours was a professional violinist. When in the garden I could often hear him practising. He played in one of the well-known national symphony orchestras but, strangely, never offered us tickets to any of the concerts in which his orchestra was taking part – except once. These were two tickets for a concert at the Royal Festival Hall on 4 February 1957. With great boldness, I invited one of the girls from the church youth group who I knew liked classical music to come with me. Marion King and I enjoyed the performance of Sibelius's violin concerto and also enjoyed holding hands underneath the programme!

In the summer of 1957, a group of about twenty of us went on holiday together to the Keswick Convention – a gathering of Christians from all over the world in the Lake District town of Keswick and renowned for the high quality of Bible teaching given. We stayed in a farm about eight miles from Keswick, attended many of the meetings and were inspired and challenged about our commitment to Christ and His service. I learnt a lot and re-committed my life to God for whatever purpose he might have for me.

While all these changes were going on, I was also working my way through sixth form at Latymer. Following my successes in the O level exams, I had elected to study maths, physics and chemistry for my A-level subjects. I found sixth-form life very much to my liking. No longer were we treated as schoolchildren but more like responsible adults. There were private study periods – usually referred to as *free* periods – when I could choose between spending time in the library studying, catching up on homework or neither! We had a delightful sixth form library overlooking the Thames and I would sometimes sit there and write letters to my sister, who had now gone to a missionary training college just a couple of miles down the river at Chiswick.

I did well throughout the two years and in due course passed the A-level exams in chemistry, physics, pure mathematics and applied mathematics, gaining distinctions in the first three. On the strength of these results, I was awarded a state scholarship to take the course of my choice at an appropriate university. No doubt influenced in some measure by a desire to follow in my father's footsteps, I soon gained a provisional place at King's College in the University of London to study for an honours degree in chemistry.

One event sticks in my memory from those sixth-form years. One of the maths teachers was a retired army sergeant major. He looked like a sergeant major and when he chose to, he could shout like one and usually put the fear of death into the boys, especially the younger ones. On this particular occasion, I was in the canteen eating my lunch when the major got up from the staff table and bellowed at the top of his voice at the first- and second-year classes who had been allocated the same lunch period, telling them to stop talking and be quiet. I was incensed. (I had never liked the major simply because of his association with the armed forces. He had tried to get everyone, including me, to join the Cadet Corps, but I have always considered that life in the forces degraded people and took away their personal dignity and I would have nothing to do with it.) Amidst the hush that followed, I got up from my seat, approached the ogre and told him that I thought he was being unreasonable. It was lunchtime, an opportunity to relax and chat with friends and no one should be forced to eat in silence. He seemed absolutely flabbergasted that anyone should question his authority and for almost the first time ever, lost for words. I returned to my seat, and a few moments later, he very grudgingly conceded to the junior forms that they could talk, but quietly. I mention this incident not because it was a victory won, but because it reflected an aspect of my character which I think I have retained – an anger and intolerance towards any kind of injustice. I also think it reflected how much self-confidence I had gained in just a couple of years; before my conversion I would never have done such a thing.

Although I had been accepted at King's College to study chemistry, I also enjoyed maths and was undoubtedly very good at it. I was therefore persuaded by my maths tutor to remain at school for an extra year in order to take a scholarship examination in maths at Cambridge University.

King's College London was and is a very fine college; but there is something special about Cambridge as the leading university in the country. I thought it would be nice to say to people that I went to Cambridge, and so I agreed to stay on at Latymer to study advanced mathematics. But to be honest, I struggled. In the middle of December 1957 I spent two or three days in residence at Emmanuel College, Cambridge, while taking the examination. I failed.

Looking back, I feel sure that this was what God wanted for me. If I had gone to Cambridge, I would have had to get to know a whole new bunch of people and also find a new church. Because of my shy nature, this could have been difficult for me and the effort required might well have distracted me from more important things. As it was, when I went to King's I was able to live at home, continue my involvement with many of the people and activities in the Baptist church and thereby grow stronger both in my faith and in my new-found confidence as a person.

When I returned to Latymer after the Christmas break, there was a new headmaster. For seven years and one term, I had appreciated the strong Christian ethic of the school which was largely due to the personality of the head – a most gracious and kindly man by the name of Wilkinson. Now he had retired and the whole atmosphere felt different. I didn't like it! The prospect of staying there for another two terms with nothing particular to do was not attractive. I decided to leave and get a job for six months to earn some money and to fill the time usefully and interestingly.

I wanted to do something which might give me some insight into areas that I would be studying when I went to King's, and was therefore delighted to secure a position as a junior technician at the British Aluminium Company's research laboratories at Gerrards Cross. I was to carry out studies on the thermal conductivity of various forms of carbon which were used as electrodes in the manufacture of aluminium from crude ores. This was a challenging problem because the work involved heating carbon blocks to very high temperatures but without them catching fire or burning. Temperatures at different points along the block were measured and analysed using a complicated formula. Within my first week, I uncovered some faulty calculations made by my predecessor and from then on I was something of a 'blue-eyed boy' in the eyes of my supervisor. I enjoyed the work very much and was quite sad that I never saw the project through to its conclusion. However, there was some compensation.

Marion King also worked in Gerrards Cross as a pastry cook and confectioner in a small patisserie. Basically, this meant that she made cakes and decorated them. She started very early in the morning but her finishing time was not dissimilar to mine and we found that it was quite convenient to travel home to Ruislip on the same train. We soon became close friends. I would have liked it to be more than that and I suspected that Marion felt the same way, but in my shyness, I didn't really know how to make such a transition.

But the summer was coming and I decided that I would organise a holiday to my beloved Lake District for some of my newfound friends. In all, seven agreed to come: John, the classical music fanatic; myself; two other fellows and three girls, including Marion. We were to spend a week together at a youth hostel just outside Ambleside with the primary intention of walking the fells. I wanted so much to show my friends how wonderful it all was. There was one slight problem. Marion had to work on the Saturday morning when we were due to travel; so whilst the rest of the party caught the morning train, I offered to wait and accompany Marion on the afternoon train. It was about five hours from Euston to Windermere and I was very happy being in her company for all that time. We read a book together which, of course, meant snuggling up fairly close to each other. By the time we had joined the others at Iveing Cottage, I was feeling pretty optimistic about the week ahead.

It was a great time. The weather was reasonable, we did lots of walking and generally had a lot of fun. There was one incident which was not so pleasant, although looking back it had its funny side. Having been back to the Lakes with my parents in 1951, '53, '54 and '56, I felt I was getting to know the area quite well and was therefore well qualified to lead the walks. On this particular day, it was necessary to climb a rather steep slope – on which there was no actual path – in order to reach the top of a ridge. There were complaints that it was too steep and one of the girls insisted that she could not do it. It just happened that I was carrying the rucksack containing our packed lunches at the time. I therefore raced off up the fell-side, deposited the lunches at the top of the ridge, came down again and announced that if they wanted any lunch, they would have to climb. It worked, but not without the aforementioned young lady having to be almost physically pulled up the slope. It was not that hard and I was cross at all the fuss she had made. Later that evening I said, 'If I'd been a dragon, there would have been fire coming out of my mouth!' I am often reminded of that quote and we laugh about it now.

Because of the potential danger of getting lost on the fells, especially in bad weather, I had stipulated that we should always keep together as a party. Marion and I broke the rule one day and went off on our own. It was a very special day when we admitted our feelings for each other and agreed that when we got home, we would continue to go out together; we became an item! It was 17 July 1958 – the start of a life-long love affair. But it would be almost four years to the day before we would be married.

More Decisions

When we got home after the holiday, everybody was talking about us and not without reason. Marion was a very outgoing person: noisy, talkative and friendly – indeed, she was everyone's friend. By contrast, I was quiet and shy. I was also about to go to university whereas Marion had been to a secondary modern school, left at sixteen and since then had a number of jobs in the poorly paid catering trade. All in all we were so very different that our friends imagined that we had simply had a holiday romance and that our relationship would only last a few weeks.

There was another problem. Ruislip was (and still is) divided by the Metropolitan Line of the London Underground system. As a broad generalisation, the homes on the north side of the railway are distinctive and expensive, whereas those south of the railway tend to be much cheaper, often terraced properties. This resulted in an element of snobbery between the two halves of the town which may not be so evident today. I came from the 'posh' side of the railway while Marion came from 'the other side'.

It certainly didn't bother me, but it did bother my mother, who expressed the view that Marion was not a suitable partner for me because she lacked polish! Understandably, Marion found this opinion offensive and for about six months she refused to come to my house. The impasse was ended only when Mum, realising that our relationship was here to stay, invited Marion to tea one Sunday. She came and behaved as if nothing had ever happened and nothing more was ever said. But as time went by, Mum recognised that Marion had much more depth of character than might first be apparent from her noisy, bouncy exterior and her initial doubts were soon replaced by acceptance and in later years by real appreciation and affection.

Whilst we were hopelessly in love with each other, there was a great deal more to our relationship than explosive chemistry! We might have been complete opposites as far as temperament was concerned, but we shared the most important thing in our lives – our faith in Jesus Christ. For both of us, it was not just an extra to be tacked on to an otherwise normal lifestyle. It was central to our thinking, planning and living. Because Marion worked in the baker's at Gerrards Cross and bakers begin work early, she had to leave home before seven o'clock most mornings and even earlier on Saturdays. This meant that she needed some early nights. At the same time, I needed to study hard most evenings and so for much of the time, seeing each other was restricted to Saturday evenings, Sundays and Tuesday evenings. The latter was so that we could attend the Young Peoples' Fellowship meeting (YPF). We were both members of the committee which planned and organised YPF and so it was a priority. More often than not, our Saturday evenings and Sundays were also largely spent at church, where we wanted to grow in our faith and where we met our friends. We had observed that many couples tended to isolate themselves and become lonely 'twosomes'. Right from the start, we sought to avoid falling into this trap. We tried to mix freely within a wide circle of friends from YPF. It was here that Marion's gift of friendliness immediately helped me. With her free and easy manner, she was able to make me feel more at ease with people so that I could gradually enter conversations and break down the shyness that had always plagued me: this was to be a feature of our life together for many years to come. Within a few months of going out together, I felt very sure that Marion was to be my future wife, but first there was the prospect of three long years at King's College.

Some people have the impression that university life is an easy option with just a few lectures a week and lots of spare time to enjoy the social life. That is certainly not the case for anyone studying chemistry. It is a huge subject and expanding at an incredible rate as new discoveries are made. So many things from our everyday lives depend on chemistry or the application of chemical processes – drugs and medicines, plastics, printing and photography, soaps and washing powders, dyes, pesticides – the list is endless. Furthermore, in order to understand chemistry, it is necessary to be familiar with ideas from advanced physics and mathematics. Thus, my course involved all these three subjects for the first year, chemistry and physics for the second year and chemistry alone for the third. It was also necessary to study elementary German for a year to make possible easy translation of articles written in that language. (A huge number of journals are published worldwide dealing with different aspects of chemistry. English is the most frequently used language, but German and Japanese are probably not far behind. I am so glad I didn't have to learn Japanese!) Don't imagine that the reduction in the number of subjects by the third year meant an easier life – far from it. We had at least one and a half days a week of practical chemistry in the laboratory and throughout my whole course, there was virtually no free time except for Wednesday afternoons which were left vacant so that those who wanted to could play various sports. Apart from a couple of inter-departmental cricket matches, I never used this facility.

But there was one feature of King's which was a great boon to me. In addition to the science faculty, the college had other departments, including theology. At nine o'clock on Monday mornings, there was a course of lectures in theology that were open to students from all the faculties. To accommodate those wishing to attend, normal lectures began an hour later that day. At the end of each academic year an optional exam could be taken and if, at the end of three years, one had a good attendance record and had passed the exams, one received the award of AKC (Associate of King's College). This may not have stood for very much when trying to find a job, but for me it was a wonderful opportunity to learn about things which would normally only be taught at Bible College. What I learnt during my AKC course about textual criticism, comparative religion, a scholarly approach to the New Testament and much more besides, proved invaluable in later years when I became a preacher.

Because I had chosen to live at home in order to maintain all my involvements at the church, I missed out on any university social life. But I did not mind. It was apparent from the start that this mainly revolved around two things – drinking and 'hops'. It was a while before I discovered that the latter were dances. I didn't drink as a matter of principle and I was far too inhibited to be able to dance. (In later years, I found it just as difficult. I simply didn't know what to do with either my feet or my hands. The exception was barn dancing or square dancing where a caller tells you exactly what to do.) So I tended to steer clear of the Students' Union building for fear of getting dragged into one of these activities by well-meaning fellow students. I got on well with most of the fellows and girls in my year but would only count two or three as real friends. Peter Melrose was a lovable rogue who worked with me as a partner in practical physics and Yvonne Rees was a plump but not unattractive girl who was easy to get along with. But my feelings towards them were never in the same league as the Christian friends at home. The only other thing I did at university apart from study was to play chess. This might not have happened but for a fortunate coincidence. In my year group of about thirty students was a young Jewish man who I had met when playing inter-school chess. He was chess mad and was soon playing at Board 1 for the college. Because we were together every day, he encouraged and cajoled me until I agreed to play as well and before I left King's I had reached the heady heights of Board 3. I also played occasionally for the University of London – a much higher standard – but still played in the top fifteen places. It is a matter of regret that so few young people play chess these days. It is such a good intellectual exercise for keeping the brain in trim.

When you are in love, things can get out of proportion and one's thinking can become distorted. I was in love and wanted to be with Marion whenever I could. But in spite of this, I quite enjoyed my time at King's. Physics and German were a bit of a trial, but I found chemistry more and more interesting as time went on. Three years of concentrated study could have seemed a long time but fortunately there were other things going on. At the end of my first year, I got a holiday job at the famous Selfridges store in Oxford Street selling kitchen gadgets – everything from potato peelers to egg whisks. To my surprise I did really well, which was to my advantage because my pay was linked to the value of goods that I sold. During that same summer of 1959, Marion and I were allowed to go on holiday together. We stayed for a week with Marion's Auntie Edie who ran a boarding house in Babbacombe near Torquay. She was rather a fearsome lady who kept her eye on us much of the time but it was better than being apart. Whilst at the seaside, there was an opportunity for Marion to try to teach me to swim. Unfortunately the result was just the same as it had been at school: I always ended up cold, shivering and sinking. It was my last attempt; after this, I simply gave up.

A month or so later, I was asked to take over the leadership of the Witness Team. In view of my studies I hesitated, but eventually agreed, on the understanding that Marion and I would do it together. She immediately displayed a real gift for organising both events and people. We could plan together but she was able to make sure that everything about the visit happened as it was meant to happen. We made a good team.

Our next step was to get engaged. I proposed to her overlooking the River Thames outside the Royal Festival Hall where we had enjoyed that first date nearly three years before. We chose and bought rings for each other and made the announcement to our parents on Marion's twentieth birthday, 6 December 1959. In those days, twenty-one was the age when people were considered to become adults and not eighteen. Consequently, our parents were slightly surprised and possibly a bit hurt that we had taken this step without consulting them. To be honest, it had never occurred to me. We had already made up our minds and there seemed no reason not to let the rest of the world know our intentions.

The following summer saw some more important events. First, my sister got married. Malcolm and Barbara had both been to Bible Colleges with a view to becoming missionaries; but Malcolm's health had subsequently ruled this out and so he was to become a Baptist minister here in England. Marion's brother also got married with Marion as a bridesmaid. Once again Marion and I were able to go on holiday together, returning to the youth hostel in Ambleside where our romance had all started three years before. But it was not a very happy return for me. A party of schoolboys aged from about twelve to fourteen were also in residence in the hostel and Marion, in her usual friendly way, made a great fuss of them. Because of their age, there was no way they could have been a threat to me, but I still felt jealous of the attention she lavished on them and this merely reflected the basic insecurity from which I still suffered.

Insecurity really springs from the feeling that one is not good enough. Not good enough in whose eyes though? My own, actually. My geography master's old adage that if a thing is worth doing it is worth doing well meant that I always sought to excel in whatever task I attempted. This was the positive side but unfortunately there is something in me that wants to go beyond this and be perfect. I was a good student with a good brain, but never likely to become a university professor; I played the piano in a way that was greatly admired and appreciated, but was never going to be a concert pianist; I played chess really well – but only at Board 3; I was quite a useful cricketer but would never play for England. I seemed to be successful at whatever I put my hand to, even selling kitchen gadgets, but I still felt that I was a failure because I didn't actually make it to the top. This kind of insecurity was to dog my thoughts for many years and still rears its ugly head occasionally, even now in my sixties. Gradually, I have had to learn the lesson that it is for God to decide what is good enough. He made me the way I am and only expects me to perform to the level of ability with which He has equipped me. I have to accept myself and not insist on being something that God never intended me to be.

The most significant event of the summer of 1960 was my holiday job. Selfridges had been an interesting experience but as I approached my final year at King's, I wanted to find something which might be of real benefit to my future career. I wrote to Glaxo, the huge pharmaceutical firm whose laboratories were only a short train ride away in Greenford, and was pleased when they offered me a short-term job in their Physical Chemistry Research Division where I worked with a delightful man called Bart Taylor. He was studying the oxidation of Vitamin A and in the course of the two months I was with him, I learnt to apply and use many of the new analytical and instrumental tools which I had only heard about in theory at lectures. Suddenly, chemistry took on a reality that was exciting and stimulating. Bart had a dry sense of humour which always amused me and he was a good teacher. He had no time for fools and if I did or said something stupid, he would let me know. But he gave great attention to detail and his logic and reasoning were impeccable. I saw what was needed to be a good researcher and I was attracted by what I saw.

As I returned to college in October, time was slipping by and it would soon be necessary to make vital decisions about our future. This had been on our minds and in our prayers for a long time. In the late 1950s a book was published which became a bestseller among Christians. *Through Gates of Splendour* told the story of Jim Elliot, a young American missionary with a burden to take the gospel of Jesus Christ to a tribe of savage Indians, the Aucas, living in the jungles of Ecuador in South America. He and his companions were killed by the Aucas but their sacrifice opened the way for others to follow and convert the Aucas to Christianity. The book contained sections of Jim Elliot's personal journal including the now famous quotation: 'He is no fool who gives what he cannot keep to gain what he cannot lose.' One result of reading this book was that some folk started their own journals and I was one of them. Between 1958 and 1961, I made occasional (not daily) entries containing comments on Bible passages I had read, notes from sermons I had heard, personal thoughts, prayers and aspirations. I still have the journal and some of the entries clearly reveal what shaped our thoughts and plans for the future.

As early as June 1959 I wrote:

> I seek not for a life of comfort, leisure and wealth. But I will sacrifice the treasures of this world that I might expend all my energies in the service of my Lord.
> I give Thee back the life I owe,
> That in Thine ocean depths its flow
> Might richer, fuller be.

It was an expression of how I really felt but it needed to be worked out.

Marion and I had discussed Fiji and certainly warmed to the possibility of going there. Perhaps 'warmed' is a good word because undoubtedly, the idea of a warm climate and an almost idyllic south sea island was very inviting. Perhaps we were in love with the place rather than having a sense of calling. But there were other factors to consider – I was only too aware that God had given me a good brain and it seemed unlikely that He would have put me through university to waste all the knowledge that I had gained there. Moreover, we felt no desire or calling to go to Bible College – a compulsory step towards being accepted by most missionary societies. It therefore seemed appropriate to think in terms of being what was called a non-professional missionary. We were advised that in many countries of the world, the rise of nationalism meant that Christian missionaries from abroad were likely to be barred from entry, if not now, then in the near future (this has since proved to be true). A better option was for Christians to take jobs in teaching, medicine or industry where they would be welcomed and spend their spare time assisting and encouraging the local indigenous church.

This seemed to be the right line of approach, but where did we start? I was painfully aware that I had no gift for languages and so having narrowed the search down to English-speaking nations, we wrote to the Colonial Office. They recommended Tanzania (known then as Tanganyika) and Zimbabwe (then called Rhodesia) as the only likely places for the type of openings we sought. It seemed that Fiji was not an option. I remember writing off for a job in a chemical complex near Lake Nakuru in Tanganyika but nothing came of it. The Baptist Missionary Society (we belonged to a Baptist church) suggested a number of teaching posts in India. Apart from the salary, which seemed derisory, I didn't want to teach: I had no inclination in that direction whatsoever.

And so, gradually, one door after another seemed to close. But it was then that some words spoken to us by a wise man, Ben Peake, began to take on some significance.

> Sometimes, God calls us out for service by showing a particular need; but then, having once gained control of our wills, He may use us in another sphere.

It is interesting to note from my journal in February 1960 that we had a great burden for those in the YPF. It deeply concerned us that so few were bothered about prayer or were willing to serve on the Witness Teams. They seemed so full of apathy and were interested only in pleasure seeking. Maybe even in those early days God was re-channelling our zeal into new spheres, although we didn't realise it at the time.

But it was now 1961 and my three years at King's were almost at an end. Because of my state scholarship, all my fees had been paid but because Dad had a good salary, my maintenance grant – what the government gave me to live on – was just £27 per year, not even enough to pay for my season ticket on the Tube from Ruislip to London. In other words, I was still dependent on my parents to keep me. I always felt that the so-called 'means test' was very unjust. Dad had worked hard to achieve success and I could not understand why he should be penalised for this by having to look after me until I was over twenty-one. My two holiday jobs had given me a little spending money but there was no way Marion and I could consider getting married at the end of my course. Quite simply, we hadn't enough money.

Because of my experience the previous summer, I decided to write to Glaxo – to the head of the department where I had worked before – to ask if there were likely to be any permanent vacancies. To my surprise and delight, I was told that a member of the research staff had just resigned and that an application to be his replacement would be favourably considered. God was opening a door! The interview was almost a formality. They had obviously been impressed by my activities a year earlier and gave me the job. I was to stay with Glaxo for sixteen years.

Meanwhile, Marion had moved on from Gerrards Cross to work at a patisserie in Pinner, but now decided that she had had enough of the long hours and low pay associated with this trade. She therefore found a job as a wages clerk with Strand Hotels Ltd, a chain of hotels in London's West End owned by Lyons. This was something of a surprise. Marion would be the first to admit that she is mathematically challenged, yet here she was working in a wages department. However, her main task was writing letters dealing with queries connected with national insurance contributions. The only time she handled any money was when she travelled to each of the hotels once a week to hand out pay packets to some of the staff. She coped well with her new responsibilities and duties and thoroughly enjoyed the 'buzz' of working in central London, surrounded by all the people, the noise and the bright lights. So now we had two reasonable salaries coming in and could plan our wedding and also look for somewhere to live after we were married. We also had more time to pursue all our activities at church than we had known during the previous three years.

Property has never been cheap in the London area and Ruislip was almost certainly beyond our means. But two of our best friends from church, David and Margaret, had recently married and moved to Northolt about three miles away, becoming involved in a Baptist church there. Although slightly closer to London, Northolt had a somewhat rural feel about it in 1962. There were fields, a pretty village green with a quaint parish church and even a public house with a thatched roof. I think that it was only the second or third property we looked at that we decided was just right for us and we agreed to go ahead and buy it. This in itself was remarkable; many people look at dozens of houses before they find the right one.

93 Eastcote Lane was a ground floor maisonette just 150 yards from the Baptist church which David and Margaret attended. It looked out on an avenue of elm trees with the entrance to a park immediately across the road. It was just six minutes' walk to the Underground station from where it was only one stop to Greenford for Glaxo, and twenty-five minutes to Marble Arch for Marion. It had a light and roomy lounge at the front, a reasonable sized bedroom, a small second bedroom that we planned to use as a dining room and of course a kitchen and bathroom, which both seemed adequate. The price was just £3,000 – ridiculous by today's standards but still plenty of money in those days. My parents generously agreed to loan us £500 to go with the equal amount we had saved and we managed to arrange a mortgage for the remaining £2,000. We were in business! We then had the pleasure of visiting all the furniture shops in the area (there were about four in Harrow town centre, all of which have since closed down) choosing dining room and lounge suites, a bed, wardrobes, carpets, curtains and so on. We couldn't afford top quality goods, but we did well. Our bedroom furniture, our dining table and

chairs and our bookcase are still going strong after forty-three years. Things are not made to last like that today! Our only problem was that the maisonette would not be vacant until a month or more after our wedding date. Again, Mum and Dad came to the rescue and invited us to live with them for a few weeks after we returned from honeymoon.

Our wedding took place at 3 p.m. on Saturday 14 July 1962 at Ruislip Baptist Church where we were so committed. The service was conducted by our then minister, Reverend Arthur Thompson. Marion's bridesmaids were Judy, her next door neighbour but one, and Sylvia, one of our closest friends from YPF. I would have liked John to be my best man, but he had upset some people at the church and was under a bit of a cloud at the time. So I opted for Martin, another close friend from YPF. As Marion and her father arrived at the church and some photos were being taken, big spots of rain started to fall and as the service got under way, there was quite a thunderstorm; we hardly noticed. We had determined that we were going to savour every moment, every word, every hymn and above all, enjoy the occasion to the full. I think we did. The church was packed – probably a reflection of Marion's popularity as much as anything – but all our friends were there along with a sprinkling of relatives (mainly from Mum's side of the family, I need hardly add) and Marion's neighbours (an indication of the greater communal spirit encountered south of the railway!). Were we happy? You bet we were!

The message which Arthur Thompson brought to us was based on I Timothy 6:6. 'Godliness with contentment is great gain.'

This verse was to remain firmly in our memory in the years ahead. In many people's eyes, our future lifestyle would be devoid of the very things which supposedly bring happiness, yet those same people are rarely satisfied and frequently searching for more. By comparison, we were indeed to find great contentment in seeking to live for God.

By the time the service was over, the storm had also passed and the sun was shining – a good omen for the future perhaps? Our reception was held at the Cavendish Club in Eastcote – not terribly grand, although today it has been redeveloped and is a delightful venue. But it didn't matter. We had waited four years for this day and it was all about being joined together as one flesh for all our tomorrows. Marion and I were what mattered and the externals were not that important. We were convinced that God had meant us for each other and that God had a plan for our lives, even though as yet, this was unknown territory. We had no idea what the future might hold but we had spoken the words 'for better, for worse, for richer, for poorer, in sickness or in health' and we were absolutely convinced that God was with us and that we could trust Him implicitly. If either of us had entertained any pre-wedding-day doubts, this assurance of God's presence had completely dispelled them and given us the best possible start to a marriage that anyone could ever ask for.

A Home of Our Own

It is as well that we entered married life with such confidence in God, because the first six months were to bring us some shocks and surprises, most of which we would not have chosen.

We spent our honeymoon in Penzance – the first time either of us had been to Cornwall – and then returned to live with my parents for three weeks until our maisonette was ready for occupation. It was probably during this period that our son Martin was conceived. We had waited four years to get married and had looked forward to a time of just enjoying each other in every way. Up until then we had given no thought to having a family. Suddenly we were confronted with a whole new situation. Marion was pregnant and things were going to be very different. Perhaps we were comparatively naïve about sex and contraception. Certainly we had not planned to start a family, but having once got over the initial shock we concluded that this must in some way be part of God's plan and purpose and gradually got used to the idea. It did, however, mean some fundamental changes to our lives. We had anticipated continuing our involvement at Ruislip Baptist Church, but now this did not seem such a good idea. We had no car, and although we could use buses for a while, the time would obviously come when carting a small baby around in this way would be far from ideal. We therefore turned our attention to the church along the road. Knowing David and Margaret meant that we could immediately feel at home and have someone to introduce us to new people, and it was a key step to a new beginning.

Whereas the church in Ruislip had over 300 members, Northolt Park Baptist Church had barely fifty, and the youth group consisted of about a dozen teenagers. It was a whole new ball game, but an exciting one, especially for me. At Ruislip, I had always felt that I was living in Marion's shadow. She was everyone's friend and I wondered if people had accepted me because of my association with her, rather than because they saw or liked anything in me. This was probably a false picture, born of my own insecurities, but at any rate Northolt provided me with a fresh start because people did not know either of us and so could accept us as they found us with no previous history to cloud their judgement.

About a month after we had moved into our new house, we were approached by one of the young men from the church with a request. Ron was an art teacher at the secondary school just down the road, opposite the church. In his mid-twenties, he had just returned from Europe having spent a month or so doing evangelism with an organisation called 'Operation Mobilisation' (OM for short). Today, OM is huge with workers in many nations all over the world and even owns a couple of ocean-going ships which visit ports with Bible exhibitions. But the summer of 1962 had been the start of all that. Teams of students had volunteered to give up their summer holidays and go to France to distribute Christian books and literature house to house in many towns and villages. Ron had been thrilled by what he had experienced and wanted to have a prayer meeting to pray for this work and especially that there would be positive results from the summer mission. He needed a home in which to hold this meeting and asked us if we would be willing. I had never forgotten those wonderful Friday nights at the Paynes' and Marion and I had also been greatly helped and encouraged in another home – that of the parents of my best man Martin. So we had determined that when we had a home of our own, it was going to be an open home; a place where folk could feel welcome, and find warmth, friendship and hospitality. Here was an opportunity to make just such a start – so we said yes. What we had not realised at the time was that this was not to be a one-off meeting – Ron's intention was to hold a regular weekly gathering. We went along with that too!

But colder autumn evenings soon arrived. We had no central heating and as we were both at work during the day, could not switch on our electric fire until we got home. This meant that the house was still pretty cold for the meeting. Ron overcame the problem by bringing along a portable oil-burning heater which warmed up the lounge very rapidly. One evening, he arrived early and so, after lighting the heater, we all retired to the kitchen to finish clearing up after our meal and prepared some coffee mugs for later in the evening. About half an hour later we returned to the lounge to find flames leaping into the air from the oil stove. Evidently, it had been left on too high a setting. Miraculously, nothing had caught fire but the room was enveloped in black smoke and the ceiling and walls had turned the colour of soot!

Needless to say the meeting was cancelled, but the young people who arrived immediately joined in the task of hoovering the upholstery and the carpet, washing down the surfaces and stripping the blackened wallpaper. Within a couple of weeks, with some help from Mum and Dad and a number of others, the room had been completely redecorated and looked as good as new. The great thing to come out of this incident was a community spirit – many people lending a hand to get the task done as if they had a share in our home. We had started to get to know some of the young people in a way that was much more than superficial.

The winter of 1962–'63 was one of the worst on record. In early December, there was a freezing fog which lasted for days on end and then on Christmas morning we awoke to find about four inches of snow on the ground. A real white Christmas sounds wonderful but there was a serious downside: no running water! Evidently the pipes had frozen. Being in a ground-floor maisonette meant that access to the loft was only possible from our upstairs neighbour's flat. Mrs Annabel was a sweet old lady of about seventy and of course she had no water either. I decided to investigate the cause of the problem, but needed some assistance with holding a torch. I could hardly expect Mrs Annabel to clamber into the loft and Marion was four months pregnant. Kathy, a fifteen-year-old from the church who had befriended us, volunteered for the part. The news was not good. A pipe from the cold water tank ran under the eves of the house and had not merely frozen but cracked: to thaw it out would result in a flood! To make matters even worse, Kathy managed to miss her footing and her legs came crashing through Mrs Annabel's kitchen ceiling. Looking back, it is quite amazing that Kathy was unharmed and that our elderly neighbour was more concerned for our young friend than about her ceiling. As the freezing cold weather continued, plumbers were in great demand and it soon became apparent that we were in for a long wait. It eventually transpired that not only had a pipe burst but the tank itself had also cracked and would need replacing. In the short term, all we could do was to empty the water system as best we could and then wait for a thaw before the necessary repairs could be attempted. This meant that we could not light the boiler and our only source of water was the direct mains supply from the kitchen tap. We could boil up some of this in a kettle for washing and washing-up but that was the limit of our hot water. We even had to fill a bucket from this tap for flushing the toilet.

This was the nightmare situation that faced us in the early part of 1963. We hoped it would only be a couple of weeks at most. But the cold worsened. The old Christmas carol came true: 'snow had fallen, snow on snow'. Even the sea froze at several places around the coast of Britain. Eventually the temperature started to rise and the snow began to thaw around 8 March, almost ten weeks after Christmas. By mid March, the tank and pipes had been replaced and thoroughly lagged to make sure that nothing of the kind would happen again. But I vowed that if ever there was another winter like it, we would emigrate, or at least move to Devon or Cornwall, the only parts of Britain which had escaped the severe freeze.

During those ten weeks, life had gone on regardless. We had gone back to our Ruislip homes for baths and folk from the church took pity on us because of our predicament and assisted us with our laundry and other things too: this probably helped us to get more integrated into the church community. Throughout these months we had been getting more and more involved with the teenagers. For some reason, they seemed to like us and would frequently come to visit. Of course, we were not that much older than them and so there was no generation gap. As a result this meant that although they looked up to us, we could also be friends. Within six months of our arrival at Northolt, we were asked by the minister to take on the leadership of the youth club, which meant organising a weekly meeting mainly for church youngsters (some of whom were certainly not Christians) and which included some Bible teaching.

Even before this happened, there had been a youth weekend in the autumn at which a young man from Poplar in the London docklands was the speaker. We had met and heard Doug Barnett a year or two before and been impressed by his zeal for Christ and his natural and unreligious way of communicating with young people. In the intervening period, he had become a full-time evangelist with an organisation called National Young Life Campaign (NYLC). We talked at length to Doug during that weekend and evidently our love and concern for young people came through to him. He suggested that we became members of NYLC and he would then try to give me opportunities to serve God through that organisation. In particular, he recognised my musical gift, which was important because some of the churches he visited had very inadequate pianists/organists which did nothing for the credibility of the missions he was conducting. (Guitars were not known at that time as far as church worship was concerned. The Beatles had just arrived on the scene and many young people were seeking to copy them in the hope of finding fame and fortune. This resulted in the formation of a few Christian bands but in most churches they were frowned upon and it would be a few years before they acquired general acceptance in Christian circles.)

One of the first missions on which I accompanied Doug was in March 1963 at a church in Ilford. For nearly two weeks, I caught the Tube straight after work each evening, travelling across London on the Central Line to play the piano for the meetings and sometimes accompany a solo singer. It was tiring work but a fine experience. At the weekend, Marion agreed that I should stay over at Ilford rather than waste so much time and effort travelling back and forth. I stayed at the minister's house and on the Saturday afternoon, was invited to join him and Doug on a visit to Upton Park to watch West Ham United play football. When I was quite a small boy, my father had taken me to watch Brentford a couple of times but apart from that, I had never been to a professional football match. The atmosphere was electric, the game exciting and West Ham (the local team for both my companions) won. From that day on, I became a life-long supporter of West Ham. This has not been easy. There have been plenty of ups and downs (rather more downs than ups!), but being a supporter of a certain team is a bit like marriage – it should be for better or for worse! I have little time for the supporters of teams like Manchester United who, unless they live in Manchester (it seems to me), choose to support the club simply because they are successful: that's too easy. I sometimes wonder just how many of these fair-weather supporters would change their allegiance if, by some unimaginable turn of events, Manchester United were to find themselves struggling in one of the lower divisions! But I must not get on to one of my hobby horses.

Back home in Northolt, spring was on the way and the next most significant event in our lives was imminent: our baby was nearly due. Marion had a very long-drawn-out labour in the Central Middlesex Hospital lasting nearly three days before our son was born on the morning of 14 May 1963. He was whole and healthy and we chose to call him Martin David Lewis. We liked these names but in particular, Martin had been my best man, David was another special friend and Lewis just sounded right.

Having a baby in the house seemed very strange at first. Because I was at work all day and therefore needed my sleep at night, Marion took on most of the responsibility for Martin in those early days (well, if he woke up in the middle of the night, I couldn't exactly breastfeed him, could I?). I had no experience and no training in handling babies and I suspect that most men at that time felt much the same way I did – that things were best left to the mother. I remember one occasion when I was left in charge for an hour or more on a Saturday while Marion had to go out. Martin decided to cry and try as I might, I could find no reason for this and no way of stopping it. The sense of frustration grew and grew to a point where it just boiled over into a mixture of anger and helplessness. Fortunately, I recognised that on no account could I harm this small, innocent person in my care, but I had to vent my feelings somehow. The nearest inanimate object was a waste-paper bin which was well and truly stamped on, leaving it dented and crumpled beyond repair.

Martin hated going to bed at night. From an early age, he would stand up in his cot, gripping the sides and bounce up and down until the whole cot actually bounced on the floor and moved gradually across the room. The perpetual banging noise was exceedingly irritating, and if we went into his room and laid him down again, it would only be a matter of minutes before the process would start all over again. I think he thought it was a big joke. We eventually learnt to ignore him until he got worn out, or maybe just bored with the whole thing and went off to sleep. Apart from this phase, he was a remarkably trouble-free child. There were no health problems of any kind and he had a very placid temperament. We could leave him with a whole variety of babysitters with confidence that they would not have any trouble and I can never remember him having any kind of tantrum. All of this was a great blessing to us. It meant that we were able to continue with our lives and get involved in all kinds of activities rather than have everything revolve around Martin. This was probably good for Martin too. He was certainly not neglected but he grew up with a broader view of life than might otherwise have been the case.

Throughout the first couple of years, Mum and Dad were a tower of strength. They were always there if we needed anything and although they occasionally indicated that they did not entirely approve of the way we were bringing up our son, they were gracious enough not to force their views on us. In August 1963 when Martin was just three months old, Mum looked after him for several whole days to allow us to have some time out in lieu of a holiday. The following summer, they looked after him for a whole week, while Marion and I enjoyed a break at a guesthouse in Keswick – the Lake District again. We were so grateful. No doubt Marion's parents would have liked to be equally supportive, but her mother had been an invalid for many years and her father therefore had his hands full looking after her as well as working full time as an engineer with the electricity board. Marion's mum died in 1965.

But Martin's arrival soon heralded the next phase in our lives which was truly remarkable, although it resulted from two very simple things. First was the fact that teenagers, especially teenage girls, seem to have an inbuilt fascination with babies and toddlers. The second factor was the topography of Northolt. Ruislip was and is a sprawl, as evidenced by it having no less than five Underground stations (Ruislip, Ruislip Manor, South Ruislip, West Ruislip and Ruislip Gardens). Many of our friends in Ruislip lived far apart and, as we have already mentioned, in areas where property values and therefore lifestyles differed enormously. On the other hand Northolt was more of a community, especially our part. We lived on the edge of a council estate known as the Racecourse Estate because the site had been a pony racing course until about 1952 when redevelopment had commenced. I had visited the area in my early teenage years and can still remember the grandstand and the white railings marking out the perimeter of the course. All the roads on the estate are named after famous racecourses: Newmarket Avenue, Epsom Close and Doncaster Drive, for example. There was a small parade of shops on the estate, an old people's home, a small Anglican church, the Baptist church which we attended and the secondary school immediately opposite. Everything was very compact. Nearly everyone who lived on the estate went to the same school, the same shops and generally travelled from the same station. If you went out, it was highly probable that you would see someone you knew. This sense of community was something new in our experience, although sadly it has largely evaporated over the years as Northolt has expanded with new housing, new roads and an influx of immigrants who tend to maintain their own culture rather than integrate into local life.

Of course, Marion had left work and was now at home all day. In the autumn term of 1963, a couple of the girls from the church youth group who also attended the school entered the sixth form which gave them the privilege of being allowed off the school premises at lunchtime. It was only about two minutes' walk from the school gate to our maisonette and so they started to call on Marion. I have no doubt that the presence of little Martin was an added incentive not to mention the fact that they probably got a free cup of coffee! It was a small beginning but as the weeks and months went by, some of Barbara (yes, another Barbara) and Janet's classmates started to join them on the walk down to 'Marion's', and the whole thing gradually snowballed. Of course, I was at work and only knew what was happening second-hand from Marion's reports. I was absolutely astounded when, on taking a day's holiday (I forget the reason) I found about a dozen sixth-formers wandering around my home as if it was a public place. We have a group photograph which Marion took in the front garden showing no less than eleven of these teenagers and another which even includes a member of the teaching staff. But there was even more to come. Marion's unceasing friendliness meant that more and more of these kids from the school started to think of her as a friend and wanted to visit of their own accord without being brought by anyone. Sometimes, they would call after school, but before long a few started to call in the evenings, a consequence of living close by in the Northolt community to which I have already referred. The prayer meetings had more or less ended when Ron, the art teacher, had married an Indonesian girl he had met in France with OM and moved away to Cambridgeshire. But some of those who had previously come to pray continued to come, presumably because they liked our company and so with young people from church and those from the school we were inundated with visitors almost every night of the week. We had started a visitors' book when we first moved in to our home and it is instructive to look at it today and realise the extent of our involvement. For example, in the four months from June to September 1964, no less than seventy-five different young people from the Northolt area passed through our home and of course many of them came a lot more than once. Fortunately, one or two of the older ones like Barbara showed a degree of maturity in realising that Marion and I rarely had any time to ourselves and it was decided that one day a week should be visitor-free unless there was an emergency. The first week, a notice was pinned to the front door to this effect, but it was incredible how quickly the word got around that Chris and Marion were not to be disturbed on Mondays. We were grateful for our 'day off'.

Why did they come and keep on coming? There were many reasons. For some, it was escape. Home life was relatively unhappy and it was somewhere to go to be away from the influences they didn't like and into an environment that was radically different from what they were used to. For some it was a case of doing what their friends were doing. Teenagers have always responded to peer pressure and want to conform, rather than be left out of things. For others it was a case of looking for genuine friendship. Perhaps some were actually lonely, but for the most part, they just seemed to like us and wanted our friendship. A further group wanted to talk and it was particularly exciting that they were willing to talk about Christianity. We could share and discuss our beliefs and they had genuine questions which we tried to answer. As a result some of them started to come to church and became genuine seekers after God. For others, our home was a place where they could come with special needs. Among these were Brian, whose beautiful girlfriend died suddenly while still in her teens, and Sue, who went on a student expedition across Asia and was involved in a horrific coach crash which killed many of her companions, making headline news and leaving her emotionally scarred.

Whatever the reason, I like to think they found something different in our home even if they failed to recognise what it was. Because we had no television to divert our attention, we were able to give of our time and our emotional energy to each and every one of them. We sought to demonstrate the love of God, who welcomes everybody regardless of their background or what they have done. Because our home was always open, our lives were constantly exposed to scrutiny. Our visitors could see how Marion and I lived, that we treated each other with love, consideration and dignity; that our lifestyle, the way we talked, the books we read, our attitudes to various issues reflected in large measure what we said we believed. Of course we were far from perfect and I think the Lord must have blinded their eyes to some of our howlers, but in the best way we knew how, we were seeking to live out in practical terms the faith we claimed to have.

Generally speaking, we don't know what became of many of these young people. But we dare to believe that at least some of them were touched by what they experienced and maybe this affected the way they lived in later life. Certainly, looking back at the list of names in the visitors' book over the period from 1963 to 1967, there are a significant number who became Christians and who have remained as friends even to the present time. If we had delayed starting a family and Marion had remained at work, it is probable that none of this would have happened. God's ways are past finding out.

Crusades

It was because of my involvement with NYLC that we first heard about Crusade '65.

John Blanchard was born and bred in Guernsey in the Channel Islands. He had been on the staff of NYLC and now felt a burden to hold a mission in that other channel island, Jersey. It was to be a fortnight-long crusade leading up to the Easter weekend and covering the whole of the island. John and our friend Doug Barnett were to lead it but they wanted a team of about a hundred young Christians from mainland Britain to join them to enable the crusade to reach out to every town and village throughout the island.

Marion and I felt very keen to help but there were two problems. Because the holiday year at Glaxo ran from April to April I found I had no holiday entitlement left to me and in any case, what could we do about Martin? Mum and Dad agreed to look after him but that left the problem of time off work. I approached my departmental head, and boldly declared my Christian faith and my conviction that I should take part in the Jersey mission. To my delight and amazement, he agreed to my taking a week of unpaid leave, something that just never happened at Glaxo. The way was clear.

It was an unforgettable experience, the first time we had been involved in such a large-scale Christian mission. Each morning, the whole team assembled together in a hotel in St Helier for a time of preparation and prayer. John Blanchard always gave a short Bible study and then we talked and prayed about the plans for the rest of the day. We had been fortunate to attend Ruislip Baptist Church before our marriage as this had given us an excellent foundation of sound Bible teaching which was to prove so vital for the rest of our lives. However, as we now listened to John Blanchard, we found that he had a quite exceptional gift for making the scriptures come alive and explaining things we had previously found obscure; we could have listened to him all day. Much of the rest of our time was taken up with walking the streets of St Helier talking to people about Christianity and inviting them to the evening meetings. One high spot was the opportunity to preach in an Anglican church for the first time. The place is known as 'the glass church' because of its architecture and is well known on Jersey. In accordance with their traditional practise, they wanted to dress me up in long robes before entering the pulpit, but I wouldn't have any of that! There were some good people among the team members and in particular we befriended a couple who came from near Leicester – a policeman and a nurse. In later years, they were to travel extensively to Eastern Europe taking the gospel of Jesus Christ behind the 'Iron Curtain' at considerable personal danger. We were among those who supported them in this ministry for almost thirty years. The trip to Jersey had been the first time Marion or I had ever flown in an aeroplane and the final memory of Crusade '65 concerns this. For some crazy reason, Jersey airport is built on the highest part of the island and is therefore frequently subject to low cloud and fog. The day of our return flight was no exception and we suffered a delay of about three hours until the fog cleared sufficiently to allow us to take off.

A year later, John and Doug planned a similar large-scale mission. Yes, you've guessed it – Crusade '66. This time it was to be in North Devon based in the town of Barnstaple but covering quite a large rural area. Those who had assisted in Jersey were invited to join the team once again and this year we had plenty of time to make all the arrangements. Martin was to come with us – his first mission at the age of just two years and ten months. The three of us were to be accommodated in a hotel at Heddon's Gate, a very quiet spot on the coast about ten miles from Barnstaple. Two other team members were staying there. Peter Smith, a tall and very gentle man who treated Martin very caringly, was a singer with a wonderful deep bass voice and we were to become good friends. In later years, he worked in a children's home. The other young man was Eddie, who had a car and acted as chauffer for the five of us on our daily trips into Barnstaple.

Now it may have been only ten miles as the crow flies, but the journey was much longer than this. The first part was over unclassified roads – really nothing more than narrow country lanes and even the main roads turned out to have a continuous sequence of sharp bends and steep gradients. This would not have been so bad if it hadn't been for Eddie's mode of driving, which alternated between hard acceleration and drastic breaking, designed to make even the most seasoned car traveller feel very sick! It was a nightmare. We used to open all the windows so as to breathe in as much fresh air as possible. We even suggested to Eddie that he might drive a little bit slower, but I don't think he knew any other way to drive. We all survived the week without actually being car-sick but I think this was more an answer to prayer than anything else.

In a week of hectic activity, one event has stuck in my memory which taught us a biblical truth in the clearest possible way. A team had been invited to visit a youth club in one of the small towns. We started by showing a film which spoke about the death of Christ as the means of salvation. We followed this up with several team members sharing their actual experience of how they had found Christ as their own personal Saviour. There was then a short talk which further reinforced the message already given. Finally, to the accompaniment of light refreshments, we were let loose on the young people with a written questionnaire which posed such questions as 'Why do you think Christ died?' 'What is a Christian?' 'How do you think a person becomes a Christian?' along with more general information. Later, when the results were analysed, it transpired that most of the youngsters had no idea about the three crucial questions. This was hard to believe since we had just spent half an hour explaining the answers in three different ways. No, I don't think they were mentally subnormal; and nor do I think they were being deliberately awkward in their responses. The truth is that a person comes to faith in Christ only by revelation. In other words God has to open their inner eyes for them to understand the message, otherwise it is just as if they are blind and deaf!

Between Crusades '65 and '66, there were two other occasions when I assisted Doug Barnett with missions. In October 1965, we went to Rayners Lane Baptist Church, and in January 1966 we were at Roxeth Green Free Church (where we were to become members some fifteen years down the line). Both churches were local, being less than three miles from Northolt, and in both cases the events were directed at young people and were termed 'coffee bar evangelism'. This style of evangelism was being pioneered by Doug and offered free refreshments and music to entice young people in to chat around the coffee tables and later listen to the gospel message being preached. A spin-off from the Rayners Lane mission was that we got to know a whole new group of young people. Yet again, they seemed to like us and the feeling was mutual. Because the Northolt group was still comparatively small, we felt it might be useful to encourage links between the two groups. After all, we were anxious for our Northolt youngsters to find boyfriends or girlfriends who were Christians and we hoped this would widen their choice. It was a nice idea but in fact no lasting relationships ever came about.

The music at both these missions was provided by one of the first, good Christian rock bands – the 'All One'. This consisted of Bernard, the lead singer and guitarist, Ken on drums, Dave on lead guitar, Rob on bass and Mel on backing vocals and miscellaneous percussion. They were a great bunch of guys and we were to get to know Bernard and Ken very well in the near future. But that story is reserved for the next chapter. There were bigger things coming up in the summer of 1966.

Every football fan knows that England won the World Cup at Wembley on 31 July of that year. They may also remember that it was largely thanks to West Ham United, my team! The goals were scored by Geoff Hurst and Martin Peters and the captain who lifted the trophy was the late Bobby Moore. All three played for 'the Hammers'. Strangely enough, I missed it, although I watched the whole match on film when this was released later that autumn. On the Saturday afternoon in question, I was doing one of the things I loved best – playing cricket. A young man called Cliff who had joined our church was a fine batsman and having discovered my enthusiasm for the game, arranged for me to join the team he played for – Perivale Nomads. (I subsequently played for West Ealing Baptist CC, a team which had originally been a church team but had changed over a period of time so that few of the members then had any connection with that particular church. Years later I played regularly for Ruislip Baptist Church CC, one of my team-mates being the man who had married us – an ageing Arthur Thompson who still did an excellent job as wicketkeeper.) I was not bothered that I missed the England versus Germany game. It was such a pleasure to be playing competitive cricket and to be bowling, batting and fielding for real most Saturdays throughout the summer. On the afternoon of the World Cup, we happened to be fielding, but the batting side had their radios on and whenever a new batsman came to the crease, he would relay to us what was happening and the latest score. Victory came just as we broke for our tea interval and so we celebrated with tea and cakes rather than champagne.

But even before this momentous occasion there had been another event of great significance: Billy Graham had returned to England.

His 1966 crusade was held throughout the month of June at Earls Court in London. Each evening about 14,000 people packed in to the arena and every evening, literally hundreds went to the front when Dr Graham gave his appeal to those who wanted to receive Christ into their lives. These enquirers then went to a separate room where a counsellor spoke with them, prayed with them, left them some literature to read and took down personal details for passing on to local churches for follow-up purposes. There was a choir about 1,000 strong, of which Marion was a member, whilst we both signed up as counsellors. Obviously we couldn't be present every night as we needed to find babysitters and sometimes we would take it in turns to attend. But we just didn't want to miss out: it was so exciting to be there. It wasn't that the preaching was so great, but clearly God was doing something and we were both amazed and thrilled to see so many people becoming Christians. The music was also great – we'd never been part of such a huge congregation. The choir was superb, as were the soloists who sang each evening. One of these, a black American girl by the name of Myrtle Hall, particularly appealed to me and at that time I started to nurse an ambition to be able to accompany her, which of course never happened. But something else did that really was amazing.

The counsellors used to sit together in a block facing the stage but in front of them was an advisor with his back to the stage looking at the congregation. When the appeal was made and individuals started to move out of their seats to go to the front of the auditorium, the advisor would beckon to a particular counsellor to follow someone of a similar age and sex down to the front. He or she would then be the person to be spoken to in the counselling area after the meeting was over. On one particular evening, following this practise, I finished up talking to a young man in his early twenties and in due course came to record his personal details. His name was Dave and then came the surprise. His address was... 56, Eastcote Lane, Northolt!

Of all the people in the auditorium that night, I was talking to someone who I had never seen or met in my life before but who lived in the same road as me – barely 200 metres away! Dave didn't become a Christian that night. He had some unanswered questions that he needed to pursue, but because he lived so near it was easy to keep in touch, to invite him to come along to our church and to our home to talk through some of his problems. Within about three months, he had invited Jesus into his life and was to be a friend for quite a few years until he moved away from the London area. Was it just a huge coincidence? I hardly think so.

Another memorable night during the Crusade was when Cliff Richard, at the time famous only as a chart-topping pop singer, was interviewed on the platform and openly declared that he had become a Christian. On that same evening, Marion had taken Rod, currently the head boy at our local high school, to the meeting and he was one of about 1,000 who went forward to accept Christ into their lives. Nearly everybody knows about Sir Cliff and his powerful Christian testimony the past forty-odd years. Rod too is still on the Christian pathway and a leader in the church he attends, and then there are about 1,000 others... It was quite a night!

1967 brought more exciting times. In the spring, John Blanchard kept up what was becoming an annual tradition with Crusade '67. This time it was a much smaller event in Southall, just a few miles down the road from Northolt. The team consisted of only four people and once again, I was the pianist. Then in the summer, Billy Graham returned to Earls Court for another long crusade. This was virtually a continuation of what had happened the year before, but amazingly, the momentum seemed to increase and the number of enquirers going forward each evening reached staggering proportions.

In September, I was involved in yet another mission, this time in Ireland with Doug Barnett, Gerald Whittingham (previously unknown to me) and Pete Smith, the singer with the deep bass voice. For two weeks we held a programme of extremely varied events at a church called Sydney Hall in Mount Merrion, some six miles from the centre of Dublin. Pete and I stayed in the same home where there was a superb grand piano and on those mornings when we had no engagements, we spent a lot of time together recording a large selection of songs. Accompanying a soloist is quite an art. It is not just playing the notes but seeking to be creative so as to balance the instrument with the voice and also enhance the message of the words. I had learnt a lot with our friend David at Northolt Park, who also had a great voice, and I had frequently accompanied him as far back as the Witness Team days at Ruislip. Sadly, he and his wife Margaret and their two young children had emigrated to Australia in April 1965, but my previous experience now proved invaluable. Pete and I made great music together and I think we were both disappointed that the quality of the tape recording was not good enough for us to have submitted it to a recording company.

This was my first experience of Ireland and it was quite an eye-opener. Ireland was and still is a Catholic country; that is to say, Roman Catholicism is the officially recognised religion. As a consequence, the church had a very strong influence on people's lives. Catholic principles and a Catholic lifestyle were expected and any departure from this was severely frowned upon. In other words, religion was much more strict than in mainland Britain. Sydney Hall was a Protestant church and so we had an uphill task to get people to come to the meetings. But we did find, particularly among the younger people, that they were tired and generally disillusioned with all the strict rules and regulations of Catholicism and were looking for greater freedom. They were quite open to the gospel message, which is not about rules but about a personal relationship with a loving God. We also had a few opportunities to explore. Dublin is a very attractive city, in my view much nicer than our capital city of London. Only a few miles outside Dublin, the countryside begins and much of it is very beautiful. I particularly loved the Wicklow Mountains, but then I would, wouldn't I?

Whilst I was in Ireland, Sandra, one of the girls from the church youth group, had started work at Glaxo in one of the offices. I had flown back on the Sunday night and on my return to work on the Monday, I hoped to see her to find how she had been getting on. Probably about 1,000 employees used the large and airy canteen each day and inevitably there were certain characters who caught the eye. There was one particular girl who, if you were a man, could not possibly have escaped your notice. She was quite tall, slim with pretty features and long chestnut brown hair which fell to below her waist. She had long legs which were accentuated by her high-heeled shoes and ridiculously short mini-skirt (I think it was probably called a micro-mini!). As I scanned the canteen on this particular day, I could hardly believe my eyes. This girl was sitting chatting away to Sandra! In my shyness, I almost felt embarrassed to join them, but join them I did and was soon introduced to Christine as Sandra's youth leader. It transpired that the two of them worked in the same office and were becoming good friends. As we talked, it also came to light that Christine was currently getting involved with a lady who was a Jehovah's Witness. We warned Christine against following in this direction by pointing out that although Jehovah's Witnesses might be very sincere, they were considered to be a sect and were therefore not accepted by the overwhelming majority of Christian churches. We suggested that it might be better if she looked at the real thing before getting sucked into something which was possibly a distortion of the truth. She agreed and we arranged for her to come round to our house one evening to talk about what it meant to be a Christian. Sandra came too and arranged for her brother Chris to pick up Christine in his car from her home in Hanwell. It was a wonderful evening which finished up with Christine praying to ask Jesus Christ into her life as Lord and Saviour. She was soon to become Marion's best friend. In less than a year, she was to marry Chris (Sandra's brother) and they moved into a maisonette just around the corner from ours. Subsequently they were to become missionaries in Portugal, but that's another story for another chapter.

Baptised in the Holy Spirit

While all this was going on in the external world, something else was happening to me on the inside which was probably of greater significance. It all started when I met Bernard and Ken of the band All One.

They were different from any Christians I had ever encountered before. Whenever we met, they would always greet me with the words, 'Are you rejoicing, brother?' In the normal course of events I was not unhappy, although I still retained a measure of shyness and introspection which meant that I was not exactly a bundle of fun; but I couldn't say I was rejoicing! That was a bit over the top. But Ken and Bernie really did seem to be full of an inner peace and outer joy. Moreover, they were able to talk about Jesus and spiritual things as if they were all part of everyday experience. In short, they appeared to be naturally spiritual – or maybe spiritually natural! One of the songs they had written contained the line 'I've got a fire in my bones' and it was obvious that these were not empty words but a true expression of the passion they had for Jesus. To be honest, I found all this rather threatening. I recognised that what I saw in them was what I ought to be; but although by this time I was a deacon at the Baptist church as well as a youth leader and occasionally did a bit of preaching, I knew that I did not match up. Marion felt the same way but whereas I was curious but cautious, she was hungry to find out what it was that they had and which she wanted.

Shortly after the two local missions at which the band had played, Ken and Barbara – the same Barbara who had started the procession of sixth-formers to our house – started courting. One result of this was that Ken, usually accompanied by Bernie, started to make regular visits to our home. They always brought their Bibles with them and gradually we started to learn what it was all about – the Baptism in the Holy Spirit.

Although I had been brought up at Ruislip in what was widely acknowledged to be a church with thoroughly sound teaching, I had never heard anyone preach about this and so I was understandably sceptical at first. But there it was in the scriptures.

This is not a book on theology and so it would be out of place to deal with this in very great detail; but for the sake of any readers who are as puzzled as I was by this teaching, I will try to explain how I gradually came to an understanding of the whole business. Before the day of Pentecost in Acts 1, the disciples of Jesus had been rather fearful, full of doubts and character weaknesses; in fact, pretty much like me. I could relate to them. But after Pentecost in Acts 2, they suddenly become like Super-Men, unbelievably bold, doing the impossible and completely undaunted by every form of opposition. What caused the transformation? Well, Jesus had said that they would be baptised in the Holy Spirit and that this would mean receiving power to enable them to live for God. I knew about this from Sunday school days but what I hadn't realised before was that this kind of thing happened again and again as one worked through the book of Acts. In chapter 8, when some people from Samaria received the gospel message, Peter and John were sent there to lay hands and pray for them to receive the Holy Spirit. When Paul met with Jesus on the road to Damascus, within twenty-four hours a man called Ananias is doing the same thing for Paul. In chapter 10, we have the same pattern with a man called Cornelius and in chapter 18, there was the amazing report of Paul visiting some Christians in Ephesus and immediately asking, 'Did you receive the Holy Spirit when you believed?' It was as if Paul recognised that something essential was missing. All of this really made me sit up and think. If the difference was so obvious, then all the evidence seemed to point to the fact that the problem was promptly put right. This meant that in all probability, all believers in New Testament times were baptised in the Holy Spirit. Perhaps that was why the church at that time seemed so powerful and resilient, so different from the church in the twentieth century. But then again, I thought, maybe that was by design, just to get things started. Once again, I found a scripture that disproved my own argument. Acts 2:38–39 clearly states that the promise of the Holy Spirit which the disciples had enjoyed at Pentecost was '…for you, your children and everyone whom the Lord our God calls to Him.' I had to face it: that included me! There were other things for me to learn too. In New Testament times there were supernatural gifts in use: believers prophesied, spoke in strange tongues, healed the sick, had supernatural knowledge and more besides. It seemed to me that these gifts were inextricably tied up with the experience of Baptism in the Holy Spirit, that they were all part of the package. Once again, I recognised that in my experience, the church at that time was all the weaker for their absence and if they were still available today, then I wanted some of them.

It took a long while and a good many visits from Ken and Bernie for all this to sink in and for me to overcome my scepticism. Perhaps it was because I was a scientist that I had to examine the evidence so carefully before jumping to conclusions. Marion had no such problems. She was eager and had more faith than I did. During the summer of 1967, she had received this blessing from God, was speaking in tongues and had clearly moved up a gear in her Christian life. This was even more threatening for me and the next seven or eight months were actually quite strained as I tried to come to terms with the change in Marion and my own stubbornness and resistance to what was going on. Eventually I was convinced that this was biblically OK, but there was a further problem – my pride. I didn't like to admit to my inadequacies. I prayed that God would baptise me in the Holy Spirit quietly and privately so that I could then move on, while pretending, of course, that it had always been like this. God was having none of it! We were in our own lounge where about a dozen of our young people from church had gathered for a time of prayer, Bernie and Ken were there too, and I felt a desperate urge that this was the time. Was I serious about living for Christ? Then I dare not delay. I asked Bernard to lay hands on me and pray for me, right there in front of some of those who I was supposed to be leading.

It is hard to describe what happened that night. I felt a lightness in my spirit to the extent that I felt I could literally jump for joy. I wanted to shout and sing. It was as if someone had unlocked something in me and set me free to be the person God had always intended me to be. As the weeks and months went by, I became different. Much of the residual insecurity and self-consciousness which had often made me a distinctly moody sort of person was disappearing. I felt secure in the knowledge that God loved me and knew me. Where I had been extremely introverted, I was now much bolder, less afraid to speak to people, and as time went by, human relationships became the very stuff of life for me. I could now truthfully say in response to Ken and Bernie's question, 'Yes, I *am* rejoicing!' Shortly afterwards, I received the gift of tongues and this further added to the sense of freedom I felt: a few weeks earlier I would have been much too embarrassed to admit to such a thing.

The question of 'what next?' now arose. Ken had only one piece of advice: 'Get into a meeting.' We were later to hear of a meeting in a home in Northwood, six miles up the road, but at the time, we could only point out that there wasn't a meeting to get into. But then something else happened. Cliff, my cricketer friend, had elected to train for the Baptist ministry. He phoned us one day to say that he had been baptised in the Spirit at, of all places, the theological college where he was now studying. His advice was the same; that we needed to get into a meeting. A week or so later, Rod and Sandra went away together on a weekend conference and whilst there, they too were baptised in the Holy Spirit. It was all happening. (Rod was the young man who had been converted at the Billy Graham crusade on the same night that Cliff Richard had given his testimony, while Sandra was the girl who still worked at Glaxo. They had been going out for a while and later got married.) Suddenly we had our answer: if five could constitute a meeting, then we were in business.

The five of us started to meet whenever we could find the time, which usually meant about once a fortnight. We had no idea what we should do or what was going to happen but it seemed reasonable to start by praying. We soon learnt that prayer is a two-way communication and we needed some times of silence in which to allow God to speak to us. And He did. We learnt to prophecy – bring messages from God which had direct application into the lives of one or other of us. Sometimes this was embarrassing, as bad things and wrong attitudes were unearthed and then sorted out in repentance and prayer. God was getting rid of much of the rubbish which had accumulated in our lives over the years and telling us to use each other to smooth away our coarse rough edges, rather like stones rubbing together in the sea. We came to realise that the power that we had received was to help us to clean up our act as well as to serve God more effectively. We were also being taught what it really meant to be 'the body of Christ'. Each one of us could contribute to what was happening and each one was necessary if God was to accomplish anything amongst us.

This was an exciting time. Rumours spread quickly and some of our young people started to ask questions. 'What is baptism in the Holy Spirit?' Perhaps they had their spies out, but word soon got around that the five of us were meeting together and it was only a matter of months before others asked if they could join us. This meant that the meetings started to include some Bible study as we sought to explain the scriptural basis of what we had come to believe and experience. Before long, quite a few others had entered into the same experience and we were all meeting regularly on Thursday evenings, but with no idea where this would lead us in the coming years.

It was around this time that we encountered Norman. He was a young man from the north-east with a strong Geordie accent. He was a student at one of the smaller colleges which make up the University of London and he was in difficulty. His sister was at college with one of the girls from Eliots Green School (our grammar school up the road) who had come to know us well and it was in the course of conversation between these two young women that our names came up. It was suggested that maybe we could help him. And so it was that Norman turned up on our doorstep one evening and started to talk.

That is a bit of an understatement. He would talk for hours on end and we would listen and occasionally make a comment. He became a regular visitor, often coming two or three nights a week and usually staying until midnight before catching the last Tube train back to London. Sometimes he missed the train and would spend the night on our sofa. His problems were emotional, intellectual and psychological. Probably today we would recognise some of the symptoms as clinical depression, but we were naïve although we were also learning all the time. We had enough faith to believe that Norman needed God and that God could solve his problems and bring about the healing he needed. And after months of late nights, exhausting conversations and much prayer, Norman did come to faith in Christ and his problems gradually resolved themselves. He was a new person and became a good friend, a regular at our church, getting involved and even going out with one of the girls for a time. A few years later he returned to his native Teesside, married a local lass and we three Sharps had the joy of attending his wedding. I especially remember Martin looking unbelievably smart in a new jacket and long trousers bought especially for the occasion. Nearly forty years on, Norman and his wife are still there and active in their local church; we hear from them every Christmas. God is good!

Meanwhile, Martin had been growing up, the way kids do. His bedroom was small and as he got older and collected more toys, it was clearly inadequate for his requirements. I had been doing well at Glaxo and with my steadily increasing salary the time seemed right to consider moving to a bigger house. But therein lay a problem. As I have already explained, we lived on the edge of a council estate and so we assumed there was no point in looking there. There were a few other roads around but these contained either bungalows little bigger than our maisonette or standard type houses with two reception rooms. What was wrong with that? you might ask. Simply that we were aware that the meetings in our house were expanding and we considered it expedient to have a single large living room to accommodate them. Because of our involvement at Northolt Park Baptist Church, there was no way we would even think of moving away from the area and so, after a fruitless search over some months, we resigned ourselves to staying put. All we could do was to make improvements and so we had new double-glazed windows fitted at the front of the maisonette.

Then in February 1969, I had an attack of mumps. The illness I should have contracted from my sister as a small child had finally caught up with me after nearly thirty years. For almost the first time ever, I had to take sick leave – two weeks off work. By the Wednesday of the second week, I considered that I was no longer contagious so we invited a young couple for a meal. Kathy, who had fallen through the ceiling in the big freeze of 1963, was now married but she and her husband were living with her parents. However, that afternoon they had been out house-hunting. As they arrived, they quipped, 'Do you want to buy a house?' They had seen one on the council estate which they felt might be just what we wanted. We had not realised that some of the council houses had been purchased outright by their tenants and were now available as freehold properties. This particular house was exactly that, and although Kathy and her husband had been very enthusiastic about it, they had decided it was not suitable for them because it had no garage for their car. We, on the other hand, did not possess a car.

On the Thursday morning, we wandered down to the estate agent to get some details and make an appointment to look at it. Having resigned ourselves to staying where we were, we were not very optimistic, imagining that Kathy had possibly exaggerated. Indeed if I had not been off work at the time, it is very unlikely that we would have bothered.

That afternoon, we went to look at 3 Doncaster Drive. We were amazed. The selling point was the L-shaped lounge, a really big room perfect for meetings. Other things were all bonuses. The kitchen was bigger than the kitchens of any of our friends and had fitted units, including a built-in eye-level oven (both quite unusual at that time). There was a downstairs toilet (which would save all our visitors having to go up and down). The bedrooms were all good sizes; Martin would have plenty of room for all his toys, and even the smallest room could serve as a guest room or study. All three bedrooms had built-in wardrobes and there were other extras that we could not have expected. The owner was obviously a keen DIY expert and he had built shelves in various useful places, a small cupboard under the stairs and a large veranda at the back of the house so that washing could be hung out to dry even if it was raining. We simply could not believe our good fortune!

We returned home and that evening invited our usual Thursday evening group to pray with us about this exciting new development. The overwhelming view was that we should go ahead. We even received a prophetic word saying that 'the glory of the latter house would exceed that of the former'. In view of all that had happened at 93, this was quite a promise, but one that was to be wonderfully fulfilled. On the Saturday morning we made an offer on the house, which was promptly accepted. On Monday we therefore returned to the estate agent to ask him to put our maisonette up for sale. This was done and within a couple of days folk were coming to view. It was almost heartbreaking to hear a prospective buyer discussing with his wife how they would make various alterations, particularly when they said they would build a bar in the lounge! However, they made an offer which we accepted and incredibly, we had bought and sold property in just one week. The price we were to pay for our new home was £6,100. At the time of writing it is valued at about £240,000. Now that's inflation!

We later discovered that the owner had in fact sold the house some six months previously for £6,250 but the sale had fallen through. We really felt that God had kept it especially for us as part of His plan for our lives.

The next three months were exciting as we planned for our move. Because we would have more rooms and more space, we needed to buy extra furniture and fittings. Apart from that, everything went remarkably smoothly. I measured up each of the rooms and then made scale drawings of them. I also measured all our furniture and cut out shapes in cardboard corresponding to each item and on the same scale. It was then easy to shuffle the pieces of cardboard around to work out the best arrangement to fit everything in. Consequently, on the day of the move, we knew exactly where each item was to go. The smaller items went into tea-chests, most of which we packed ourselves, and these were labelled according to which room they needed to be left in. It was all so easy, I don't know why people claim moving house is so difficult.

On the day of the move in late May, Mum and Dad helped us with small and light items, transporting them in their car. The distance involved was only about 300 metres. We arranged that a carpet fitter should come and lay the new lounge carpet in the morning before the removal lorry arrived later with the large items of furniture. As the morning progressed, I looked in to see how the carpet fitter was getting on. I was really pleased with the appearance and said so. He seemed surprised at this and explained that because carpets were usually selected from small samples in the showroom, customers frequently remarked on seeing them laid in a room that they didn't think the carpet would look like that. About two hours later, Marion arrived, having spent the morning cleaning up at our old house. She drifted into the lounge and promptly remarked, 'Oh, I didn't think it would look like that!' But we liked it anyway and it lasted thirty-six years.

Our first visitors were two fourteen-year-olds from the church youth group, Sue and Carol, who came round after school and helped with ironing and putting up curtains. By the end of the day, nearly everything was shipshape and we felt very comfortable in our new home.

As things turned out, we were going to need every inch of space in the new house. Indeed, we had no idea what God had in store for us.

Later that year, my father retired early from the Autotype Company and he and Mum sold up the family home in Ruislip and moved to Seaford on the Sussex coast. It was a surprise move, leaving all the familiar people and places after almost thirty-five years. But it turned out well. They bought a delightful bungalow with a view of the Downs and joined a lively church where they made a lot of new friends. It seemed to be one of the best things they could have done and we were pleased that they had found a new lease of life despite their advancing years. Of course, we missed having them close to hand but in the coming years we spent quite a few holidays with them exploring the lovely Sussex countryside. A few years later on one of these trips, we were to meet someone who was to be of great help to us at a time of crisis; once again God seemed to be a step ahead in laying plans for our future.

Into the Seventies

The move to 3 Doncaster Drive was to herald the most thrilling yet demanding decade of our lives. If what had gone before was exciting, the next ten years were to far exceed that, whilst bringing about a great many changes, some of which were to be rather frightening.

At this time, there were two principal strands to our lives which were nevertheless closely interwoven, the first being our work at the Baptist church. During the sixties, there had been a number of changes to the youth work. When we took over as youth leaders in 1963, there was just a weekly youth club with a short 'God slot' or epilogue, at which we would try to present some facet of Christian teaching. As time went by, an increasing number of unchurched youngsters had come in to the club and discipline had become a major problem. Trying to control this unruly element occupied most of our time and the church kids, some of whom were Christians and who wanted to learn and make progress in their faith, were in danger of being neglected. Eventually, a decision was taken to close the club down altogether and concentrate for a while on building up the faith of those who wanted to come to a prayer and Bible study evening, similar to that which we had been brought up in at YPF in Ruislip. Inevitably, this meant starting with a very small group, but in the long term, the strategy worked. During this period, there was a steady increase in the number of Christians attending, most of them coming from the school as a result of their contact with us in our home. It meant that when we eventually reopened the club, we had a nucleus of strong Christians to set the tone and atmosphere. We even created a rule that the number of young professing Christians compared to those who did not profess any faith had to exceed a certain ratio at all times. This meant a constant check being kept on new members. I cannot imagine such a thing being allowed in today's world but once again, it worked.

As a result, by late 1969 we had a thriving youth project on our hands. Our responsibilities had been enlarged so that we were now known as leaders of the church's Youth Department, which meant we were trusted to do almost anything we pleased. Club night had become a balanced mixture of recreation and more spiritual activities. We arranged an evening for parents to talk about our vision for their children; we had a youth choir to sing at special church events; we arranged rambles and outings at bank holidays. And the numbers steadily grew.

The new decade seemed like a good time to move forward once again and on 1 January 1970, we sent a letter to all our young people entitled 'Into the Seventies' in which we outlined the basic elements that we considered essential for the ongoing work of the department. Let me quote from that document:

> We believe that the aim of the Youth Department should be fourfold.
>
> 1. Fellowship – not just being together but building relationships in which Jesus is central. We must give ourselves to one another in service ... learn to share our experiences, learning from and helping each other. We must pray together and above all, we must come to love each other...
>
> 2. Growth – we must make spiritual growth unto godliness and we therefore need to be well grounded in God's word ... everyone should be given the opportunity to minister ... spiritual gifts for building up the whole group.
>
> 3. Recreation – God knows that as young people we want to 'let off steam' and enjoy ourselves. This is natural and good, provided we are neither selfish nor allow recreation to take too large a place in our lives to the exclusion of more important things.
>
> 4. Evangelism – the essential task of the church is to tell others the gospel of Jesus Christ. We must endeavour to do this by every means open to us. Above all, it is our hope that in fulfilling the three aims above, we shall create a fellowship which is so Christ-centred, that when we invite strangers to come in, they will sense His presence and see their need of Him.

The letter continued by outlining new plans for the administration of the department. We had appointed a committee with about seven members, each of whom had responsibility for a particular aspect of the work. We had realised that delegation is vital if leaders are not to burn themselves out and that taking real responsibility is an important step towards training future leaders.

It will be apparent from this letter that we were setting very high ideals. Some of these had been formulated in our minds because of the second strand of our work – the Thursday evening meetings. It was here that we were learning new values and ideas and we wanted to apply them to the larger scenario: but we had to do so with some caution. At this time, baptism in the Holy Spirit, speaking in tongues and the other things I have written about were still viewed with grave suspicion by many traditional churches and that included Northolt Park Baptist (NPBC). More and more youth department members were joining us on Thursday nights but we had to regard this as something quite separate and independent from anything we did at the church and this was not always easy.

However, there was one more event for which we were responsible at NPBC and which proved a great success. I had read a book called *The Davidson Affair* by Stuart Jackman in which the events surrounding the first Easter are presented in a modern setting as seen through the eyes of a television correspondent. The idea was brilliant and it seemed to me that this would be a good way of presenting the message of the resurrection of Jesus. I set about dramatising the book to form a play lasting about an hour and a half. Having never tackled anything like this before, I have to say that I was delighted with the result. One of the older men in the church, Jack Mitchell, who was a natural when it came to acting, was very enthusiastic about it and together we set about producing the play for public performances in the church. Many of the young people proved to be brilliant actors and actresses whilst Jack and I played the two major roles of the correspondent and his office chief. Remember that I had declined to join the Guild at Latymer and so had never done any acting; yet here I was, taking a leading role. Here was very clear evidence that my experience of the Holy Spirit had released me from much of my self-consciousness.

One particular incident sticks in the memory. Phil played the part of Thomas, one of Jesus' disciples, and in one scene he was meant to describe one of the healing miracles performed by his master in the words, 'There'd be a blind beggar by the synagogue, propped up against the wall, covered in flies and whining for a handout with a tin mug in his fist.'

In one rehearsal, what actually came out was that the beggar had a tin fist in his mug. The tense atmosphere of the scene was broken and we all fell about laughing, much to Phil's embarrassment.

When our new friend Norman had fully recovered, he moved to Harrow and regularly attended NPBC. In late 1969, he hired a couple of cottages in the Yorkshire village of Thwaite in Swaledale and persuaded about twenty of us to go on holiday there together. It was a great success and so, in the following year, Marion and I decided to be very brave and organise a holiday under the umbrella of the Youth Department. During the sixties, we had been on quite a number of holidays organised by NYLC, so we had plenty of ideas about what to do and how to do it. We elected to go to a place we already knew well, the hostel at Ambleside in the Lake District where we had first fallen in love back in 1958. We planned to go walking most days either in the mountains or by the lakes and we invited a Baptist minister friend to join us to lead times of worship and Bible study each morning and evening. Amazingly more than fifty young people booked in, including a few couples who had been recently married and a few non-Christians who had been invited by friends within the group. In theory it should have been a tremendous week, but in practise it only served to show how far short we fell in realising our ideals of Christian love and fellowship.

From the start, we had arguments. Those who were more energetic wanted to climb the highest mountain peaks in the area and needed one of our hired minibuses to get them to their starting point. Most of the girls wanted a more relaxing time – perhaps a tour of the lakes or a shopping expedition. The poor drivers were caught in the middle. It seemed that no one wanted to give way for the sake of others except very grudgingly or under pressure from me. It was a case of selfishness through and through and one or two, having been unable to get their own way, showed their displeasure with either biting, caustic remarks or a fit of the sulks. The Lake District weather was typically perverse and during several very wet days, people became bored and irritable and vented their feelings on others who were simply minding their own business. Some of the married or engaged couples had rows. A group of about a dozen spent every available minute playing cards and they along with some others insisted on staying up late into the night, making a lot of noise without any consideration for those who were trying to get to sleep, including the hostel warden and her family. In the midst of all this, my minister friend was faithfully expounding the scriptures in a way that was really inspiring. Yes, the meetings were great, but we had compartmentalised the holiday into spiritual and secular. In the meetings we were as Christian as anyone could desire, but the rest of the time our behaviour denied what we said we believed. It was not surprising that the 'unbelievers' among our number showed little interest in what they heard and rapidly disappeared from the scene once we got home.

A year later, in July 1971, we tried again. This time the group was much smaller, twenty-nine in all, and we hired two cottages at Obley in the wilds of Shropshire. They were not large cottages, but the upstairs rooms had been packed tight with beds to enable fifteen to sleep in one and ten in the other. The remainder of our party were to be housed in a four-berth caravan parked at the rear of the larger cottage. There was no room for wardrobes and so everyone literally had to live out of a suitcase; there was no sense of privacy at all. There were a couple of other houses and a farm in the vicinity but that was all. The nearest village with shops or a pub was a three and a half mile drive along a narrow country lane. Cooking was by means of an Aga – a solid fuel cooker – and water was pumped from a nearby spring and passed through filters before we could drink it. There was no mains gas. The buildings were of stone construction, old, extremely dirty and full of dust and cobwebs: all of this I had known in advance. The previous February, before making the booking, I had visited the place and seen for myself what a primitive set-up it was. I had explained my findings to the group and done my best to dissuade them from choosing this particular site, but everyone was convinced that it would be fun! Not until the party actually arrived did they realise that I had not been exaggerating. Quite a number felt like taking the first train home. A few of the girls almost wept. But we determined to stick it out and make a success of it. It proved to be an unforgettable experience.

From the start everyone set about making the place more habitable. We had arranged washing-up and cleaning rotas, but these were immediately forgotten as everyone lent a hand where it was most needed. Out came the carpet sweeper and brooms. People were soon wielding dishcloths or potato peelers, whilst others went out gathering flowers from the hedgerows to put into vases to brighten the cottages. No one complained and the spirit of cooperation was such that by the time we had cleared away the dishes from our first meal and gathered for our first evening meeting, we all felt very attached to our new home. In the space of a few hours, we had come to see that people matter more than things; that the presence of nearly thirty Christians all working together and acting with unselfish love could transform the most forbidding surroundings into a place where it was good to be. But that was just the beginning!

Twenty-four hours later, disaster struck in the form of sickness. Since Marion was doing the cooking and I had complete confidence in her, I am convinced that it was nothing to do with the food that we had eaten. I suspect that some micro-organism eluded the filters and got into our water supply. Whatever the reason, the result was horrendous. As we sat together in the lounge of the larger cottage, one after another made a beeline for the row of toilets at the top of the stairs and were violently sick. A few didn't make it in time – with unpleasant consequences. I shall never forget Adrian, a normally very quiet and studious young man, fighting the symptoms for a while before haring up the stairs with the words, 'Hell's bells and buckets of blood!'

Looking back we can laugh, but at the time it was definitely not funny. About half our number were affected and a few others, including me, felt slightly unwell. It is bad enough being so ill at any time, but when you are away from the comfort of home and the security of family and know that there is no way a doctor is going to be found until the next morning, everything becomes much worse. But the response of the group was amazing. Those who felt reasonably well sought to bring comfort to the rest by praying with them or at the least by putting an affectionate arm around them. Some read aloud, in relays, words of reassurance from the scriptures – mainly from Psalms. Still other attended to the less pleasant tasks of mopping and cleaning up where folk had vomited and disinfecting those areas of floor or carpet. Most of us stayed up all night to meet the needs of those who were still feeling or being sick. All this was done without any coercion; it was seemingly motivated by love for one another.

By the morning almost everyone was back to normal and the services required of the local doctor were minimal. But what had happened affected us for the rest of the week. When people have seen you at your worst and you have lost all sense of decorum, there is no point in trying to pretend any more. You can be yourself, open and honest, and it is this condition which makes for real communal life; we found this to be the case, at least. As the week progressed, the marks of Christian love continued to be seen. Two lads got up early each morning and nearly choked to death trying to light the Aga so that it could be used to cook breakfast. There was a scraggy mongrel from the farm up the road who raided our dustbins at night and left the contents strewn across the road. Several of the fellows cheerfully cleared up this mess day after day and without complaint. The rotas continued to be ignored, and the meetings were refreshing, dovetailing completely naturally into all our other activities. Whether worshipping, eating, doing household chores or walking and enjoying the beauties of the countryside, we were learning to be a company of God's children living as God intended us to – in love.

Incidentally, the weather throughout this week was wonderful so that we were even able to have some of our meetings out of doors. My final memory of the holiday relates to our last night. Because we were miles from any streetlights, the darkness was really intense and the stars in their millions a fantastic sight. But as we watched, for almost half an hour there were flickering lights in the sky as if a barrage of laser beams were being directed at it. We heard no thunder, but we guessed that a storm was probably brewing many miles away and we were seeing some lightning flashes reflected in some way in the upper atmosphere. Whatever it was, it was beautiful; as if God was giving us a firework display to celebrate what we had experienced.

The seventies marked all sorts of changes on the national scene. On 14 February 1971, the United Kingdom changed to decimal currency: no longer did we have twelve pennies to the shilling and twenty shillings to the pound. It was now one hundred new pence to the pound – pure and simple. The mathematics was now so much easier but for many citizens, it was quite a problem: old habits are hard to break. Fashion-wise, there were also changes. The sixties had been the era of the miniskirt. Suddenly, 'minis' were out and the 'maxi' was in. Young women and older ones too were to be seen in long, ankle-length dresses and skirts, some of which were exquisitely pretty and very feminine. They were not just for special occasions either but worn even to work and certainly to church. It is sad that we have now reverted to casual clothes which do not have anything like the same charm or beauty. Other changes were for the worse. The so-called Swinging Sixties had been a time of moral decline. The advent of the contraceptive pill had resulted in casual sex becoming acceptable and experimentation with mind-expanding drugs was also gaining popularity, following the publicity given to them by the Beatles and other pop groups. It was a time when previous standards of behaviour went out of the window and an 'anything goes' mentality became prevalent.

A Christian man called Peter Hill returned to Britain around 1970 after living for nearly a decade in India. He was both amazed and horrified by the changes which had occurred in our society while he had been abroad. With help and advice from a few church leaders, he decided to do something about it and the result was the 'Festival of Light' in September 1971. It was a series of events designed to make a public stand against the darkness and depravity permeating every area of British life but also to be a positive declaration for truth, purity and light. On Sunday 19 September, Christians throughout the country were called to a day of prayer for a spiritual awakening in the nation and for moral standards to be reinstated: such a day of prayer had not happened since the bleakest days of the Second World War. Then on the following Thursday night, beacons – huge bonfires – were lit at key sites across the country, reminiscent of the days in the sixteenth century when such an action had been used to warn the nation of the threat of an invasion. Finally on Saturday 25, there was a huge rally in Trafalgar Square when thousands met together to read and present a proclamation to the government and to pray for the nation. This was followed by a festival of music in Hyde Park with well-known artists like Cliff Richard taking part. Groups carried banners with the names of their towns from every corner of the country. Other banners declared 'Moral Pollution needs a Solution' and still others that stated Jesus Christ was that solution.

It was a remarkable sequence of events. It had all started with one man who was a complete nobody but his efforts had awakened Christians throughout the country to realise that all things are possible with God and that ordinary people can make a difference. For our part, we joined in the lighting of a beacon on Horsenden Hill, a couple of miles from Northolt, and we were in London for the main festival. We had never encountered anything like it and it was a great encouragement to believe that although we might be up against strong forces of evil, we could still stand up and be counted. The festival was repeated in 1972 with even greater support and it was possibly the forerunner of a similar movement in the eighties and nineties when millions of Christians simultaneously 'marched for Jesus' in cities all over the world.

The early years of the seventies were also a time when some of the young people we had encountered and worked with since moving to Northolt decided to get married.

One particular couple – Pam and Martin – did not have much money and so we helped them to organise their wedding reception 'on the cheap'. Marion's experience working in the catering trade before our marriage meant that she now regularly made wedding cakes for friends; but preparing a sit-down meal for about eighty people was a new challenge. However, with help from a good number of the young people, the task was successfully accomplished and at a fraction of the normal cost. Indeed, we even considered the possibility of doing this sort of thing on a regular basis to make a little money but it wasn't really a very practical idea. Subsequently, Pam and Martin became the first people to stay in our new house. Like us some eight years earlier, the property they were buying wasn't ready on time and so they moved in with us for about a month. It wasn't a problem. Pam was another Glaxo employee and so she was able to give me a lift to work in her car each morning, and we all got on well together. Their staying with us prompted us to buy our first refrigerator because we needed to keep more food in the house to feed the extra mouths. (Yes, amazing as it may seem, we had managed without this everyday commodity until July 1970! Bear in mind also that we did not have a car or a television, yet we coped with life perfectly well and never felt hard done by or deprived; our life had always been rich, exciting and rewarding, as I hope I have shown.)

Meanwhile, our Thursday night meetings were becoming more widely known. Young people came from all over Northolt. Their names fill page after page in our visitors' book but sadly, we have since forgotten who many of them were. Possibly some were associated with the school or were friends of members of the youth group. Many of them only came once or twice, probably out of curiosity, but their names are there and occasionally in more recent years, we run into someone who tells us that they came to a meeting in our lounge years before. There were others, however, who started to come from local and not so local churches. During 1971, about fifteen young people from Greenford Baptist Church turned up on various Thursdays. Some of them were quite regular. A similar situation occurred with our old church – Ruislip Baptist – and we particularly remember praying with one young man for him to receive the baptism of the Holy Spirit. Today, he is a bishop in the Church of England with a high media profile! Another group of frequent visitors came from St James's Anglican Church in Alperton. One of those young men subsequently went to work full time with OM (Operation Mobilisation) and thirty years on, is one of their leading lights with the official title 'International Minister at Large'.

For some years, I myself had been preaching spasmodically at Emmanuel Church in Hounslow. On one occasion, I was daring enough to speak about the baptism in the Spirit and after the service, Ruth, the organist, told me that she had received this blessing but felt very isolated as no one else in her church understood this teaching. I invited her to join us on a Thursday evening and before long, two or three others from her church also started to come. A similar thing happened at a church in Hanworth, near to Heathrow Airport, resulting in two more fairly regular visitors. We were also having an impact close to home among our new neighbours. Teenagers from three neighbouring homes in Doncaster Drive all became regulars both at NPBC and on Thursday nights. Perhaps most surprising of all was the arrival of a young Canadian couple, Peter and Agnes Braun, who were studying at London Bible College about five miles down the road. Whilst studying there, Agnes gave birth to their first child David, and because they were unable to find suitable accommodation, they came to live with us for a couple of months. We became good friends. They subsequently returned to Canada where Peter was ordained a minister and we have remained in contact and still communicate regularly with the family by email. Because David spent the first couple of months of his life under our roof, he looks upon us almost as second parents and came to stay for a while in 1996 and again in 2003 with his lovely new wife, Svea. They too are working full time for God, mainly among the young people in the church of which Peter is the pastor.

In the summer of 1972, in addition to another fellowship holiday, this time in South Wales, Marion and I had a week together in the Isle of Wight, staying at a guesthouse at St Lawrence near Ventnor. The intention was to be on our own for a change but as it turned out, there were a few teenagers staying there with their families and almost inevitably, we were drawn to them and they to us. Lizzie from Sussex was a bit of a rebel but we built up a really good relationship in just a few days and remained in correspondence with her for some years, during which time she became more settled in her faith. Another girl, also named Liz, was probably not a Christian, but the time we spent together during that week was sufficient for her to want to make the journey from Finchley to Northolt on quite a few Thursdays during the coming years and we believe she became a Christian.

But things were coming to a head. With the knowledge about Thursday nights spreading far and wide, it was inevitable that sooner or later word would get back to the minister and church officers at NPBC. What subsequently happened is sad to relate and merely illustrates how easily we can be confused by things we don't understand. The news that reached them was that people spoke in tongues at our meetings. This was actually a very small part of the meetings, but for them it was too much. Some had formed an idea that such behaviour could only result from falling into some kind of trance and they imagined that we had people rolling around on the floor and frothing at the mouth, all of which was completely untrue. Almost overnight, everything changed. Instead of 'doing a grand job with the young people', we were 'leading them into error'. In fact, nothing had changed; it was merely false impressions which caused the problem. Immediately, restrictions were put on me and Marion as to what we could and could not do in the life of the church, most of which were completely illogical. Finally, it was said at a church business meeting that this was a Baptist church and if people didn't like the Baptist way of doing things perhaps they should go elsewhere. This statement was so pointed and obviously aimed at us that after much prayer and discussion with people like Ken and Bernie, whose advice we sought, we felt there was no real alternative but to resign our membership and leave NPBC. It was not an easy decision to make. We had no desire to cause a split there and made it clear to the Thursday night regulars who were also at NPBC that because we had left, it didn't mean they had to. We also faced criticism from folk like my parents who just couldn't understand why we were leaving the church.

The real reason can be summed up in the words of Jesus in Matthew 9:17: 'You can't put new wine in old wineskins.' The experience of the Holy Spirit which we had enjoyed was something new and in order to express the new quality of life that we had discovered we needed a new format or pattern of church life. We had seen the need for a deeper fellowship based on loving relationships. We had seen the need to use the gifts of the Spirit to build each other up and that this also meant that everyone had a part to play rather than one person being the minister. We had discovered a new dimension and enthusiasm in worship which made the traditional Sunday hymns and prayers seem dull indeed by comparison. And there were other things too. It was tough, being misunderstood and almost persecuted for what we believed; but we looked at the history of the Christian church and saw that this was nothing new. Many times over the centuries, when God had started to do something new, the establishment had rejected new ideas and tried to get rid of those who were fermenting change. We were in good company, but still – we hoped we wouldn't actually finish up as martyrs!

The Northolt Fellowship

It is one thing holding a meeting in your home: it is quite another being responsible for the spiritual growth and well-being of nearly fifty adults. But that was the situation which confronted me in July 1973 after we had made our official departure from NPBC. In spite of our warnings, the overwhelming majority of the young people there decided they wanted to come with us – more, I believe, out of a sense of loyalty and commitment to me and Marion than from any real understanding of what the future might hold. Suddenly, we were an independent body of Christians – in other words a church – and the first thing we needed was a name. 'The Northolt Fellowship' showed a marked lack of imagination but it was simple and it stuck.

As a next step, those from other places who had been in fairly regular attendance on Thursday nights had to make a decision as to where their commitment lay – in their existing churches or at the Northolt Fellowship. We never had a membership roll as such, but various folk made it clear that as far as they were concerned, Northolt was now their home church and they were looking to me as their pastor and leader. As someone with no formal training as either pastor or church leader, this could have been a frightening and daunting prospect but for things that had happened during the previous twelve months.

At a youth weekend at NPBC, we had started to share with the speaker about the developing problems between us and the church due to our experience of the Holy Spirit. He was sympathetic and told us of someone living in Seaford who might be of help to us. The following spring, while spending a weekend with Mum and Dad, we tracked down the person concerned who was the leader of a growing church in Vale Road. Mum and Dad were members at the local Baptist church – a friendly place – and we normally accompanied them to the service on a Sunday morning. However, on this occasion we made our apologies to Mum and

Dad and went to Vale Road, where we found lively worship, spiritual gifts and lots of people taking part – in fact very like a larger version of Thursday nights at our house. We had several talks with the pastor about our situation and the impending break with NPBC. He seemed to understand our predicament very well and went further to make a suggestion which was to have a tremendous impact on our lives for years to come. He told us that there were other groups like ours at Northolt and some of the leaders of these groups met together on a regular basis at the Bonnington Hotel in London for worship, teaching, fellowship and general encouragement. He thought I would find these meetings invaluable and invited me to the next gathering. The name of the pastor was Terry Virgo.

Our first visit to the Bonnington Hotel was just wonderful. Marion and I had felt somewhat marginalized at Northolt, but now we discovered that there were hundreds of small fellowships like ours and that we were at the heart of something new and exciting that God was doing. There were men there who, although not belonging to any of the recognised denominations, had great maturity and wisdom and seemed to be very much in tune with God. We were introduced in the first instance to Hugh Thompson, who headed up a fellowship near Bristol. He promised to keep in touch and to be available to help and advise if ever we needed him. What a blessing and what a relief! Later on, he was to relinquish these duties because of the travelling distance involved; but he found someone more local who was prepared to give both me and the fellowship all the support we needed. That person was Gerald Coates, who lived at Cobham in Surrey. Another acquaintance I made at the Bonnington was a young man called Clive Calver and this was to lead to yet more exciting developments. In subsequent months and years, the Bonnington meetings moved to other locations and expanded dramatically to include almost anyone who wanted to attend. We remember with great pleasure a number of gatherings at the Friends' Meeting House in Euston Road where we met other like-minded Christians; leaders like John Noble who later came to minister God's word at Northolt and a new generation of singer/songwriters like Dave Bilborough from whom we learnt many new worship songs. The five men behind these meetings, often referred to as the London Brethren, also produced a bi-monthly magazine containing much new teaching about issues like relationships, spiritual gifts, the Body of Christ and much more, which kept groups like ours in line with what God was doing on a much bigger scale around the country.

In the first year of the Northolt Fellowship's independent existence, so much happened that it is difficult to know where to begin. Since people matter more than anything else, I will start by mentioning some of the folk who joined us. Of course there were still plenty of visitors who came from all over west Middlesex. Our visitors' book has little groups of names mainly at seven-day intervals and clearly these were Thursdays. They came from Harrow, Hayes, Uxbridge, West Drayton, Isleworth, Edgware, Stanmore, Watford, Ealing, Finchley, plus of course Ruislip, Greenford and Hounslow. On many occasions we had more than fifty people packed into the lounge and spilling over into the hall. I think the record was sixty-one. We used to move all the furniture except chairs and the piano out of the room and also took the door off its hinges. Fortunately we had mainly young people who are not averse to sitting on the floor, but even so it was quite a squeeze; no one seemed to mind, though.

Corinne was a striking redhead who worked in the Chemistry Department at Glaxo. One of her colleagues was the secretary of the Glaxo Christian Fellowship and through him, I learnt that she had recently had some unfortunate experiences in her personal life which had left her rather depressed, disillusioned with her church and feeling spiritually rather low. We had scarcely spoken before but I invited her to come to one of our Thursday nights and from then on she was a permanent fixture.

George was another member of the Chemistry Dept, but he was not a Christian. He worked closely with Corinne and she became aware that he too was depressed and generally unhappy with his life. At her suggestion, he agreed to come along one Thursday night and over a period of time, God met with him and set him free from most of his problems. He became a Christian, a committed member of Northolt Fellowship (NF) and actually lodged with us for several months while he was looking for new accommodation.

John, yet another recruit from Glaxo was one of my own laboratory assistants. We often talked about Christianity whilst working together at the bench and he too came and found Christ at the Northolt Fellowship. From then on it was especially nice to be able to sometimes start our day's work with a prayer together.

Paul was found by two guys from Gerald Coates' fellowship in Cobham. They were both studying at London Bible College and at the time were engaged in street evangelism in Watford. After talking with Paul, they prayed with him and he received Jesus into his life. However, because he had a drug problem, it was clear that he needed to be linked up with a group of Christians who could show him some love and help him to keep out of trouble. The Cobham guys passed him on to us. As a first stage in his rehabilitation, two of our young men who shared a flat agreed to let Paul join them. But he still had a drugs offence hanging over him and a court appearance which might well result in him going to prison. For the first time in my life I went to court, to speak on his behalf. I explained to the magistrate that he had become a Christian and that his lifestyle and ideas had dramatically changed. I further explained that as a fellowship, we were committed to helping Paul to become a good member of society and that we took this responsibility seriously. The magistrate was obviously impressed and agreed to let Paul off with a small fine but with a warning that he wouldn't be given another chance. It meant, in effect, that we at NF had a duty to see that Paul never went back to drugs or his old way of life. Praise God, he never did and thirty years on he is still involved in church life in his native Newcastle.

Mike came to us from Hayes Methodist Church. He just turned up one Thursday and enjoyed himself so much that he came back the following week with his guitar under his arm and never left us. Mike was quick to learn and had a very sensitive spirit. There were other guitarists amongst our number who were very capable of accompanying our singing, but I chose to have Mike sitting alongside me most weeks to lead the group in times of worship as I played the piano and Mike his guitar. He was always ready to trust the Holy Spirit for something new and I could always rely on him to be in tune with whatever we felt God wanted to say or do among us on any particular evening. Mike was the only 'member' of NF who actually had his membership officially transferred from another church. He was a single man with no romantic attachments who just loved spending time in our home and reckoned that he learnt as much about life from watching the way Marion and I behaved together as he did from my Bible teaching. He also got on really well with Martin. We all became the very best of friends and when he eventually did find someone to love, he invited me to be best man at the wedding.

Clive worked part-time in a garage near Aylesbury. One day, Chris (Sandra's brother and now married to Christine) stopped off at this garage for petrol and started talking to him about Jesus. The outcome was that Clive went to Chris's house that evening and gave his life to Christ. He then took his girlfriend Helen along and she too became a Christian. The following Thursday, they both came along to number three and they too became committed members of NF.

I have already mentioned Ruth, the organist from Hounslow who had become a regular member of NF. Amongst others she subsequently brought along to us was her future husband, Mike Alexander. Mike was a very gifted artist and musician, and together with Ruth and several others from the fellowship, he formed a small band called 'Portico', which was always closely associated with NF until its demise in about 1980. Ruth and Mike later emigrated to Australia where Mike eventually became the pastor of a small church. Many years later he wrote to us to say how invaluable he had found the spiritual foundations we had laid in his life during the NF years.

Rick and Lyn were comparatively late arrivals in May 1975. Like so many before them, they just turned up out of the blue. They were also in need of permanent accommodation and so, with slight hesitation because we scarcely knew them, we offered them our spare room as a temporary measure. Amongst their belongings was a pet hamster going by the name of 'Enterprise'. On their first night at our house, the cage containing Enterprise was left on the sideboard in the lounge. This seemed a reasonable idea at the time – much better than having him in the bedroom where he might keep Rick and Lynn awake by playing on the various gadgets in the cage. However, next morning, we discovered that the darling creature had stretched a paw out between the bars of his cage, grabbed a bit of curtain, hauled it into the cage and set about chewing it. Such was his enthusiasm for the task that a strip about six inches wide and about two feet long had been ripped from the bottom of the curtain. It was not a very auspicious start! Some people are easier to live with than others. We liked Rick and Lynn, sufficiently to take a week's holiday with them in North Wales but their stay with us was not always easy and no doubt they found us difficult at times too. Perhaps God used this experience to teach us all patience and tolerance.

There were many more and space does not permit to relate all their stories but our visitors' book is a great source of memories.

While we were still finding our feet as a new church, exciting events continued to pour upon us. We had a fellowship holiday in Pembrokeshire at a self-catering centre called Langton, near Fishguard. This had been arranged six months before but it was a good opportunity for us to gel together and we even managed to fit in some of the newcomers. One young man who came with us was not a Christian and during one of our evening meetings, he started to behave very strangely. Along with four or five of the more mature men in the fellowship, we took him into another room and tried to pray with him. It soon became obvious that he was under the influence of some kind of evil spirit as he started writhing around and speaking in a deep voice which was definitely not his own. We had read about such things but never actually encountered it first-hand. We kept praying, commanding the spirit to leave him and eventually, calm was restored and the young man appeared to come out of this and be himself again. He had no recollection of what had happened! So we explained that if he was not to suffer the same fate in the future, he needed to fill the void left behind by whatever it was that had taken him over. He gave his life to Christ there and then and we prayed for him to be filled with the Holy Spirit. The next morning, we went down to the beach and had an open-air service in which this fellow and a couple of others were baptised in the sea. It was a bit rough and because I do not swim, Duncan, one of my right-hand men, carried out the baptisms. At the time, Duncan was training at Bible College and got a severe reprimand for his involvement when news of it somehow got back to his college tutors. We could never understand why!

Shortly after this, in September 1973, 'Come Together' burst on to the scene.

An American called Jimmy Owens had felt deeply grieved by the divisions in the church caused by denominational prejudices, the generation gap and the general lack of loving relationships between Christians. He had therefore written 'Come Together' which he described as a 'musical experience in love'. At the time, it was a new and unique type of presentation involving music for both choir and congregation interspersed with teaching, but also with an interactive element when those present were invited to talk and pray together and encourage one another. The music was upbeat and lively, led by a small band and incorporating half a dozen solo singers.

It was Keith, one of our most loyal members, who first told us about it. He had bought the recording and then researched details of a national tour which was about to take place. Apparently, a nucleus choir had been recruited from some of the new churches (including Cobham) but the plan was to augment this with other singers at each of the venues around the country. It was too late in the day to join the nucleus group, but we were soon infected by Keith's enthusiasm and so a couple of car-loads of those of us who had decent voices and could read music went to get a taste of what it was all about and actually took part in performances at Bournemouth, Reading, Birmingham and the Westminster Central Hall in London.

We always came away walking on cloud nine, thrilled and overwhelmed by a sense of love uniting God's people and full of praise to God for what He was doing. It was wonderful – no other word will do – and obviously thousands more thought so too, because they clamoured for more. Accordingly, by popular request, a further three performances were arranged at London's Royal Albert Hall in December. As before, Pat Boone, an American pop singer who was well known for his overtly Christian beliefs, was narrator and compère. Marion and I and several others sang in the choir and because it was near to home, many of the fellowship came along too, including our Martin.

Marion had arranged that she would meet up with him after the performance at the stage door but, as can so easily happen, she got talking and completely forgot about her son. Now, the Albert Hall is a frighteningly big place when you are just ten years old and Martin was somewhat upset when Marion eventually met up with him about half an hour later than planned. At that precise moment Pat Boone also made his exit and noticing the anxious face, enquired what was wrong. The outcome was that Marion, Martin and a white-suited, bronzed and handsome Pat Boone walked off down the street together with Pat holding Martin's hand. Marion was so jealous. Why couldn't it have been her hand?

On another evening, someone else got lost. John, our neighbour from Doncaster Drive, found a girl called Pam in tears after the performance because she had somehow missed the coach conveying a party from her church. John reassured her that she could go home with him and that his friends Chris and Marion would put her up for the night and she could sort out getting home the next day. So, at about 11 p.m. we were confronted on the doorstep by John with a sixteen-year-old from Sidcup, the other side of London from Northolt. After she had phoned home, we started to talk until well into the early hours of the morning. We discovered that Pam had been suffering from mental health problems for some time and that she had an appointment with a psychiatrist the following day. Before eventually retiring to bed, we asked if we could pray for Pam to be healed, and she agreed.

She didn't make the appointment the next day, but as we kept in touch with her, we sensed that things were getting better. We later visited her at university and she came on a fellowship holiday with us in 1976. Many years later, she told us that her healing had commenced that night when we prayed for her. Well done John. He may not have known exactly what to do, but he knew people who would!

1974 marked a further consolidation of the Northolt Fellowship as Gerald Coates came to commission me as an elder. If you read Acts, you find that Paul appointed elders in each of the churches that he established. Gerald, as a kind of overseer to our church, took it upon himself to do the same thing. It was simply a recognition of what I had already been doing but it was good to have that formal declaration and for the members to pledge their support.

As an elder, there were now many duties and responsibilities to which I gave my attention. First I wanted to train and disciple suitable men for future leadership. I used to meet about once a month with half a dozen of the likeliest characters, teaching them about lifestyle as well as using their gifts. I would share with them my hopes and aspirations for the fellowship, including any detailed plans, and in a way allowed them to advise or correct me if they felt I was off track. There was no way I was going to be a one-man band.

Following 'Come Together' I was anxious to see churches doing just that and it seemed that as a starting point, it would be good to bring leaders together to build love, trust and confidence between them. Frank Gamble from Roxeth Free Church, Chris Wood from Sipson, Dave Shaw from a fellowship in Ealing and the curate of the tiny St Richard's Anglican Church on our estate were amongst those who I invited to meet with me for fellowship and prayer every once in a while. We didn't exactly see the walls of denominationalism collapse but I think it helped to give us all a broader picture of what the church was meant to be. A great many churches are so caught up with their own agendas that they have no time to see that other local churches may need all sorts of practical help which it is within their power to give.

The front room of our house was now bursting at the seams but we still wanted outsiders to be able to join us and so we instituted what came to be known as 'All Saints Nights'. In principle, this was an enlarged version of our meetings at home but held approximately bi-monthly in a local church hall, with a group of musicians, a speaker (sometimes from outside the fellowship), and open to anyone sufficiently interested to come. Gerald was a regular speaker and others included some of the men we had met at the Bonnington Hotel, including Clive Calver, who brought with him a young musician called Graham Kendrick.

Sooner or later, young people tend to get married and here was another role for me – officiating at weddings. Many people

The author, age four, with his sister, Barbara, in the back garden at Ruslip

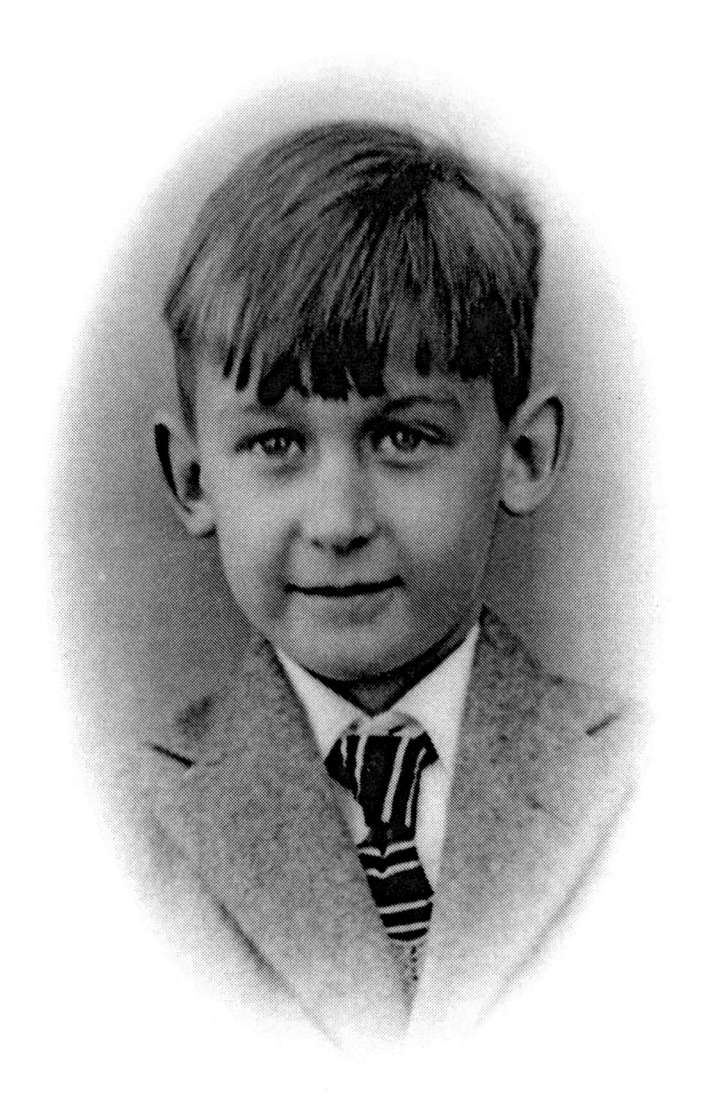

School photo, age seven

Class Upper 5A, Latymer School, 1955
(author is third from the left, in second row from the back)

On holiday with Mum, Dad, Barbara and her fiancé, Malcom, Lynton 1957

Engaged to Marion,
1960

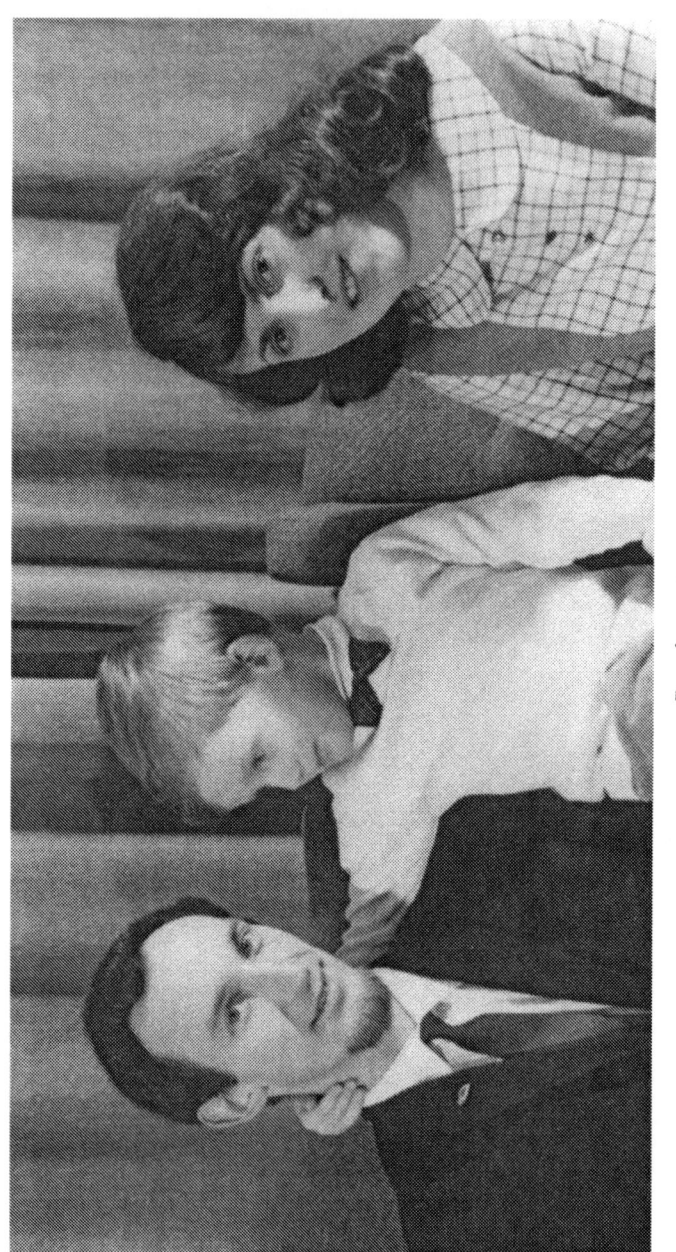

Proud parents, 1966

*A group from the Northolt Fellowship days,
Wendover, Bucks, 1973*

Conducting a wedding during the Northolt Fellowship period

Patch

Mike and Martin leading worship at a house party at Bernard's Acre, September, 1982

With Esther,
1984

*Still playing cricket at forty-seven (author at extreme right),
West Ealing Baptist CC, Summer 1986*

*Silver wedding,
July 1987*

March for Jesus,
1989

*Church youth group in our back garden,
October, 1996*

With Cecile, one of our first foreign students, 1997

*Mountain climber,
Scafell summit, Lake District, 1997*

*Retirement day with collegues from PEL,
December 2002*

*With Rob Frost on the Three Peaks Challenge,
August 2003*

At a Sri Lankan wedding,
2005

do not know that you don't have to be a clergyman to take a wedding. Anyone can do it, provided there is an authorised representative from the registry office present. As church elder, I conducted more than a dozen weddings over the years and thoroughly enjoyed the privilege. Perhaps the most memorable was that of Sue and Alan, which took place on 26 June 1976. It was a very hot summer and up to that time, this was the hottest day of the century! Throughout the ceremony, we sweltered and it was so hot that one of the bridesmaids fainted. Never has it felt so good to remove jacket and tie at the reception once the service was over.

A less pleasant duty involved a middle-aged lady with a rather nervous disposition who joined our fellowship. She was a widow, living alone in Southall. She complained of strange noises and happenings at her house and was convinced that it was in some way haunted. I'm not sure what I believe about 'ghosts'. There are enough documented cases to say that they exist but my own theory is that they are evil spirits impersonating people in some way. However, we needed to take the problem seriously and along with Keith and one of the other young men I was discipling, we went to the house and sought to banish whatever it was in the name of Jesus. Perhaps it was auto-suggestion, but there did seem to be something there that sent shivers down the spine. However, after a couple of visits, the house felt much better.

Amongst other tasks was the need to prepare to teach from the Bible most Thursday evenings. I would also try to meet up with Gerald as and when I could, to pray and discuss how the fellowship was doing. This was a very informal relationship but Marion and I will always be grateful to him for his input into our lives. His teaching was fresh and radical, calling into question things which were cultural rather than Christian and making us think about what we were trying to do. One of Gerald's favourite topics was the Kingdom of God. Indeed, for some years the church at Cobham held a kind of annual festival entitled 'Kingdom Life'. It was all about seeking to bring the rule of God into people's lives so as to create a bit of heaven on earth. We learnt so much from him about lifestyle, not least about showing appreciation by letter writing and unsolicited gifts. A few years later, the fellowship gave me some stereo equipment, Marion an electric food mixer and even Martin was not left out, receiving some Airfix models on which he was keen at the time. These gifts, coming at a period when we had a comparatively small monthly income, showed us how much we were loved and appreciated and we understand it was Gerald who initiated the idea.

There were occasional difficult situations to resolve, such as when one young couple separated prior to a divorce and when an unmarried girl became pregnant. It was sad that in a Christian group these things should have happened at all, but at least they were the exception rather than the rule, and I am happy to say that of all the marriages I conducted, not one has ended in divorce.

Because, we were now a church and not just a group gathering for meetings, we started to get together on a Sunday afternoon as well as on Thursdays. This was to benefit couples with young children. At the time, this only applied to one couple, but the principle seemed right. In any case, old habits die hard and Sundays would have seemed very strange if we had not met together with fellow Christians. Often, these would be fairly informal times, following which a few folk would stay to tea and then spend the evening playing board games or relaxing and listening to music. In the summer, it was not unknown for some of the fellows to play football on the green at the back of our house or cricket with a tiny bat in our back garden. In retrospect, it never ceases to amaze me that our neighbours were so tolerant and understanding. Having perhaps fifty people arriving, singing and then departing every week for many years was hardly what they could have expected in a residential area. But we never had any complaints.

Another decision that eventually had to be made involved splitting the overcrowded Thursday night meetings in two, with half the people gathering at another home about a mile away. In theory, this should have helped the second group to develop spiritually without having to lean or rely on me. After all, I had learnt that part of my job as a leader was to make myself redundant. In practise, the two meetings were never quite so exciting as when we were all together but maybe we needed to learn that excitement is not the only criterion of what is best.

In the midst of all this routine activity, there were plenty of highlights. Several times a year, a large group from the fellowship would go out, often on a cheap-day rail excursion, and enjoy time together relaxing and walking. There were memorable trips to Cornwall and to Settle in Yorkshire when we got lost on the moors and nearly missed our train home. The fellowship was invited to perform 'Come Together' at Carisbrook on the Isle of Wight and I was given the task of emulating Pat Boone as narrator but without the white suit (the best I could do was a white check jacket). But I will especially remember 1974 for my first ever visit outside the British Isles. Chris and Christine, who by this time had two young babies, had left Northolt and after a brief spell of training in Ipswich had moved to Portugal to join another missionary couple living just outside the city of Oporto. As a fellowship, we had agreed to support them in their missionary endeavour and that included their financial needs. In a double sense they were therefore our missionaries and so it seemed only right that I should visit them, to get a better idea of what they were actually doing and offer them encouragement in their work. The fellowship was in full agreement with this plan. In addition, Sue (who had helped us with our move), now eighteen, wanted to visit her friend Christine and so it was agreed that we should make the trip together.

It was a bit alarming arriving at Oporto airport to see soldiers armed with machine guns patrolling the terminal building, but there had been a revolution in the preceding months culminating in the overthrow of a dictator and a return to a more democratic form of government and obviously things had not totally quietened down. Oporto is a beautiful city, with buildings in a striking architectural style very different from Britain. It sits astride the River Douro and is the centre of the port wine industry. As you travel inland along the Douro, the valley sides are terraced and the terraces covered with vines. Even in the city and its suburbs, every house seemed to have its own vine. If there was no garden, the tiniest of patios still boasted a vine. I wish we had been there in September rather than mid-summer in order to see the grape harvest.

As the days passed, I was able to make an assessment of the

situation facing Christians in Portugal. The revolution had brought about huge changes. Instead of a secret police there was now great freedom but as often happens, this had resulted in a breakdown of moral standards and a rise in lawlessness of various kinds, including an upsurge in pornography. Thus the churches were starting to realise what a great opportunity was theirs if only they would wake up from the very formal religion that was the norm. These stirrings were reflected in posters in the streets boldly proclaiming 'RELIGION IS NOT ENOUGH – YOU NEED JESUS'. This was an ideal scenario for Chris and it was apparent that he had built good relationships with a number of churches and that his forceful preaching on issues such as the baptism in the Holy Spirit was being warmly welcomed and embraced. His grasp of Portuguese had also improved so that he did not always need an interpreter when he preached.

On the Sunday of our stay, we all went to a church where I spoke through an interpreter – another first. Afterwards, the leader invited us to return to his home to sample his port! I confess that I had never tried port and Chris and Christine rarely drank anything alcoholic. The same was probably true of Sue. Nevertheless, we felt it was only polite to accept the invitation. After all, it was really no different from an Englishman inviting us back for a coffee. He was obviously a connoisseur of port and very proud of his collection. Amongst the sample bottles he brought out was one that was seventeen years old. He proceeded to pour tots of various ports for us to try and we proceeded to drink them. They were excellent and I got quite a taste for the stuff. Unfortunately, Christine just could not handle it and became more and more giggly as the evening went on, causing the rest of us to feel more and more embarrassed. Fortunately our host did not seem to notice, or perhaps he was just thinking what strange people the English were!

Bearing in mind that I had an eleven-year-old son at this time, it may not come as a surprise that I was very keen on railways. Martin was an avid locomotive spotter and at home we both loved watching trains as well as travelling on them. So it was a great pleasure to go on a train excursion inland to a place called Villa Real where we encountered at close-hand some steam engines.

(Steam locomotives had been discontinued on British railways almost ten years before and so this was a special treat.) We also travelled by car to the northern town of Braga and the mountainous terrain near there. It was all very enjoyable and a real bonus to the visit; but there was a downside to the whole trip.

Sue had been a member of our youth group at NPBC since she was eleven and it is sometimes easy to forget that young people grow up. I suppose I felt responsible for her in a foreign country and was overprotective of her to the point where she felt understandably inhibited, especially so when we were accompanied on some of our excursions by a close friend of Chris and Christine, called Fred. Fred may be a very English sounding name, but in fact he was the son of a Portuguese count, wealthy, handsome, charming and spoke excellent English. There was obviously a bit of chemistry going on between him and Sue and I suppose I was thinking how dangerous it might be for her to fall in love with a comparative stranger who was a foreigner as well! (It's just as well I never had a daughter or I would never have had a good night's sleep for worrying about her!) We got to a point where Sue was scarcely talking to me and having realised the error of my ways, I had to make my apologies to her on the plane home. We are still good friends today so all's well that ends well.

Whilst I was away, the fellowship had looked after Marion and Martin in every way possible and to my amazement had repainted the outside of the house. I was thrilled, not so much because it was a job that had needed doing but because this demonstrated the sort of love and commitment that I longed to see amongst the members. It was not an isolated incident either. There were many occasions when we were offered lifts in cars or when those with practical gifts helped us out with mechanical or electrical problems around the house. One young man helped with some gardening at a time when I was particularly busy.

If Portugal was the high spot of 1974, the following year was especially memorable for another musical from Jimmy Owens entitled 'If My People'. This had a similar style and format to 'Come Together' but was based around the scripture verse from II Chronicles 7:14: 'If my people which are called by my name, shall humble themselves, and pray, and seek my face, and turn from their wicked ways; then will I hear from heaven, and will forgive their sin, and heal their land.'

The programme aimed to focus on the failure of Christians to be a powerful influence for good in the nation because of their own sins. There were acts of repentance based on each phrase of the verse and interactive prayer for the nation. As such it was much more serious in content and tone than the earlier musical but was nevertheless very challenging and brought people into a deep experience of God's love and forgiveness. After consultation with my trainee leaders, they were happy to release me from my duties at Northolt for the whole month of February to go on the national tour as part of the band. Some years earlier I had swapped my piano for an electronic organ and at this time owned a Hammond with an external rotary speaker cabinet. The sound was superb. Bravely I agreed to my Hammond being used on the tour to save the expense of hiring another instrument.

The nucleus group of singers and musicians amounted to about seventy people – a coach full in fact – and surprisingly, at nearly thirty-six, I was one of the oldest present. I cannot adequately describe the thrill of playing with a band and choir at presentations in major concert halls across the land. Today, I sometimes hear mention of the De Montford Hall in Leicester, the City Hall in Newcastle or Liverpool Cathedral and say to myself, 'I've played there!' We started in London, travelled down to Truro by way of Paignton, and then gradually made our way up to Glasgow. At the end of two weeks, we returned to London's Royal Albert Hall for three days and the remaining venues were all in the south-east. This meant that I was able to get by with just two weeks' holiday from work as I could reach these latter venues in time after going to work first. In all we did twenty-two performances. Naturally I made a good many new friends and we had some fun times together; but the best thing was being a part of a nationwide movement where Christians were sorting out their lives and committing themselves to pray for the country as a whole. The only disappointment was that my Hammond did not enjoy being transported around the country in a lorry and suffered some severe dents to the woodwork. I managed to remain philosophical about this and shortly after my return, traded it in for a brand new piano.

It was a great blessing to me that the folk in the Fellowship recognised my gifts and were happy for me to be away from time to time. Two particular areas of ministry loom large in my memory. The first was an invitation from Clive Calver. At this time Clive was heading up a ministry team called In the Name of Jesus (affectionately known as ITNOJ for short). They were a group of Christians mainly in their twenties with a wide variety of gifts and bound together by their love for God and each other and their desire to share that love with others. They were able to conduct missions in schools, universities, churches, prisons and so on. It was not dissimilar to what I had been involved in during the sixties, but theirs was a permanent team with all the advantages that could bring – being able to work very closely together knowing each other's strengths and weaknesses. Amongst the group was a young singer–songwriter by the name of Graham Kendrick who had recorded a couple of albums but was still relatively unknown. I could hardly believe it when Clive asked me to join the team for a weekend in the Isle of Wight and actually give them some Bible teaching to build them up in their faith. I felt very inadequate, but somehow the Lord made it possible and I had the privilege of joining up with them on more than this one occasion. I got on very well with Graham and one outcome of this was that I actually played the organ at his wedding a couple of years later – one of my few claims to fame. There were several other couples from ITNOJ with whom I built good relationships but one of these was very special: Rob and Gill Buckeridge became lifelong friends to me and Marion and we constantly thank God for all that they have done for us over the years.

The second area of ministry involved my musical gift. I cannot remember how I first met Trevor Martin, but he was the leader of a fellowship in Ewell, Surrey, and God had given him a remarkable gift of healing. Once a month, there was a healing meeting in the local Bourne Hall at which Trevor and his wife Shirley would pray for all manner of sick people with some very encouraging results. (I don't believe there has ever been anyone with a 100 per cent record of healing, apart from Jesus of course. In practise, 10 per cent is pretty good going, but that doesn't mean we should stop trying!) Presumably because there were no capable musicians at Ewell, Trevor asked me if I would play the piano for the Bourne Hall gatherings and I was happy to do so. Initially I anticipated playing for just a few worship songs but in fact, Trevor wanted me to play throughout the period of well over an hour when he and Shirley were praying for the sick. He said that he felt the Holy Spirit was released through him in greater power because of the anointing in my playing. It was quite exhausting but at least it was a grand piano.

This question of anointing is something I don't really understand but it does seem that when I play the piano, it brings people closer to God. It is not that I am technically brilliant – no way; but there is something about the way I play which is a gift from God to His church and I can only marvel and say, 'Thank you, Lord.'

Of course, we believed in healing at the Northolt Fellowship too and it was not uncommon on Thursday nights to pray for those feeling under the weather. Generally speaking young people do not suffer from serious illnesses, but there were several healings which as far as I'm concerned were exceptional. From as far back as I can remember, I suffered from hay fever every summer. It was usually at its worst in June and early July, which was particularly annoying when I was at school because it coincided with examination time. I would have fits of sneezing which would go on for several minutes leaving me totally exhausted and feeling like a limp rag. My eyes would also irritate to the point where I felt like plucking them out. Over the years, I had grown to accept this situation but around 1971, I came to the firm conclusion that this had to stop. It was not honouring to God if I was feeling washed out and unable to get on and do things and it wasn't doing me much good either. Having become convinced of this, I became equally sure that God would heal me and so I requested prayer one Thursday evening in May. June came and then July and the hay fever did not return. Occasionally, when the pollen count is exceptionally high, I may get a mini fit of the sneezes but for all practical purposes, hay fever became a thing of the past from that day onwards.

The second healing concerned a young woman who was a nurse. A committed member of the fellowship, Linda suffered from back trouble which was obviously a serious impediment in her job, where she often needed to lift patients in and out of bed. On one Thursday evening, the back was so bad that she had been forced to sleep on a board, was in constant pain and had been told that her career was in jeopardy. A group of us gathered round to lay hands on her and pray for total healing. The following day, she phoned to say that the pain had gone and she was able to touch her toes. Amazing! She carried on nursing for many years.

The third healing concerned Gill, a young woman who had been diagnosed as unable to have children. She and her husband were visiting us for a meal I think, when this information came to light. I prayed that God would heal her condition. I confess that I quite forgot all about this until a couple of years later, when a letter arrived, announcing the birth of their first child and thanking me (and God) for praying. They finished up having four children, all of whom are keen Christians today. God does not work by halves.

Marion also experienced God's healing work in her body. She had suffered with colitis for a number of years and was making regular visits to a specialist at Northwick Park Hospital. After prayer at a meeting in London, her condition dramatically cleared up. The specialist was honest enough to admit that the hospital had done nothing towards this and merely asked her to make an annual visit to check for any recurrence. There never has been and the visits have been terminated.

Before concluding this survey of the years 1973 to 1976, there is one other story which must be told. Because a fair number of Northolt Fellowship members had got married and needed time on their own, we discontinued the fellowship holidays after 1975. But in future years, we often found ourselves going away with smaller groups, mainly single folk. Thus in August 1976, a dozen of us set off for a self-catering holiday in the tiny village of Strete, near Dartmouth in South Devon. During one of our planning meetings, when we agreed to hire a minibus to take us there, I had seriously asked the question, 'Where will we stand if the minibus breaks down?' to which, amidst great hilarity, I received the answer, 'At the side of the road, of course!' Many a true word is spoken in jest and, just before we reached the Exeter bypass, that is exactly what happened. Our good friend Mike was driving and while the rest of us just stood around, he had the bonnet open trying to ascertain the cause of the breakdown. Try as he might, there was no way he could restart the engine. Foolishly, we had not anticipated trouble and none of our party belonged to the AA or RAC. We had no other vehicles and still had nearly fifty miles to go. We found a garage about half a mile down the road, but it was late on a Saturday afternoon and they were closed. In our desperation, we decided to try the only thing we knew – to pray. We all laid hands on the bonnet of the minibus and prayed both aloud and silently for about five minutes. Mike then tried the starter motor once again and the engine spluttered to life. We piled back in and continued our journey without incident, even climbing some moderately steep hills.

Next morning when we wanted to drive down to the nearest beach, the minibus was completely dead. We had to have it towed in to a local garage for some major repairs before our return journey the following Saturday. I am not a mechanic and so did not understand the details, but the diagnosis of the problem was such that there was no way the minibus could have travelled those last forty-odd miles. But it did! Who says prayer doesn't work?

Full-time Elder

Whilst all this had been going on, I had been working five days a week at Glaxo. The Physical Chemistry Department was within the Research division and of necessity worked in close cooperation with the Chemistry, Pharmacology, and Development sections. My work was very varied and for the most part quite interesting. In order to give an indication of the scope of my research, let me outline in very simple terms just a few of the projects on which I worked.

Dehydro-emetine was a drug used at that time to cure amoebic dysentery, a very unpleasant disease caused by parasites getting into one's body and breeding. The drug acted as a poison to the parasites but the problem was how to administer it in such a way as to obtain maximum benefit and minimum side-effects. We absorbed the drug on different types of ion-exchange resins – similar to those used in water purifiers – and measured rates and mechanism of release under conditions designed to simulate the intestinal tract.

Most solids exist as crystals if you could only view them under a microscope, but some exist in a variety of different crystalline forms or shapes. I attempted to prepare as many different crystalline forms of a particular antibiotic as possible and then compared their long term stability to heat, air and moisture. Obviously this is very important since medicines need to have a significant shelf life, without losing their usefulness because the active ingredient has partly decomposed.

In today's world of factory farming, pigs are frequently bred in concrete pens where they are unable to root around in mud and vegetation for essential minerals. Consequently, piglets suffer from iron-deficiency anaemia which drastically affects their general health and growth rate. To combat this problem, injectable iron preparations have been used. But the iron needs to be in the form of a water-soluble but extremely stable chemical compound which will be absorbed from the muscle tissue into the bloodstream rather than break down in the muscle and simply leave a dark brown stain which would make the meat or bacon unsaleable. I spent some time trying to develop and test new iron preparations for this purpose. It was whilst I was engaged on this project that I had the most embarrassing moment of my career as a chemist.

Testing on animals was not my job. You have to have a licence for that. In this particular project, the testing was carried out by the senior pharmacologist using rabbits. (Only after the products were shown to be promising would they be tried on the pigs: pigs are expensive animals.) I would prepare a batch of new compounds, pass these to the pharmacologist who would inject them into rabbits' legs. The animals would be looked after in a normal manner for about three weeks and then killed in order to examine the release of the iron from the muscle. Normally, I was merely invited to observe the isolated muscle tissue after the messy work had been done, but on one occasion, I bumped into the pharmacologist in the corridor just as the three weeks' test period was up. He said he would go and 'do it' right away and insisted that I accompany him. What he didn't know was that I have always been terribly squeamish when it comes to blood and even the mention of blood in conversation makes me feel distinctly queasy and the sight of it or the loss of it, especially if it's mine, has even more devastating effects. It is one of those things I just have no control over.

I tried to make excuses why I needed to be somewhere else, but he insisted that it would only take a few minutes and so I was literally led to the slaughter! The rabbit was placed and secured inside a special type of wooden box with just its head emerging and a barbiturate drug injected into a prominent vein in its ear. One moment the rabbit was bright-eyed and cuddly but within seconds, the eyes had glazed over, the head slumped and the rabbit was dead. Immediately, the bolts were loosened on the box, the animal was lifted out and my colleague took out his scalpel and started to remove the skin from the legs. He then cut into the leg to expose the muscle into which the iron preparation had been injected for me to observe the stain or lack of it. It was all over in less than a minute, but I was struggling madly with feelings of nausea, telling myself that in spite of the blood all around, I was only looking at joints of meat. I managed to hold myself together sufficiently to show some interest in the result but then hurried away to find some fresh air at the exit of the building, where I sat down on the steps with my head between my knees for several minutes hoping against hope that I wouldn't actually faint. Fortunately no one came along but when I returned to my own laboratory, someone did ask if I was feeling all right because I looked very pale!

Perhaps my best achievement for Glaxo resulted in my name getting on a patent as the joint inventor of a process which significantly increased the yield and therefore the cost efficiency in the manufacture of a potent antibiotic. You can read all about it if you are interested by visiting the Patents' Office in London and looking up patent specification no.1,189,306.

For the most part, my fellow researchers were a good bunch and easy to get along with. Bart Taylor, with whom I had worked on that first holiday job, was ever present throughout my stay and always a good companion. One of the female laboratory assistants was a motorbike fanatic who regularly rode as sidecar passenger at the Isle of Man TT races. My departmental head was an amiable man but tended to reject any ideas I might have on the progress of my projects. However, I soon discovered from my colleagues that if you could put an idea into his head so that it appeared to be coming from him, then it would probably get the go-ahead. I don't normally believe in manipulating people but I learnt to make an exception in this case.

One good thing about research was the lack of stress. Most projects were long term with no particular deadlines or time limits for their completion. One just carried on for as long as was necessary. This made it much easier to cope with my extracurricular activities at NPBC and later with the Northolt Fellowship. There would be times when an experiment was running and required little or no attention so that I could even prepare a Bible study. In retrospect, I'm not sure whether this was right or not, but I don't think I ever neglected my work and always sought to do my best. Another benefit was the need to write reports. When you have been working at something for maybe a year and need to collate the results and make valid conclusions, it takes a lot of thought and planning to present everything in a logical and concise manner. I believe that the experience of doing this over sixteen years proved a great help in the task of preparing sermons, enabling me to present and develop truths from God's word in a straightforward and logical sequence which the listeners can easily follow and understand. There is no room for waffling in a scientific report, or in a sermon.

On the negative side, research can be very frustrating and not in the least the glamorous occupation it may seem to be. Sometimes, I could carry on for months at a time getting nowhere and seemingly hitting my head against a brick wall. Then I might come up with an idea which would work and I could then move on to the next phase which probably meant another long, fruitless period. Someone has very rightly described the life of the researcher as 5 per cent inspiration and 95 per cent perspiration!

Glaxo had an excellent sports and social club but in my early years, I was much too shy to get involved and in any case, my spare time was all taken up with the young people at church. However, as time went on and especially after I was baptised in the Holy Spirit I started to loosen up and I shall always be grateful to some of the other Glaxo Christians in the group who really helped me in this. Pam enjoyed playing table tennis and discovered that there was a table available at lunchtime for those keen enough to wait and take turns to play. She introduced me to this and before long I was playing for one of the Glaxo teams in a regular league (not the first team I might add; I was never that good). George invited me to the clubhouse to play snooker with him – a game which I now really enjoy and play as often as time permits. Corinne encouraged me to take advantage of the facilities at the club to play badminton with her. She was a star player and much too good for me; but it got me started and Marion and I subsequently enjoyed playing with various friends at local leisure centres for some years. Best of all was the inter-departmental cricket tournament and I am proud to say that I was a member of the Research Team which won the trophy in 1977. I have a photograph and a medal to prove it.

Another aspect of life at Glaxo was the introduction in the early seventies of flexitime. This was a brilliant scheme whereby one could work flexible hours. It was required for each employee to work a stipulated number of hours in a four-week period, but by working slightly longer each day, it was possible to build up enough time to enable one to take a maximum of one complete day off in that period. This was great and for many years I took advantage of the scheme to enjoy days out in the countryside, walking and taking photographs – both things I loved doing. At that time, we still did not have a car but I was earning enough to be able to afford train fares and travelled all over southern England: Shaftesbury, Guildford, the Cotswolds, Watership Down (near Newbury), the Chiltern Hills, Savernake Forest, the Kennet and Avon Canal. All these places and many more are recorded in my photograph albums and were happy days indeed. But I had never been to Scotland.

In the spring of 1977, British Rail were offering a special 'Freedom of Scotland' ticket which enabled the holder to travel anywhere on the rail network in Scotland over a period of seven days at a very reasonable price. Because Martin was approaching his fourteenth birthday, after which he would no longer be able to claim a child's half-fare, we decided to take advantage of these tickets as a family and enjoyed a whistle-stop tour of many of Scotland's most beautiful places. The railway lines from Glasgow to Fort William and Mallaig, from Kyle of Lochalsh to Inverness and from Inverness to Edinburgh via Perth are probably the most scenic lines in the British Isles and sitting in the comfort of a railway carriage is certainly a great way to see what the Highlands of Scotland are really like. For Martin the trainspotter, it was also a wonderful opportunity to see many diesel locomotives of types never seen or used in England.

As well as visiting the towns and cities mentioned above, we also spent forty hours on the Isle of Skye. Not for nothing is it known as 'the misty isle'. For all but five minutes of our time there, the sky was overcast and the hills largely covered in cloud. On the one occasion when the sun appeared and the clouds lifted for a few minutes to reveal the majestic mountain known as Blaven, I was caught without my camera. By the time I had shot into the house, found it and returned to the viewpoint, the sun had gone and the cloud descended once more. Ah well. Whilst in Fort William we also attempted to climb Ben Nevis, the highest mountain in the British Isles. Marion felt this was just too energetic but Martin and I set off with high hopes until, by the time we had reached about two thirds of the way up, we were trudging through quite deep snow merely following in the tracks of other walkers who had gone before us and hoping that they had known the way! But then a snowstorm blew up and it was clear that even the tracks would soon be hidden. Someone had been killed on the mountain the previous day so we knew it was potentially dangerous. There was no alternative but to turn back: it would be another twenty-five years before I climbed it again and actually reached the summit.

Even in Scotland, we could not avoid encounters with people. As we travelled around, we kept meeting up with a young American student who was also 'doing' Scotland. We chatted and even gave him our address in case he ever found himself in London. Sure enough, he did come and see us and subsequently we received an invitation to his wedding in 1980 when he married a lovely English girl in Lichfield; we still keep in touch.

It was around this time of our lives that I started to seriously consider the possibility of leaving work in order to have more time for my duties as elder of the Northolt Fellowship. For the most part, I had enjoyed my time at Glaxo but it was a job rather than a calling; a means of making enough money to live on whilst doing what I really wanted to. Chemistry was not half as satisfying as many of the things I had been involved with over the previous few years and if I was to continue to extend and enlarge my ministry, then I needed more time. Marion was not sure that she wanted me at home but the fellowship were quite enthusiastic and willing to support me financially as best as they were able although this would be well below the level of my Glaxo salary. The decision was taken and in July 1977 I gave three months' notice of my intention to leave. My work colleagues were surprised but interested to know my reasons and this provided good opportunities to share some aspect of the gospel with a few of them. At the same time I found wonderful support from many friends outside as well as inside the fellowship. At the time of my actual departure in October, I received about thirty greeting cards wishing me well in my new life and assuring me of prayerful backing. In fact, this new phase of my life was to last less than two years but it was no less exciting for all that.

In many ways, life now was both a continuation and extension of what I had been doing before. But there were changes too: I made sure that I spent most mornings in prayer and study. One can never pray too much and I would be the first to admit that I have never prayed enough. But being at home provided the opportunity and it was good for me to exercise the discipline. There are far more books in the world than there is time for reading them, and I needed to study if I was to be able to teach not just young people any more but discerning young adults. Afternoons tended to be free or given over to visiting. There were quite a number of our members who did not go to work and in particular there were some who came to the meetings but were nevertheless struggling with their faith and needed much encouragement. I am sure most people like to be visited, for it makes them feel wanted and appreciated. Equally, we found that being hospitable was crucial if folk were to feel loved and cared for and know that we were interested in them as real people; so we frequently invited members and friends for meals.

My being at home, however, meant stress for Marion. When I was at work, she had been tremendously supportive in looking after me and maximising my free time by leaving me with very few domestic duties. Now that I was at home, things ought to have been different. However, if I wanted a cup of tea mid-morning, I expected Marion to make it because she had always done so. But this was a hindrance if she was in the middle of doing something else and in any case, what was wrong with me doing it myself? It took a while for me to realise how busy a housewife can be and it was a long learning curve for me to become more of a help and less of a hindrance around the house. But by the end of the two years, I had come to a far greater appreciation of my beloved wife than ever before and we had both made adjustments which in subsequent years have made for a more harmonious and happy domestic lifestyle than might otherwise have been the case.

With more time available, I was able to considerably enlarge my activities outside of Northolt. On the very first weekend after leaving Glaxo, I led and spoke at a house party organised by the Northwick Park Hospital Christian Union. During this two-year period, I also spoke at two house parties of the Whitelands College Christian Union. This was a teacher training college in Putney and I formed a good relationship with some of the students there and was a regular visitor to their CU. I also visited a village in Yorkshire on at least two occasions, once with a team of folk from the fellowship. Adrian (who I mentioned in connection with the events at Obley in 1971) had got married, moved there and was involved in a small but struggling Baptist church. We were invited with the hope of injecting a little bit of new life into this church while spending time with our friend. On a subsequent visit on my own, I found myself talking to the minister only for him to share with me some serious personal problems. I also found myself meeting regularly with another married couple nearer home in Wembley to sort out marital problems. He too was the minister of a church and I can only thank God that by acting as a kind of neutral referee in their disputes they came to a better understanding of each other and their marriage was repaired and renewed.

I started to have an increasingly close association with Gloucestershire. After the break-up of the ITNOJ team, Rob and Gill Buckeridge had moved to the tiny village of Shipton Oliffe near Andoversford and we often went to visit them. They were to introduce us to a place called Paradise Pottery, where the lady owner used to hold occasional meetings not dissimilar to those at our home. I was invited there to lead a seminar on worship and took along a group from Northolt, including a few musicians, to help me. The lady had also arranged for me to stay overnight with an Anglican vicar from Hardwicke, another Gloucestershire village, where I was to preach on the following Sunday morning. The seminar was very well received and led to invitations to several other churches in the area to do something similar. But my visit to Hardwicke had other far-reaching consequences. Geoff Stickland was (and is) a vicar with a difference. He was a larger than life character, bold and outspoken in his views and boisterous by nature. When first introduced to Marion during the Paradise seminar, he remarked, 'Dear lady, I would far rather be looking after you!' He regularly drove heavy articulated lorries to eastern Europe as a sort of hobby and also rode a powerful motorbike. I was welcomed by him and his wife Ruth with great warmth and their hospitality was exceptional.

In many ways, we were as different as chalk and cheese. He was a life-long Anglican who always wore his robes and vestments with pride when conducting church services. I had no denominational links and was convinced that the distinction between clergy and laity was completely out of order. I wasn't one for dressing up either. Geoff smoked cigars and frequently enjoyed a pint at his local. I never smoked or drank beer. Nevertheless, being present at one of his services was a complete revelation to me. Ever since my junior school days, I had thought of the liturgy of the Church of England as being boring and repetitive; but Geoff brought it to life by his extravagant gestures and intonations. Suddenly it was not empty words but full of rich theological truth and I found it inspiring and uplifting. Geoff and I formed an instant friendship, and over the years we have spent much time discussing spiritual issues to our mutual benefit. It is an example of Proverbs 27:17: 'As iron sharpens iron, so one man sharpens another.'

I started to make regular visits to Hardwicke, preaching in the church and getting to know a fair number of Geoff's parishioners. I was welcomed into other homes for meals and at every turn there was opportunity to share something of my faith in Jesus.

Although, as I have said, I had no time for robes and vestments, on my first visit following the seminar at Paradise I had been wearing white shoes, and I was never allowed to forget it. On subsequent visits, Geoff always referred to the famous white shoes and I felt obliged to wear them when preaching there, if only to humour him. Geoff subsequently moved to the adjacent town of Quedgeley and will probably stay there for ever. We still go and visit him and Ruth and enjoy great food and good fellowship spiced with plenty of laughter.

If Hardwicke removed some of my prejudices about Anglicanism, something was also needed to deal with my antipathy towards Roman Catholicism. Following my visit to Ireland in

1967, I had looked into some of the precepts of the Catholic faith and come to the conclusion that they were way off beam. I often felt quite angry inside that so many people worldwide could be under such a delusion and felt frustrated that I could do nothing about it. However, now that I was no longer at Glaxo, Frank Gamble from Roxeth Green Free Church invited me to go along to the South Harrow ministers' fraternal. Amongst those who gathered together for prayer and discussion was the priest from the local Catholic church. As I got to know him, I was amazed to find that he had the same passion for God, the same desire to serve and the same aspirations and hopes for the members of his church as me – if not more so! I came to recognise that although we could not agree on everything, here was a man who was clearly a child of God, a brother in Christ and someone from whom I could learn. Since then, I have met many Catholics and count some of them among my friends.

Being at home rather than at work meant that I occasionally listened to the radio. This was an era when the monopoly of the BBC had only recently been broken and many people enjoyed the novelty of listening to the new stations. One of these, Capital Radio, beamed mainly music to the London area and was very popular. I noticed that they played a huge variety of different music styles and it occurred to me that they might therefore be prepared to play some Christian music. I duly wrote to the head of music at Capital and was invited to visit him, taking along some samples of what I had in mind. I contacted some Christian record publishers and they provided me with a selection of recordings by some of the best Christian singers and musicians and I took these with me. The interview was extremely cordial. The man was clearly unaware of the breadth of the Christian music scene and was greatly impressed by the sheer quality of many of the recordings which I had brought. In short it was an eye-opener for him. At the end of the day, Capital decided not to incorporate Christian music into their programmes but the whole experience was a good one and may have had repercussions of which I am not aware. I was glad that I had been bold enough to try.

There were other visits and trips including one to Spain, but looking back to this period of my life, I feel that the most significant events concerned the rescue of two very different individuals whose stories I shall try to tell in some detail.

Towards the end of July 1978, I had an unexpected phone call from one of the singers from the 'If My People' choir. She had been in hospital for a serious lobotomy operation and while there had encountered a Christian young woman suffering from some kind of mental illness. For reasons that were beyond my comprehension, she had decided that of all people, I might be able to help. I had considerable misgivings about this but took down some details and agreed to pray about it. Over the next couple of days, God left me in no doubt that I had to go and see this young woman and so, with some trepidation, I set off to the psychiatric ward of the Royal Free Hospital in Hampstead one Friday afternoon to meet Rebecca.

To my surprise, she was only twenty-one and able to talk quite normally about herself. But as the minutes ticked by, it became apparent that some of her behaviour was compulsive and her words betrayed a mindset that was decidedly strange: I was out of my depth and could only pray with her and trust God to do something. Perhaps I was being manipulated, but she made it clear that she had valued my visit very much and asked me to come again. I could hardly refuse.

Over the next few weeks, I went to see her every three or four days. Sometimes we went for a walk on Hampstead Heath adjacent to the hospital. Sometimes we just sat in the hospital chapel and talked. Sometimes I took Marion with me. In between visits, I found myself writing letters to her, trying to follow through lines of thought we had discussed. It usually seemed impossible to get her to fully grasp anything when we were together, but I hoped that by reading and re-reading a letter, truth might gradually penetrate her mind and thinking. I have no idea whether this worked – probably not, because mental illness is not logical and so it is unlikely that reasoned arguments will ever prevail. However, I believe I got one thing right. Whereas the hospital were only interested in treating her as a patient and giving her drugs to suppress the symptoms of her illness, I was treating her as a human being and trying hard to show her real care and Christ-like love. I felt it was imperative that Rebecca knew that I was committed to her and had confidence in God that she would one day be healed.

In mid-September, she was discharged from hospital and returned home to her parents in Shropshire. She was obviously far from cured but I continued to write as and when I could, if only to keep in touch. In November, I made a trip to Church Stretton to see her. She was pleased to see me but was obviously not feeling very bright. I met her parents who expressed their thanks for all the help I had given to their daughter but an observation of the interpersonal relationships in the home was not encouraging. It was very clear that they did not know how to treat Becky and that there were tensions that were likely to exacerbate her condition. I was not therefore altogether surprised when, a few weeks later, I was notified that she had been readmitted to hospital – this time to a mental institute in Shrewsbury.

One of the best things that had happened at Northolt about this time was the arrival of a lovely young couple, Maurice and Wendy, who were incredibly supportive of our whole family and had great spiritual strength and maturity. (In later years, Maurice was to be appointed United Nations adviser on AIDS to the governments in Zimbabwe and Uganda.) It was Maurice who volunteered to drive me to Shrewsbury on a bitterly cold December day. If the weather was bleak, it was nothing compared to the grim and forbidding building which I had come to visit. It looked more like a prison than a hospital and in many ways this was close to the truth. I had to pass through several doors to enter a room like a large lounge where Becky was to be found and then the door was locked behind me. I was on my own with about thirty people, of mixed ages and sexes, all of whom were obviously considered too dangerous to be allowed into the outside world. Some of them looked at me with strange, uncomprehending eyes. Some totally ignored me. I found Becky and very gently started to talk. At least she remembered who I was and seemed pleased to see me; but she didn't seem to remember much else and certainly did not know why she was there, probably the effect of the drugs she was being given. I was only allowed about forty-five minutes and it was an uncomfortable and anxious time as I tried to keep one eye on the other inmates and hoped that they would leave us alone. At least I was able to pray with her before the door was unlocked and I was able to leave. It had not been a pleasant experience. The journey home was not pleasant either with snow starting to fall heavily as we made our way back along the M54. I could do nothing more, except pray.

Christmas came and went and soon it was spring. Suddenly and without warning I received a telephone call from Rebecca. She had woken up one morning and seemingly been healed. She was back home and doing a part-time job in an office.

I therefore returned to Church Stretton to see her and spent an unforgettable weekend. Instead of the rather pathetic figure struggling to cope with her thoughts and feelings, I encountered a young woman full of life and vitality. On the Saturday we went on the train to Ludlow and she took me on a conducted tour of what is a very attractive town. We talked about everything under the sun and she was revealed to me as someone with insight and intelligence. We laughed a good deal too and she was fun to be with. On the Sunday, we walked on the hills and through the woods around her hometown. I especially remember the carpet of snowdrops at our feet. It was here I discovered that, like me, she loved nature and had a sensitivity to beauty which matched my own. The change in her was amazing and I realised that for the first time, I was meeting the real Becky.

Soon after this she moved to Harrow and met one of our friends, they fell in love and got married in 1980. Her husband was one of the most patient, gracious and gentle men I have ever known and as it turned out he needed to be, because in subsequent years Becky had quite a few relapses and needed a lot of care and attention. But they did have some good times too.

Sadly, this story does not have a happy ending. During one of her bouts of mental illness, Rebecca went away and disappeared. She was last seen walking on the cliffs of North Devon but no body was ever found or washed up on the beaches. Her husband made enquiries through every missing person agency he could find but there was never any trace of her. After about seven years, he decided to hold a service of remembrance for her so that he could restart his life again and I was one of three people asked to speak at this service. It was all very strange – like a funeral but without a coffin or a corpse. I found it a tremendously emotional experience as I recalled that weekend in Shropshire when through months of tears I had finally discovered a beautiful person. I finished my talk by laying a single daffodil on an empty table at the front of the church. Rebecca loved daffodils.

The second story is very different. I have mentioned working with Trevor Martin at Bourne Hall in Ewell. During the summer of 1978, he held a couple of healing meetings at a big London church and asked me to play the piano for him as usual. At the end of one of these meetings, a little grey-haired lady approached me, asking questions about the fellowship at Northolt and my role there. After a bit she told me that there was someone who lived in Ruislip for whom she had been praying for some years and who, in her opinion, was ready to hear the gospel. She also thought that the Northolt Fellowship sounded like the sort of church this person would need once he had become a Christian. The bottom line was that she wanted me to go and visit this complete stranger. I was given the name, address and telephone number and so I agreed to try to do so in the next couple of weeks.

Understandably, it was with some trepidation that I knocked on the door of a house only a hundred yards from where my old junior school had once stood (it has since been demolished and replaced by blocks of flats). It was opened by a very large man with muscular arms, a scruffy beard and ... a wooden leg! I explained that Mrs Quick (the little old lady) had asked me to call and this seemed to satisfy him that I was not some kind of con man but as he invited me through to the back room of the house, I was intrigued to note that he placed the rolled cigarette from his mouth on to the top of the door frame and out of sight. How very strange! We sat down and introduced ourselves. His name was Stan. I learnt that he had suffered a motorbike accident at the age of eighteen in which he had lost a thumb and his leg. Subsequent to this, because of the pain he had experienced, he had taken codeine tablets in such large quantities that he had become an addict. He also drank large quantities of lager, initially to deaden his senses but now as a habit. In spite of his disability, he ran a builders' business specialising in extensions, conservatories and the like. I was later to learn that the business was in deep financial trouble and that a lot of dishonest dealing was going on to try to alleviate the situation. I imagined that with so many problems, here was a guy who would be eager for some answers and I told him in no uncertain terms that God loved him, that Jesus had died for him and that by inviting Jesus into his life, things could dramatically change for the better. He was not impressed except perhaps by my sincerity. As the conversation proceeded he poured himself a glass of amber liquor and offered me one. I declined. He also rolled and lit up a cigarette and constantly puffed away at it. Suddenly, he got up and opened the window, explaining that I would not be used to whatever it was he was smoking and so we needed some ventilation if I was not to have a nasty experience! In due course we parted on good terms, as I promised to pray for him and also gave him my phone number if ever he felt the need to discuss things further.

I heard nothing for about six weeks until suddenly, early one evening, I received a phone call from Stan asking me if I would go and see him immediately. An hour or so later, I was back in the house at Ruislip but with a very different Stan. He was as big and burly as ever, but less confident and in fact was contemplating suicide as the only solution to his plethora of problems. As we talked, I sensed that he might be under some kind of demonic influence and remembered how we had exorcised the young man at Langton years before. The prospect of being alone with this huge and obviously very strong man if he was indeed under such an influence was rather frightening and I started to pray like mad, albeit silently. Within minutes, the doorbell rang and who should be ushered into the room but the little old lady – Mrs Quick.

She may have been small but she was certainly not timid and told Stan just what he needed to do, and the effect was quite startling. Suddenly he seemingly collapsed from his chair on to the floor and started writhing about. Together, we commanded the evil spirit to leave him and after a few minutes, he seemed to return to normal but with a very different attitude. Step by step we led him through a prayer of repentance and inviting Jesus into his life as Saviour and as Lord, and then we prayed for him that the Holy Spirit would come and fill him there and then. After a little more discussion, Stan gathered up his collection of pills and they were flushed down the toilet. Quite a few cans of lager went the same way.

The next day, I went to see Stan on the building site in South Harrow where he was building a conservatory. He was a changed man. He had a smile on his face, and could not stop talking about what Jesus had done for him. The following Thursday, he was at our house and joined in singing the praises of his new-found Saviour with great gusto. He was to be a regular from that day on. He spent some days in the 'detox' unit at a local hospital to free himself completely from the codeine addiction but to my knowledge never returned to the habit.

Shortly after this, he broke up with his business partner to go it alone rather than be involved in dodgy dealings and the Lord honoured him for this. Certainly, Stan worked hard but new business poured in and over the next couple of years, Stan cleared his debts and started to prosper. He did make some mistakes. He rushed into a marriage that was a short-term disaster, but in later years, after a divorce he found his perfect partner. He and Rosemary have now been married for fifteen years and they are blissfully happy. Stan suffers from arthritis and spent some time in a wheelchair. But thanks to osteopathy, exercise and joint manipulation, he is now working again, although not in the building trade. He has shared his testimony with rich and poor alike on radio in London and on television in America. He is a walking miracle and always just full of the joy of the Lord. His generosity knows no bounds and he never ceases to remind friends and acquaintances alike that when the Lord decided to save him, 'He did it Quick and Sharp!'

A Whole New Ballgame

One morning in late April 1979, a letter arrived which was to completely change our lives yet again. It was from Gerald Coates and in it he recommended that the Northolt Fellowship should close down with immediate effect. Marion and I were stunned and shocked but in retrospect we could see that this situation had been simmering for a while.

During the previous autumn, it had been apparent that the fellowship was stagnating. I did not have the vision or gifting to be able to move it on, and sadly no other leaders had emerged to do so either. It was clear that we needed outside help. Of course, we had enjoyed a good relationship with Gerald but it was one of friendship and moral support and nothing more. We decided that we needed to give someone the authority to tell us what to do and how to proceed. But who? Gerald was obviously one candidate but there were some who were not comfortable with his style and said they would like to ask Roger Price to take on this 'apostolic' role. To have held a vote would have been potentially divisive so it fell to me to make a decision. In spite of my preference for Gerald, I felt I would probably keep more people happy by going to Roger and so I had duly written expressing our wish for him to come in and bring direction and purpose to us. The reply, when it came, notified us that Roger's health had taken a turn for the worse and so he was unable to take on any new commitments. I was therefore left with no alternative but to turn to Gerald. Over the next few months, he came to Northolt regularly but detected a reticence on the part of many members to follow his or my leadership and so the call to disband had come.

No one had fallen out with anyone. We all remained friends. In fact there were a couple of meetings where everyone considered the proposal and whether to allow it to go ahead. Surprisingly, we were almost unanimous that this was the right course of action. For one thing, there had been a dramatic change in the state of other local churches during the six or seven years of the Fellowship's existence. Instead of being antagonistic towards anything remotely 'charismatic' there were now at least three churches who were moving rapidly into the areas which we had pioneered. This meant that we no longer had this independent pioneering role to play. Another thing which we could not ignore was that God seemed to be moving people away, thereby almost pre-empting the dissolution of the Northolt Fellowship. Property in West London was (and is) very expensive and so it was natural for young couples to look for jobs in parts of the country where houses would be cheaper. One couple had moved to the USA, another to Germany due to a re-posting by the RAF. All in all, we sensed that Gerald had probably got it right and that it would be pointless to try to fight against the decision to disband.

He had made a further suggestion that many of the members including me and Marion should move to Cobham where we would become part of that fellowship and be able to help with the ongoing plans and vision there. Quite a few took up this suggestion. Others stayed in the Northolt/Harrow area and joined one of the three local charismatic churches which had emerged. Others, as I have intimated, were in the process of moving further afield. At this time Cobham was a very bright light in the Christian firmament and to have become part of that fellowship there would almost certainly have led to new and increased opportunities for ministry, both musical and in teaching. But I was not happy with this. I did not feel that I wanted to be part of a church set up that had everything going for it while other churches were still struggling. I wanted to join those who were still in a battle and get stuck into the fight, however hard it might seem and however long it might take to turn things around for God. I was also aware that we still had a huge number of friends in the West London area who found inspiration and encouragement from us both and did not want us to move away.

So we declined the offer and found ourselves stranded with no church and no job. In spite of my decision not to move to Cobham, the fellowship there very graciously agreed to help support me financially for at least three months until I could either find a job or qualify for unemployment benefit. Other friends both inside and outside the fellowship also gave or sent gifts to ensure that we were well looked after.

It was a strange summer. Martin took his GCSE examinations in June and then left school, so that from sometime in July, he and I started to pay weekly visits together to the benefits office to sign on. It was the first time in my life that I had been unemployed and from a worldly point of view this sounded like a very bad backward step. In practise, I reasoned that it was summer, the sun was shining, and it was so good to have the freedom to be out in the garden or in the countryside or by the sea. Many people would have given anything for just such a privilege but were stuck in offices and factories day in, day out. I was the lucky one and I determined to make the most of it. Martin and I went on a cheap weekend rail excursion to Wick and Thurso, the most northerly points on the Scottish mainland. We also had a day trip to Cambridge taking a young French student with us and Martin trying his hand at punting on the River Cam. Marion and I went to Church Stretton to further explore the wonderful hill country I had discovered there on my visits to see Rebecca. We visited our friends Rob and Gill in the Cotswolds, and Geoff in Hardwicke. I spent a whole week in Gloucestershire. After all, with no jobs between us, we were free to go anywhere God might lead us. But, no openings appeared. There was no voice from God or blinding visions and so I concluded that Gloucestershire was not for us at that time.

We also had a holiday in the Lake District, our first visit there for nine years. We went with a group of friends but suffered with the most appalling weather. I shall never forget returning to our cottage down the valley of the upper Esk after an ascent of Scafell, a long trek of about six miles. The rain came down in torrents, the path was like a river and undistinguishable in places from the real river. But we didn't care and just marched through the water, we were so wet that we couldn't get any wetter.

Eventually we concluded that we should stay in Northolt and therefore started in earnest to look for jobs. Martin was still keen on railways and his best friend at school had obtained a job with British Rail which led to him becoming a train driver within a couple of years. Martin was rejected for a similar position because he had less than perfect eyesight, but before long he was offered a four year apprenticeship in mechanical engineering at EMI in Hayes. This was not highly paid but gave him an opportunity to learn valuable skills which would open up many different possibilities in the years ahead.

Marion had worked part-time in a Christian bookshop in Harrow for a short while around 1973 but this had been for fun rather than money. Apart from this, she had not been in employment since Martin had been born. Now, she too found a job and started us back on the road to financial viability. She returned to her old baking skills and secured a part-time position working three days a week, making and decorating cakes at a high quality patisserie in Ruislip where she had worked nearly twenty years before. The shop was now owned and run by Germans. Not famed for their sense of humour, having Marion there probably brightened things up considerably.

That just left me. Of course, I wrote to my old departmental head at Glaxo, but this was a time of recession and I was told that unfortunately all new recruitment was on hold. Because of the economic state of the country, few jobs were on offer anywhere. Nevertheless I applied for several which looked promising with companies in the chemical industry. Initially, I had no success but eventually I had an application accepted and was promised an interview. However, even before this could happen, the company wrote again to say that they had just received a directive from the top to stop all new recruitment. I was back to square one. The Post Office seemed to be worth exploring, even if only as a temporary measure until something more suitable appeared. The idea of doing an early delivery round and then being free from about lunchtime onwards seemed very attractive. I had to attend a kind of exam for prospective candidates where the questions were mainly mathematical or common sense. Not surprisingly, for someone like me with a science degree, it was a doddle, and subsequently the Post Office had no hesitation in saying that I was just the sort of person they were looking for. However, there was just one query. On my application form, I had said that I did not ride a bike. They assumed that what I really meant was that I wasn't in the habit of riding a bike or that I hadn't ridden one for some years. However, the fact of the matter was, that I had *never* ridden a bike. When I was a child, my extreme self-consciousness had meant that I was frightened of making a fool of myself or even of drawing attention to myself and consequently I had never taken up the challenge of learning to ride. So I had never wanted a bike, never asked for one, never owned one and never ridden one. I must be almost unique in this respect, but it was enough for the Post Office to reject my application. Apparently, the ability to ride a bike was mandatory for all postmen. As summer passed into autumn, another option was offered to me – Father Christmas in a local department store! Apart from bringing up Martin, I had up to this time had no dealings with young children and therefore turned down what seemed to me a most unappealing prospect. In any case, I hardly had the right figure for the job!

Then one day in October, I saw an advert in our local paper for a job with a company on the Northolt trading estate, only fifteen minutes walk from home. Planned Equipment Ltd specialised in public address and background music systems. I liked music and I knew some physics so I thought it worth following up. The next thing I knew was a phone call asking me to attend for an interview. The job on offer was very varied. Firstly, small-scale installations of PA or music systems in hotels, offices and the like had to be organised, arranging appointments with customers and ensuring that engineers and equipment were all available on time. This would also involve using a computer to generate all the necessary paperwork and check on the progress of each job (computers were still something of a novelty in 1979). Secondly, I would need to raise invoices for service calls made to customers' premises to repair breakdowns. The third part of the job was particularly intriguing. Planned Equipment rented the sound system permanently installed in the Royal Albert Hall and it would be my duty to contact every client hosting an event at the hall to arrange terms and conditions for them to use the system and also have the services of one of our engineers to set up and control all the microphones and loudspeakers. There were some perks to the job as well. My immediate supervisor would be a tall, long-legged and attractive blonde girl in her late twenties and I was told that every Christmas, staff enjoyed a free weekend away at a hotel with a dinner and dance.

Having learnt so much, I was finally shown into the managing director's office for a chat. One of the questions he asked me was, 'What do you hope to be doing in ten years' time?' I suspect my response may have surprised him. I explained that I was a Christian (he must have known this if he had read the application form and seen what I had been doing for the previous two years) and that my hopes and aspirations were therefore tied up with knowing God's will. As such, anything was possible; I could be serving as a missionary in some remote part of the world or alternatively, I might be sitting in his chair as head of the company. By the time I returned home, I felt sure that this was to be my next job and Marion had a similar conviction in her spirit. Sure enough, within twenty-four hours, I was offered the position and I accepted it. Thus, on 29 October 1979, I set out from home to start work in an office for the very first time. As I walked there, I prayed that God would make me a good witness to my new workmates and that he would prosper me in everything I did. I was forty and a graduate, yet I was to receive what was virtually a school leavers' salary. However, I felt at peace in my heart about it and was confident that God could look after all our needs.

Although I felt a bit nervous at first because everything was so new to me, I soon began to feel at home. Working in an open-plan office made it easy to get to know people and most of my new colleagues were friendly and helpful. My official title was Progress Controller. Whereas at Glaxo, I had been just a very small cog in a very big machine, Planned Equipment Ltd (PEL) had less than a hundred employees and I soon got to know the role of each person within the company, and I therefore felt significant in the overall scheme of things. Pat, my supervisor, was pleasant, patient and helpful and it was invaluable to learn some computer skills. On a couple of occasions I was able to sit with our engineer at the Royal Albert Hall or obtain free tickets for a show. What's more, the Christmas party lived up to expectations. Each member of staff could take their spouse or partner with them, and in 1979 the event was held at the Falcon Hotel in Stratford-on-Avon. Because I had no car, one of the salesmen who lived in Harrow offered me and Marion a lift to Stratford late on the Friday afternoon. The weather on the journey was horrendous – continuous torrential rain – but later that evening, the food at the dinner was wonderful and instead of staying up late to dance or prop up the bar, Marion and I were able to enjoy the luxury of our hotel room with all its facilities – and at the company's expense. After an excellent breakfast on the Saturday morning, we had been promised a cruise on the River Avon but the river was so swollen with the overnight rain that the boats could not get under the bridges. Alternative arrangements were hurriedly made to enable our party to visit some of the Shakespeare properties associated with the Stratford area – his birthplace, Anne Hathaway's cottage and so on. We just walked in and were given guided tours where the public would normally have had to queue for hours and then pay through the nose for the privilege.

While the job situation had apparently been solved, there was still the question of church. Where should we go? During the previous few years, we had developed a close relationship with Roxeth Green Free Church and some of its members. The minister, Frank Gamble, was a lovely young man who was very open to the new movement of the Holy Spirit and was seeking to lead his congregation into those things. He had gladly and willingly opened his church up to the Northolt Fellowship for some of our 'All Saints Nights' and also allowed us to baptise some of our folk there at combined baptismal services. I felt he was a man to whom I could happily submit myself and that I could be comfortable to work or minister under his leadership. Having seen the way things were moving there, it had not been uncommon for a few NF members to go along to their Sunday evening services just as some of the younger people at Roxeth sometimes came to us on a Thursday evening. We had already formed some good friendships. John and Sheila and their two young daughters Sarah and Lorraine had become so very special to us that we almost felt like part of their family and I had also found two very good friends in Sue and Dixon Upcott. Their commitment to me had been clearly shown during the period of my full-time ministry, when they had given a regular monthly amount to help with my finances. A group of Roxeth members had also been to Spain in 1978 to visit a missionary couple associated with the church and at their invitation I had been privileged to accompany them.

With all these factors to influence us, it was not really surprising that we elected to commence attending Roxeth, but we did so with great caution. It was widely known that we had left Northolt Park some seven years earlier and taken most of their young people with us. Thus we had a reputation. Inevitably, there were some who questioned our motives in coming to Roxeth. Would we cause another split? We therefore kept a low profile, attending the services, but declining any further involvement until folk could get to know us better and hopefully come to trust us. Martin came with us too and joined the Covenanter group. It was good for him to be able to mix with people of his own age group and to make new friends in his own right rather than second-hand after his mum and dad. Thus, in the spring of 1980, he had his first real girlfriend and it was his parents who had the second-hand relationship!

With three pay-packets now coming into the family, we could afford to be a little more adventurous in our lifestyle. I decided that it was high time I was able to drive. A session of six lessons at the driving school was enough for me to pass my test at the first attempt. It was then time to look for a car. When I had left Glaxo, my income had been reduced by nearly 50 per cent and I was now on a school leaver's salary. Nevertheless, I suddenly found that I was able to afford my first ever car. I am constantly amazed by God's accounting. I can't explain it but if ever there was proof that God honours those who honour Him, this was it!

Regarding finances, when I left Glaxo, I had taken on the status of being self-employed and for the purpose of filling in tax forms I started to keep an accounts book in which I entered every single financial transaction. I have continued this practise ever since. It has enabled me to check that my expenditure is not exceeding my income and also whether I can afford to give away more in terms of gifts and offerings over and above the 10 per cent I have always given, believing this to be right from my understanding of the Bible. This practise, although simple, ensured that we never got into debt and I would recommended it to anyone for that reason.

I knew nothing about cars or car mechanics but Dave Oliver, a friend from Roxeth who had asked me to disciple him in his faith, certainly did; and together we looked at a number of second-hand motors until he recommended one as being a good buy. In April, I duly took possession of a six-year-old light blue Renault 12 saloon from a private seller in West Harrow. I felt rather nervous getting into a car to drive on my own for the very first time but I was only about 200 yards away from the house of my friends Sue and Dixon, and this was far enough to assuage of my fears. I then took Sue for a short ride and I felt exhilarated, knowing that the person sitting beside me was my passenger and not my instructor.

Another luxury was soon to be ours. Although I had been to Spain, Portugal and Ireland on missions and ministry trips, Marion and I had never had a foreign holiday together. Now it was the turn of more close friends to overwhelm us with their generosity. We had known Ray and Pam Giles for a long time. As a teenager, Marion had looked after Pam as her babysitter. In later years, after marrying Ray, the four of us had greatly enjoyed each other's company but then lost touch for a while. During the years of the Northolt Fellowship, our relationship had been renewed and we had even held the odd meeting in their house in Eastcote. At this time they had been attending a very dead church and Ray used to say that spending time with us kept his faith from drying up. Apart from this we had a great deal in common, not least that Pam was artistic and Ray loved cricket. They had bought a holiday apartment on the Mediterranean coast of Spain and invited us to join them there along with their children Sally and Andrew. We only had to pay for our airfares. At the end of a week, when they had shown us the ropes and we had become acclimatised, they went home and left us to ourselves for another week. It was blissful: lots of sun, good food, wonderful walking in the gentle hills behind the development, peace and tranquillity, and very romantic, even if we were forty. We visited Puerto Banus where the rich and famous keep their yachts and spend their fortunes in the boutiques and gift shops. We spent many mornings at the Villa Carna beach club where, just like the adverts, the Germans seemed to take all the best sunbeds and the Scandinavians went topless. We went to Ojen, the perfect mountain village, and also saw the rock of Gibraltar, although the border was closed at that time for political reasons. Of course, holidays in Spain are two a penny nowadays and hardly worth mentioning, but for us at that time, it was a delightful experience.

Did we feel disappointed that the Northolt Fellowship had ceased to exist? Perhaps, but we looked at history and saw that there have been plenty of instances where men have continued with something that started off well, long after God had moved on to something new. We would not have wanted to be another example of this. What was so gratifying was that many of our members had received a solid grounding in their faith and in the coming years would take up positions of leadership in the places to which they dispersed. Inevitably there were a few casualties, those who having lost their church could no longer be bothered with faith. They make us sad, but perhaps some had never really had a conversion experience, merely going along with the crowd because they liked the people. Most of the members recognise that the days of the Northolt Fellowship were very special and look back on them with gratitude to God for all that happened. We have quite a few letters thanking us for all that what we taught them. We don't see some of them for years at a time but when we do there is a close affinity between us that has lasted the intervening years.

'Westlife' and Poetry

Following the closure of the Northolt Fellowship and the other changes which I have just recorded, it was inevitable that life would be very different from anything that had gone before. Until now, our home had been the centre of things, but suddenly, people were not coming to us in the same numbers and if we were to maintain and build relationships, we had to go out to them. Having the car made a big difference and indeed it would have been very hard to increase our involvement with Roxeth people without it. The church was about one and a half miles from our home and most of the members lived on the far side of the church from us – a distance of two or three miles.

However, plenty of good things were still happening, leftovers from our previous pattern of life. Thus in 1981, we attended the weddings of John – a neighbour and ex-NF member – and also Liz, one of the students from Whitelands College who had now taken up her first teaching post. We led a weekend house party for young people from Greenford Baptist Church and while on holiday in South Wales, we visited a member of the 'If My People' choir who lived there; we were still in touch six years after the event! We went to Shipton Oliffe for the last time before our friends Rob and Gill, now with a baby and a toddler, moved to Stroud. We also returned to the apartment in Spain, by courtesy of Ray and Pam Giles, and enjoyed another wonderful holiday in the sun. This included a visit to the ancient town of Ronda, which is built on either side of a huge gorge and also boasts the second oldest bullring in Spain. It is an amazing place and well worth a visit. Closer to home, Martin celebrated his eighteenth birthday with a party and it was encouraging to see that he had made a number of friends at Roxeth who were invited to share the special day with him.

We too were gradually becoming a part of the Roxeth Fellowship. One of the elders had a relative who led the youth group at St Austell Baptist Church in Cornwall. This resulted in an invitation to me and Marion to speak at their house party. This took place at a youth centre known as Bernard's Acre, beautifully situated on the edge of Dartmoor. We were wonderfully received and evidently our ministry was such a blessing that they invited us back the following year, when we took Mike and Martin with us to lead some worship using their guitars. Martin had first taken an interest in the guitar at the age of fifteen when we had entertained a Belgian boy on a school trip. He had been exceptionally talented and this had given Martin the incentive to improve his own skills. It was a great thrill to have my own son sharing in the ministry of the weekend in this way. We were able to sit outside in a little amphitheatre with a babbling brook flowing by and hills rising all around us and praise the Lord of creation with our music and singing.

But perhaps the most far-reaching event of 1981 concerned a young woman called Loraine West. She was just one more member of the church who we encountered as time went by, but as we got to know her we were horrified to discover her story. Her husband had recently left her and gone to New Zealand with another woman, leaving Loraine with five children to bring up, the eldest of whom was only just eleven years old. It was a frightful situation and one that demanded action and not just pious words. We started to visit her at home in West Harrow, initially to see what we could do to help. One obvious answer was to look after the children so that she could occasionally be free to enjoy some kind of life, but before making such an offer, it was clearly important to get to know the children. Here was a problem, for I had never been very good with kids. We had spent most of our life with teenagers but I had never been a Sunday school teacher and always felt that I could not get down to that level, partly because my self-consciousness prevented me from letting my hair down and partly because of my serious and somewhat intellectual frame of mind. But here was a need and so I felt I must make an effort.

To my surprise I was an instant hit. The youngest of the five were both boys and really too young for me to build relationships with but the three girls, Esther (eleven), Katie (ten) and Bonita (eight), were old enough and sensible enough to be able to play board games and such like. This was where we started and after the first few visits, they always wanted to know when I was coming again. The result was that this family and especially the oldest girl, Esther, were to almost dominate my life for the next seven or eight years!

I soon received the nickname 'Kwipiter' – vaguely reminiscent of Christopher – and became a regular visitor to the house, often three or more times in the course of a week. Board games were a particular favourite but they were not quite as straightforward as I was used to. The girls would gang up on me and with a little bit of good-natured cheating, ensure that I would never win. Having been a very competitive person all my life, and consequently rather a bad loser, this was just not fair. But I soon learnt a lesson that I should have learnt long before: that playing the game is more important than winning and that what mattered was that the girls were having a lot of fun and enjoying themselves.

Without their father, there were many areas of life where a substitute was needed. Loraine had her hands full trying to cope with everything and so the least bit of help was welcome. In the Spring of 1982, Esther was to go away for a week on a school trip to Bath. She had to be at school at 6.30 a.m. to catch the coach and because Loraine had four others to get up and get to school, I offered to take Esther. With obvious financial problems in the household, luxuries like cameras were not on the agenda, but I thought it would make the trip more enjoyable if Esther were to have a simple 'shoot and snap' camera so I presented her with one. These gestures were not meant to curry favour, but as the months went by, I recognised that I had become special to her and the reverse was also true. I was very comfortable with the other children, especially Katie, but Esther almost felt like a daughter to me. Initially, I suppose I was a sort of father figure to her, but as she grew up and passed through her teenage years, the relationship changed so that I became more like a cross between an older brother and a favourite uncle.

The activities we shared were many and varied but they also would change over the coming years. Homework was always an important area. In her eyes, I knew so much and I was able to explain so many things and give all sorts of helpful ideas or suggestions. We often went for walks, usually with Katie and Bonita, and this could involve opportunities to climb trees or play hide and seek among the rhododendrons at Old Redding, a local beauty spot. We all made occasional trips to the shops on Saturday mornings, especially when there were clothes to look at. Teenage girls love clothes and also welcomed having their photographs taken in what they considered the latest fashion. At least once a year, I would take them to the coast – usually Littlehampton – for a day by the sea, building dams, playing hand-tennis on the sand, splashing around in the sea and in later years, getting a good suntan. When it was time for Esther to change schools and four years later when she would go on to sixth-form college, I was the one who went with her and her mum to look over the prospective establishments and help her make decisions. It was obligatory for me to attend any school functions such as plays or concerts if Esther was taking any part and there were quite a few of these when she joined a steel-band. She and Katie were both reasonably musical and I was able to encourage them in this. When they took a school music exam which involved singing a duet together, they arranged for me, rather than their music teacher, to go along and accompany them on the piano. When some money was made available for Loraine to have a loft extension built to help with the over-stretched accommodation of her family, Esther wanted to consult me about the decoration and how and where everything should be put. In short, I had become an essential part of the family set-up. At times, Marion shared in some of these activities, but she was happy to let me get on with it while she pursued other avenues of activity both in and outside of the church, but she was always a very good friend to Loraine and this kept everything in balance.

Most important of all, I wanted to help with Esther's spiritual development. I encouraged her and her sisters to read the Bible and I would sometimes pray with them before they went to sleep at night. I would talk to Esther about problems she might have with people at school or at church, and tried to be patient when she went through a rebellious and difficult period during which she was not at all nice. No one was more delighted than I was when she elected to be baptised by immersion in November 1984.

Around 1985 I started to write a few poems and one of them was written specifically for Esther. Her mother subsequently wrote it out in calligraphy script for her. I suspect the style was influenced by John Betjeman, a favourite of mine, but whatever you may think of my poetry, it described our relationship so well that I am going to include it here.

> I think it was in eighty-one
> In August that I met your mum
> And you were just a child of ten.
> But I was apprehensive then
> For I'd not had much time before
> For folks with kids. They seemed a bore!
> But truth was this – I wasn't sure
> If playing games upon the floor
> Would fit my image or my name.
> I couldn't ever be the same –
> I'd never thought to use my leisure
> Bringing little children pleasure.
>
> Very soon, my life was changed.
> Days and hours were rearranged
> As my time revolved around
> West Harrow and the friends I'd found
> At thirty-six Heath Road – the place
> Where friendship met me face to face;
> Your mother, sisters, brothers too,
> But most of all, my friend was *you*.
>
> The years since then have been such fun
> With many games both lost and won;
> Treasured walks through fields and woods,
> Treading streams in wellie boots;
> Trips to Wood Green Shopping City,
> Buying clothes that were so pretty:
> Doing homework, sharing chores,
> Playing ballgames out of doors,
> Making music, singing tunes;

Days on Littlehampton's dunes;
Quarter Pounders with French fries,
Bedtime stories, dewy eyes.
Wish those days would last for ever –
Happy land of 'Never Never'.

Times have changed, you're now fifteen
You've found new friends, a different scene,
And childish things have lost appeal
But boys and discos are for real.
On Saturdays you walk the shops
And you agree that Wham are tops!
But when you're tired, it's your delight
To snuggle up to Mum at night,
And having almost lost your dad
And seeing Mum so often sad
Has made it extra hard for you
To feel secure in all you do.

And so on this uncertain day,
What is there left for me to say?
I may not always understand
But still, I'd like to be on hand
To help you cope with every trial
And maybe pray with you a while,
Help you to know Jesus better,
(Like to buy you a red setter)
Reassure you when you're fearful,
Dry your eyes when you are tearful;
Always lend a listening ear;
When you're successful, give a cheer.
Your reputation I'll defend
But best of all, I'll be your friend.

With so much time spent with this family, it is just as well that we had minimal responsibilities at church. Perhaps, subconsciously, I had substituted one for the other.

Quite early on in our time at Roxeth, I was given the privilege of playing the piano for the evening services. At that time, only organ and piano were used. We eventually applied for membership, were accepted, and a year or so later, I was invited to share the leadership of a home group which met on alternate Wednesdays. Somehow we still managed to find time for plenty of other things. We made regular visits to John and Sheila's, often on a Sunday evening after church. Their home was a favourite venue, particularly if we wanted to watch anything on television (usually cricket or football), since we still had no plans to buy one of our own. If that sounds odd, I should perhaps point out that having TV at home can offer a huge temptation to stay in and watch it regardless of whether the programmes are worth watching. We didn't have time for that and never had. I called on Sue and Dixon as often as possible for friendship's sake and a chat; and there were plenty of new people to get to know. We tended to gravitate especially towards the young people, almost as a habit, but this was for friendship only, with no leadership responsibilities. I bought a quarter-size snooker table and this provided some home entertainment with some of the young men from church. Subsequently, I became sufficiently keen on the game to join a local club where I could play on a full-size table. We made friends with a couple called Jim and Margaret and this led to another interest. Jim was a keen birdwatcher and he invited me to go out with him on a number of occasions to various reserves. I was soon hooked, became a member of RSPB and purchased a good pair of binoculars. A few years later, on my fiftieth birthday, friends joined together to buy me a birding telescope. But again, I am rushing ahead.

It will be apparent from all this that, without being unduly selfish, we were building a new life where we could do and enjoy things for which we had previously not had time. This was also true as regards holidays, where, after years of organising parties of young people, we were able to go away on our own. I have mentioned our Spanish adventures. Now we returned to the Lake District at least once every year from 1983 to 1987 and visited the western lakes, which we had not previously explored. But before that, in 1982 we had discovered a new paradise – Rhossili in South Wales. This tiny village is situated at the tip of the Gower Peninsular, jutting out into the Bristol Channel. Just offshore is the small island of Worm's

Head affectionately known as 'The Worm' because, from a distance, it looks rather like a sea monster. There is a causeway over to the island which enables one to walk there for a couple of hours either side of low tide. Rhossili sits on top of the cliffs but one can climb down steep paths into a couple of delightful bays. Fall Bay is rocky and secluded but with lovely sand and overlooked by tall cliffs where rock-climbers frequently practise their skills. Rhossili Bay is three miles long and when the tide goes out, the expanse of sand is vast. Behind the sands, Rhossili Down rises to over seven hundred feet and there are also extensive dunes where, in summer, there is a wonderful variety of colourful flowers. Because it is high up, there are fine views from the village. On a clear day, the hills of North Devon are clearly seen and at night one can sit and watch no less than ten lighthouses winking at you through the darkness. But the best place of all is The Worm.

When you struggle over the rocks, covered in slippery seaweed or crunchy mussel shells, you wonder if it is worth the effort; but you have no idea of the experience that awaits you. Here is a real island, uninhabited except for the seabirds which nest on the cliffs – guillemots, razorbills and a few puffins. There are no roads or buildings. The only sounds are the sea and the birds wheeling overhead. The ground is a mass of flowers, especially pink seathrift, and there is a profusion of butterflies. Away in the distance, Rhossili village can be seen perched on the clifftop but seeming like another world. Here is peace, tranquillity, beauty and wonder.

We fell in love with Rhossili and returned a couple of months later for a long weekend. In 1984, we went again, this time with Esther and her mother and our Martin. I have since returned on three occasions and have decided that Worm's Head is where I would like my ashes sprinkled after I die. But let's not be morbid. I wrote another poem to try to express what I felt about the place and I reproduce it here.

> Dappled sunlight on the purple down
> Above a patchwork quilt of green and brown,
> The furrowed fields where martins swoop
> And swoop again around the whitewashed homesteads of
>   the town.

> The road winds narrow round St Mary's stack
> And past the inn, a well-worn grassy track
> Threads o'er the cliffs ablaze with gorse
> And yellowhammers perched aloft sing loud and answer back
>
> We watch the lines of surf, bedecked with spray
> Roll endlessly across the white-sand bay,
> While all around is azure blue
> From Burry Holme to Ilfracombe, some twenty miles away.
>
> Across the causeway's daunting rocks we slide
> Till eagerly we reach the other side
> To gain an Eden paradise,
> The only sounds the windblown grass and booming of the tide.
>
> The clumps of purple thrift become a bed
> To watch the gulls wheel silent overhead.
> Eternity steals into time
> And holds her breath to let us find the magic of Worm's Head.

It may not be the greatest poetry but if you ever go there, I hope you will feel that I have captured something of the atmosphere of this wonderful place.

Meanwhile, there had been some interesting developments in my work life. In the summer of 1983, Marion decided that perhaps she could give up work again. She suggested that by advertising in local newspapers, she could probably obtain enough orders for making wedding cakes to earn as much money as she was receiving at the shop. Working from home was obviously advantageous because of the flexibility which it offered. At about the same time, something happened at PEL. Realising that times were hard and with recession still the order of the day, the directors had wisely decided to diversify and bought a small company specialising in electronic fire alarms. As happens in most takeovers, there were areas of overlap between the operations of the two companies – two service departments, two accounts departments, two installation departments – and some redundancies were therefore inevitable. One of our auditors supervised the whole takeover process and in the course of this work he interviewed most members of staff in order to obtain a clear picture of their individual responsibilities. Apparently I impressed him to the extent that he made a recommendation to the directors that I should be promoted to a more responsible position. They listened and in due course I was made customer services' manager for the fire alarm side of the company with a significant salary increase. In the midst of all the reorganisation and redundancies, I was the only employee to emerge better off than before. Moreover, the timing was perfect. Marion gave up her job, started working from home and the wedding cake orders started pouring in.

Other changes were afoot. Martin had completed his apprenticeship, which included receiving an Apprentice of the Year award and was still working at EMI but on a decent salary. He could now afford to have wheels and so, in 1984, after I had bought a new car, he took possession of my old Renault. With this extra freedom, he decided to move to another church. He was now twenty-one and really too old for the young people's work at Roxeth. Understandably, he wanted some independence and so we were happy when he moved to Open Door Community Church in Uxbridge where his gifting was quickly recognised and he was soon helping to lead worship.

My new car was a maroon Austin Princess but not a standard model. This one had been modified to have a soft top. It had an automatic gearbox, beige imitation leather upholstery and was in every sense a very beautiful and luxurious car. I confess that it was the image of driving along with the open top on sunny summer days and drawing admiring glances from passers-by that prompted me to buy it. But pride always comes before a fall. It was lovely to drive, but as the years went by, everything imaginable went wrong and it cost me a fortune in maintenance bills. The ultimate disgrace was when it developed a fault in the oil system and started to spew hot oil from the engine. On one occasion this caused the felt lining under the bonnet to catch fire and a fire engine had to be summoned to put it out. By the time I got rid of it in 1988, I had learnt my lesson. As far as I am concerned, a car should not be a status symbol but merely a reliable, comfortable and reasonably economic way of getting from A to B.

Another key event at this time was the marriage of our good friend Mike to Paula. I was delighted when he asked me to be his best man as this was only the second time this had ever happened to me. Mike, as the true friend he has always been, bought me a new suit for the occasion. In fact we had matching white suits, and believe it or not, I still wear mine on special occasions more than twenty years on – proof that I have put on scarcely any weight in the intervening years. It was a very happy occasion and we were especially pleased when they moved into a house less than a hundred yards from Roxeth Church. Over the coming years, Mike and I were to continue to work closely together in the music realm at Roxeth and Marion and I were to become godparents to their first son, named Christopher. The whole family remain very special friends to us and since they moved to Weymouth in 2003, we miss them very much.

Late in 1984 there was another crisis at PEL. The integration of the two companies had not gone smoothly and in the interests of economy, more redundancies were announced. 1 November was always known thereafter as Black Friday as the company shrunk in size by almost a third. Naturally there was significant reorganisation and once again, in the midst of alarm and despondency, I was promoted. A new combined service department was formed under a director – Ted Brown – who had specifically asked that I should be his right-hand man in the daily running of the department. It was another new beginning and a very exciting but demanding time.

Servicing of audio systems was largely a question of repair work, but fire alarm maintenance is mainly preventative and as such is required by law. I had to take two groups of engineers who had been working in these separate areas and gradually combine them into one force with expertise in both disciplines.

The largest preventative maintenance contract which I inherited was with Berkshire County Council, where we were required to visit around 600 sites (schools, colleges, old people's homes, libraries, council offices etc) four times a year to check and ensure that their fire alarms and emergency lighting systems were fully operational. As part of this contract, I was required to visit Shire Hall in Reading every couple of months to meet various representatives of the county council. Most of the time, this was a pleasant experience, but a bit daunting if I knew there were situations where we were failing in our commitments. There were numerous other smaller contracts of a similar nature but while I struggled to keep things under control, Ted set about gaining yet more large contracts. The company had recently started to install complex and sophisticated sound systems in large shopping centres and with our new range of expertise, we could offer fully comprehensive contracts for sound and fire systems and by carrying out the work at one and the same time with one set of engineers, handsome profits could be made. The growth and success of the new service division was phenomenal, but it was not without a lot of hard work. From the first day, I was struggling to cope with the customer workload because there were not enough engineers. The routine maintenance programme was compulsory but I decided that the only way to ease the situation was to pray that there would be very few faults or breakdowns to which I would have to divert engineers. It worked and before long the situation was under control. Ted knew that I was praying about this and he has since told me that he and the managing director joked about it. Ted has since become a Christian and now recognises that prayer probably was a key factor in our success.

Because of the extra hard work I had put in during the transition and start-up of the new division, Ted offered to take me and Marion out for a meal as a mark of his appreciation and gratitude. Not many bosses are so generous. A date was fixed in February 1985 at a hotel close to Heathrow Airport. It was a very cold night and snow that had fallen the previous day had frozen solid in places, resembling an ice rink. After I had dropped Marion off at the hotel reception, I parked the car in the car park and while walking back, lost my footing on the ice and went crashing to the ground. Instinctively, I put out a hand to break my fall and when I got back to the hotel, the pain in my right wrist was intense. In spite of my embarrassment, Ted insisted that the hotel manager provide a bandage and with this wrapped very tightly around my wrist for support I was able to manoeuvre my knife and fork sufficiently to eat my meal. But as you've probably guessed, I had broken my wrist and had to go to hospital the next morning to have it set in plaster. I was still able to write and type to a limited extent, but fortunately by this time I had acquired an assistant at work who was able to help me. However, the main thing I learnt from this incident was how dependent I was on the car, as I was unable to drive for some weeks. It was therefore with some reluctance that I had to agree when Marion suggested that she should learn to drive. I wasn't sure that she would make a good driver but I could see the logic in her argument. In fact, she duly passed her test and is a very competent driver. I repent of my male chauvinism!

Marion passed her driving test in June 1986 but in that same month we had a very sad event – a death in the family. Throughout our married life we had never had any pets. I love dogs, especially large ones, but with Marion making cakes for a living, it was essential to have a hygienic environment with no risk of getting hairs in the icing sugar. Additionally, large dogs eat a lot of food and need regular exercise, for which we had neither the money nor the time. However, our next-door neighbours at number five had a dog and three cats. Possibly this resulted in the individual animals receiving less attention than they would have liked, but for some reason one of the cats, a very beautiful tortoiseshell named Patch, seemed to prefer our company to that of her owners. I am not a cat lover, but I found an exception in Patch: she was affectionate, loyal and very lovely. Throughout the latter years of the Northolt Fellowship she was a regular at the Thursday night meetings. If she was not present at the start, she would come and sit on the windowsill outside the lounge, looking in at the assembled crowd and mewing loudly until we let her in. If we went out in the evening by car, she would be waiting for us by the kerb on our return and seemed to recognise our car.

She would then race us to the front door, and try to get in before we could stop her. Obviously she liked the warmth of the house at night. There came a time when she would climb on the veranda at the back of our house, and learnt to jump from there through a small open window to get into our bedroom. She would then sleep at the bottom of the bed, purring loudly and refusing to move if she happened to be at the spot where our feet wanted to be. She was great company and we had all the pleasure without the responsibility of feeding her or paying vets' bills. However, her owners were away on holiday when she became ill. The neighbours at number seven who had been given temporary responsibility for the animals, took her to the vet but it made no difference. She came into our house to sit under a chair in the lounge, scarcely moving for a couple of days and obviously in pain. It was there that she died. When Martin came home from work that evening, he buried her under the lawn. It was a sad day but inspired another poem.

> You waited for us night by night
> And welcomed us with sheer delight
> As we returned from visiting friends.
>
> You always raced us to the door
> And once inside, you rubbed your fur
> Against our legs,
> Entreating us with pleading eyes
> To share our food and realise
> The snug security of our bed.
>
> You talked to us in your unique, inimitable feline way
> And we conversed with you and swore
> You understood our every word;
> And you preferred our company to wandering in solitude
> And seemed to find contentment in our midst.
>
> You were an uninvited guest
> At many functions down the years;
> But always welcomed, loved, caressed.

And oft your photograph appears
An ever-present actor in the pageant of our family life,
A character in your own right.

And now you've gone,
The places that you favoured with your presence
While you watched our busy lives go by
Seem empty, colourless and sad.
We look in vain for flash of amber,
Black and white upon the windowsill
And grieve that we shall never hear your voice again
Or stroke your coat so beautiful.

But we were glad that at the end
You chose to let us care and tend
And comfort you in pain. It seems
Absurd to cry over a cat!
But many tears were shed today
For you were so much more than that:
You were a friend.

But I must move on to more important things. During the early eighties, there had been a split in the church at Roxeth. Some of the members had gone with Frank Gamble to form a new church based in Stanmore while his associate pastor, Gilbert Kirby, remained to look after those who stayed at Roxeth. The reasons for this are not relevant here. Suffice to say that while we had strong sympathies with what Frank was doing, it was quite impractical for us to attend a church in Stanmore more than seven miles away. Of our close friends only Sue and Dixon departed, but the division did leave some serious gaps at Roxeth. Over the next few years, the young people's work (Covenanters) developed a serious lack of leaders and a corresponding deterioration in both the size and vitality of this group. The situation came to a head in early 1987. Our local Anglican church, Christ Church Roxeth, were organising a week-long camp at a youth centre called Hall's Green in Kent. Their youth group was huge but someone suggested that they might invite any young people from our church who wanted to go, bearing in mind that our group was too small to do anything similar on our own. It was a nice gesture and six Roxeth youngsters showed real interest; but there was a snag. They could only be accepted on condition that a couple of leaders came from our church to share in the responsibility. At first no one was forthcoming, but since three of those wanting to go were Esther and her sisters, Marion and I volunteered for the job. Two of the Christ Church leaders, Paul and Jill Benstead, came to visit us and find out what we had to offer. My only contribution was the ability to play the keyboard, but when Marion announced that she could cook, they told us that this was an answer to their prayers.

Hall's Green is great for young people. There is a superb assault course in the grounds and a small open-air swimming pool. The dormitories are fitted out with bunk beds which were pretty comfortable and facilities for cooking, eating and holding meetings are very satisfactory. For most of the time, however, I felt redundant. We were tremendously impressed by the number of leaders Christ Church possessed and with their talents and powers of organisation. It was only when some kind of problem arose that we perceived the relative immaturity of some of these leaders whilst we were able to deal with the situation with some degree of wisdom borne out of our greater years of experience. We felt that our contribution had been minimal but the Christ Church leaders felt that we had been like house parents to them and the experience meant that we made some new friends – particularly Paul and Gill.

The repercussions of the camp were at least twofold. Having tasted youth work again, it was only a matter of months before Marion and I, along with Jim and Margaret and a couple of other folk, became the new leadership team responsible for getting the Covenanter group back on its feet again. The other result was that Esther and her sisters left Roxeth to join up at Christ Church. This was perfectly understandable. They had made many new friends at Hall's Green and of course some of them were very nice boys!

Although I must return to 1987 later, it would be a serious omission to finish this chapter without completing the story as far as Esther is concerned. I continued to visit the family regularly and usually spent at least one evening a week with Esther right up to and beyond her eighteenth birthday. Of course, our relationship was now on an adult basis and we would chat, listen to music, eat or sometimes watch TV. But it was important that I gradually withdrew so that she could spend time with the new friends of her own age. However, we always remained very close. She eventually married Andrew, one of the Christ Church young men, and I was privileged to go with her to help her choose her wedding dress and also to give the message at the marriage service. Today they have four children and after moving to the South Coast, they were actively involved in a big and lively church. As I write, the whole family are in Thailand on a short-term missionary tour. Esther and I always try to meet up on or near our respective birthdays in March and September as well as at other times and we remain the closest of friends. To what extent did all my input into her life affect her spiritual and emotional well-being? I can only guess, but if I had my life a second time, I would certainly do it all again.

Family Matters

1987 marked our twenty-fifth wedding anniversary and so it was a year to celebrate. By this time we had finally paid off the mortgage on our house and with Martin able to contribute to the family income, PEL paying me a reasonable salary and Marion making plenty of wedding cakes, our finances were looking quite healthy. We decided on a three-fold action: we purchased a new three-piece suite for the lounge; we went to the Isle of Skye for twelve days' holiday and we arranged a large party where we could invite all our friends to come and celebrate with us.

Marion didn't enjoy the time in Skye as much as I did, mainly because she was anxious about all the plans for the party which was to take place only two weeks after our return. Nevertheless, it was a good experience. Skye is like nowhere else in the British Isles. The Cuillin Hills resemble a landscape from another planet, likewise the weird-shaped pillars of rock known as The Storr, which are scattered over a hillside near the island capital, Portree. We explored much of the island during our stay. We reached the summit of one of the few mountains over 3,000 feet which do not require any rock-climbing and, amongst a variety of birds rarely found in England, we saw several golden eagles. We had an intriguing experience at an island church one Sunday where, contrary to most English practise, we were required to stand for prayers and sit for the hymns, which were sung with absolutely no musical accompaniment. Fortunately we were allowed to sit for the sermon which went on interminably. The preacher spoke on the text 'remember Lot's wife' and was very loud (he shouted), zealous and animated in his proclamation of the gospel, possibly imagining that we were sinners who needed to hear it. We felt quite intimidated by it all, but after the service the people were very friendly.

One disadvantage of Skye is the weather. On our previous visit, we had found that it was indeed 'the misty isle' as it is often called, but on this occasion we were fortunate to enjoy plenty of fine weather and there was scarcely any rain during our stay. It was particularly amusing to sit by the harbour at Uig in full sunshine looking away to the clear shapes of the Outer Hebridean islands on the horizon while listening on the car radio to the tennis news from Wimbledon where rain had caused the abandonment of play for the day! The other disadvantage of Skye is that it is a very long drive from London – getting on for 600 miles. Because of this, I don't think we are likely to return there.

The party on 14 July took the form of a sit-down meal in the afternoon followed by an informal service of worship and thanksgiving. Approximately eighty guests were present at the meal whilst about forty others who had been invited were unable to come for various reasons. Others, including many of our friends from the Roxeth young people's group, joined us for the service. The guests represented every phase of our lives. Mum and Dad were there together with Marion's father; there were people from our early days at Ruislip, including both our bridesmaids; people from Northolt Park; many Northolt Fellowship members and a goodly number of our new Roxeth friends. The event was held at Roxeth Church and it was some of the Roxeth young people who acted as waiters and waitresses. Jim Humphries acted as a kind of best man, ensuring that all the arrangements on the actual day ran smoothly. He did a great job. I gave a speech relating in ten minutes flat all the momentous happenings from twenty-five years that have taken up eight chapters of this book. Martin also said a word or two and read out various cards and messages that had been received from those unable to come. There was even a card personally signed by Cliff Richard. (No, we don't know him; but one of our friends had access to a companion of Cliff's and managed to arrange for him to sign the card, much to Marion's delight. She has been a life-long fan!) When we had sent out the invitations, we had made it clear that we did not want any presents. After twenty-five years of marriage, one has most of the things one needs and there is no point in money being wasted on 'stuff' that will be put away, never used and probably forgotten about. Instead, we said that there would be a collection box available in which gifts towards foreign missions could be donated if anyone wanted to do so. As a result of this, we were thrilled to be able to send over £300 to World Outreach, a missionary organisation we had supported all of our married life.

Our anniversary year would not have been complete without a visit to our beloved Lake District, and we spent a happy week in a cosy self-catering flat in the village of Clappersgate in October. One morning, shortly after waking up, we switched on the radio to hear the morning news only to be very puzzled by what was being said. There was no news, merely a couple of people somewhere discussing how impossible it was to get to work and how long it had taken for emergency generators to start working. As they talked about road and rail transport in the capital being at a standstill and electrical supplies out of action, we wondered what on earth had happened. Eventually, the facts emerged: it was the great hurricane which the weather experts had failed to predict but which had turned out to be the worst storm of the century, causing untold damage with literally millions of trees blown down. We looked out of the window. All was calm and still – scarcely a breath of wind! We spent the rest of the day out walking but with one eye on the weather, expecting any moment that the wind would start to rise and that we would catch the back end of the storm. It never happened! That evening, we telephoned Martin at home to make sure that our house was intact with the roof still in place. We were reassured but a little surprised that the phone was answered by a female voice. Just a friend from the Open Doors Church in Uxbridge was the explanation Martin gave us, but it soon became apparent that our son was really in love with the lovely Geraldine, and before long we would come to know and love her too.

The following May, all four of us went to the Lake District together. Gerry was introduced to some pretty strenuous climbs (Easy Gully on Dow Crag – not a place for the faint-hearted!) but seemed to cope well enough. However, most days, Marion and I did our thing while Martin and Gerry did theirs; we then met up together for our evening meal. It was a particularly good week in every way. Shortly after this, Martin took out a mortgage on a studio flat in Iver Heath looking ahead to the time when he and

Gerry would be married; but before that happy occasion, there was to be a sad one.

Mum and Dad had always seemed to be in reasonable health. Whenever we went to visit them in Seaford, we would go out walking, and in the home they appeared to cope very adequately with all the essential chores around house and garden. They were also very active in their church and seemed to enjoy life to the full. I suppose that in those circumstances, one tends to think of people going on for ever, but of course this can never be the case. However, it came as something of a shock when, in November 1988, Barbara phoned me to say that Dad had suffered a stroke and was partly paralysed down one side of his body. She had gone down to Seaford to be with Mum and help her cope with everything. At my first opportunity I took a day's holiday and went down to Sussex to visit Dad, who had been hospitalised in Eastbourne. I was only present for about an hour but it was a sad time. Superficially he seemed quite bright but the paralysis had affected his face causing his features to look somehow distorted and inevitably this had affected his speech, which was hard to understand. It also meant that it was difficult for him to eat or drink without some of the food dribbling from his mouth. I was sad because I did not want to remember Dad in these terms. I wanted him as he had always been.

A few days later, Dad had another stroke from which he never recovered consciousness and suddenly I was bereft of my father. In a way, I was glad because there seems little point in living if one's quality of life becomes unacceptably bad. I would not have wanted Dad to have lingered on for years, paralysed and maybe helpless. Nevertheless, death has a finality about it which leaves a deep impression and I was naturally upset. Perhaps the worst moment was at the funeral watching the coffin leave the church, knowing that I would not be seeing or speaking to him again. Thank God, as Christians, we have a hope of eternal life and I am sure that one day, Dad and I will meet again and I shall be able to tell him about all that's happened since his death. Or maybe he'll know already. Or maybe it won't be relevant any more. At any rate, I am confident he'll be there.

Sadly he could not be here to see his grandson get married. 29

April 1989 was dull and cold, unlike the previous day which had been hot and sunny. But happiness does not depend on such quirks of nature. Martin and Gerry got married at Northolt Park Baptist Church just across the road from us, an indication that any bad feelings about what had happened in the early seventies had been forgotten. The building was loaned for the occasion but the service was led and conducted by the pastors of Open Door Church. The reception was then held at Roxeth so in a strange way, Martin's wedding day embraced all three of his spiritual homes. Suffice to say that a good time was had by all.

Earlier in the year, I had reached the grand old age of fifty, another opportunity for a celebration. This was an ordinary working day but Ted, my boss, took me and Marion and three close colleagues out for a drink and a buffet lunch in a hotel in Hillingdon. Then in the evening, Marion had arranged a small and rather intimate dinner party at a Christian bookshop in Uxbridge. There was an excellent but inexpensive sit-down meal for about twenty people and I had selected some of my closest friends to share my birthday with me. It remains in my memory as a very special evening because my life has been so enriched by friendship and this party emphasised just how I felt about these extra special people. The fact that they had all clubbed together and bought me a birding telescope was almost irrelevant, except that whenever I went bird-watching in future I would remember them all.

My sister Barbara had not attended the wedding of the year. Actually there had been an important event on at their church in Kent that day but even so, her husband Malcolm had been suffering from very poor health for some years and she had been heavily committed to looking after him. Eventually he found it necessary to retire from the Baptist ministry and this created a problem as they had nowhere to live. At this point, Mum came to the rescue by inviting them to go and live with her in Seaford. This was a very generous gesture but one which worked out amazingly well in the next few years. Mum was now in her late eighties but I no longer needed to worry about her because I knew that Barbara was on hand. Subsequently, Malcolm had several heart bypass operations and over a period of a couple of years gradually returned to some measure of health. It was then that he was offered another pastoral job – one with a difference.

Just north of Walton-on-Thames in Surrey is a place called Whiteley Village, named after William Whiteley, the entrepreneur and founder of Whiteley's department store on Queensway, London. In his will, he left money for a village to be built as a safe refuge for retired people. The village is enclosed by high walls except for two entrances manned by security staff. Once inside, the houses are small and compact, ideal for elderly couples who do not want to spend much time on maintenance. Within the confines of the village are a couple of shops, a community centre, a hairdresser's and everything else required for a self-contained lifestyle. There are also extensive woodlands and two churches – Anglican and Nonconformist. It was this Free Church that was offered to Malcolm, one where there would be no youth work, just a regular Sunday service and the occasional funeral! There was an added bonus of a roomy and well-appointed flat in the village to go with the job. It was too good a chance to miss and Malcolm accepted it, even though it meant that Mum would be on her own again.

Barbara moved to Whiteley in January 1992 and the next year was a somewhat anxious time. Mum celebrated her ninetieth birthday in September of that same year but she had become very deaf and whenever we telephoned her, we never knew whether her failure to answer meant that she did not hear the bell ring or that she had collapsed and might be dying. It was a great relief therefore when Malcolm managed to use his influence with the authorities who ran Whiteley Village to arrange for Mum to move into an old people's home there. Unlike the self-contained houses, this home was staffed by nurses and others who were on hand at all times. Mum could have her own room and as much of her own furniture and belongings as could be fitted in; but her meals would be provided, her washing and cleaning done for her and she would be well looked after. Of course, there was a price to pay. We therefore sold the bungalow in Seaford, invested the money and used it to pay the monthly charges. It was not cheap but it meant that Mum was secure and largely content. I shall never forget her comment around the time of her move. She told me that she had prayed, asking that the Lord would use her and fulfil His purposes through her in the new surroundings in which He had placed her. What a prayer for a ninety-one-year-old! Truly, she was an inspiration to us and to many of her fellow residents and staff in the home. She never missed an opportunity to talk to them of her faith in Jesus. I hope my faith will be as vibrant if I live to be ninety!

Whilst these family matters were taking place, other changes were occurring. It seems that after the age of fifty, people often start to take an interest in gardening. Of course, there are many younger gardeners but the trend today is for more and more gardens to be converted into what the estate agents call 'low-maintenance' areas; in other words, patios, decking and perhaps a bit of lawn but nothing requiring any serious weeding or cultivation. Certainly, until about 1990, I had always looked upon the garden as a necessary evil. I wanted it kept reasonably tidy but that was about the limit of my horticultural ambition. Suddenly all that changed. What passed for a rockery had been overrun by a thorny shrub with immense prickles whose roots took so much moisture that nothing else would grow; it had to go. Once it was removed, I was able to re-lay the rocks, buy some rock plants and watch as the area developed shape and colour. It was only a start, but gardening has been a hobby and a pleasure ever since. I cannot resist visiting a garden centre and normally come away with a few new plants. I have discovered a special affection for fuchsias and am often 'collecting' new varieties. I also love geraniums, roses, hollyhocks and delphiniums, all of which now figure prominently in our garden.

Marion and I continued as joint leaders of the Roxeth young people's group and in August 1990 took about thirty teenagers away for a week-long house party to Seaford – 'camping' in the Baptist Church hall. We also had responsibility for leading one of our church's home groups.

The highlights of the following year were Esther's wedding, to which I have already referred, and a trip to the Lake District, by courtesy of BBC Radio 2 to which we were regular listeners. At this time, the Radio 2 Breakfast Show was hosted by Derek Jameson and from time to time, the show would take the form of an outside broadcast from some popular or interesting location. When it was announced that one of these was to be from a steamer on Lake Windermere, Marion wrote off for free tickets and we were amongst the lucky successful applicants. Mum had always loved the Lake District and although she was eighty-nine at the time, we felt this was an ideal opportunity to take her there for probably one last visit. We asked for an extra ticket and the BBC granted our request. We set off from Northolt around midnight and drove through the night arriving at Lakeside at about 6 a.m. Here we boarded the steamer and in due course set off along with Derek Jameson, his weather girl Anne O'Brien, various technicians, about one hundred guests like ourselves and a small jazz band led by the one and only Roy Castle. We listened to the band, enjoyed a delicious breakfast, chatted at length with Anne O'Brien and than watched as the broadcast went ahead. A couple of hours later, we disembarked at Bowness and then had to return to Lakeside by the public steamer service to pick up our car and proceed to a cottage in Troutbeck where we had booked two nights' accommodation for the three of us. Of course, Mum could not do any climbing but she was thrilled to see the mountains one more time against all expectations, and that in itself gave us great satisfaction and made the trip seem doubly worthwhile. Perhaps someone will do the same for me when I am too old to get to the Lakes by myself. Shortly after this trip, it was announced that Roy Castle was suffering from lung cancer. We actually had the privilege of hearing him play on one of his last public performances at the Ruislip Golf Club in June 1994.

There was to be one more event of great significance in 1991. On 24 May, our first grandchild, Alexandra Louise, was born by Caesarean section. May I be forgiven for saying it, but newborn babies are often very red and scrawny and unattractive. However, Alexandra was beautiful. I had viewed grandparenthood with some misgivings. It made me feel so old! But those feelings now evaporated. Marion and I had entered a new phase of our lives.

Into Europe

No, this has nothing whatever to do with our membership of the European Union!

During the Christmas break in 1992, I happened to see the film *Shirley Valentine* on TV at someone's house – I forget where. The film is about a housewife, bored to tears with her job, her marriage and her lifestyle, who decides to go to Greece to look for some adventure and romance and finds plenty of both. I was neither bored nor looking for romance but I was confronted with the fact that we had hardly ever been abroad and having passed the age of fifty, if we did not start soon we would be too old to enjoy whatever delights foreign travel might have for us.

Having always been rather over cautious when making decisions, I decided we would go to Jersey the following summer. One could hardly claim that this was 'abroad' but at least we had to fly rather than getting into the car and of course Jersey has a strong French flavour about it. The place names, the street names and the names of some of the shop proprietors all gave us the feeling of being in another country, even if we still used English currency and spoke our native tongue. So at least it was different and whetted our appetite for more adventurous exploits. The following year, we went to Majorca.

This was more like it! En route to Palma, we flew over the snow-capped Pyrénées, which were amazing and merely served to make me want to go there and climb them. On arrival, we hired a car for the duration of our stay. For someone who had never owned a car younger than six years, it was a new experience to find myself at the wheel of a two-week-old Fiat Punto with less than a thousand miles on the clock. Even more interesting was the dual challenge of driving on the wrong side of the road and sitting on the wrong side of the car. To my surprise, I soon got used to finding the gear lever on my right-hand side but throughout our stay, I still instinctively reached over my right shoulder into thin air to search for the seat belt whenever I was about to drive off.

We stayed at the resort of Puerto Pollensa in the far north of the island, our hotel being on the seafront. In the heart of the town, there were restaurants and bars frequented by mainly British holidaymakers and selling traditional British food and beer. They sounded both noisy and rowdy in the evenings and so we steered clear of these places and enjoyed eating food with a Spanish flavour out of doors at the waterfront restaurants. Our room was fine except that it overlooked a road in which there was a loose manhole cover. It seemed that every passing vehicle throughout the hours of darkness made a special point of driving over it causing a loud 'kerplunk'. We also found that the local cleansing department collected all the rubbish, nightly, at about 3 a.m. But we got used to it after a while and managed to sleep more or less undisturbed.

On our first full day, we decided to walk over the hills at the back of the town to the smaller resort of Calla de San Vicente. I never could resist hills! Our map showed the existence of a path but no one had ever warned us that foreign maps are not like the Ordnance Survey maps we are used to at home. There may have been a path once, or perhaps there was going to be a path in a few years' time when the council had got round to making one, but we couldn't find it. However, the terrain looked easy enough to find our own way and so, undaunted, we set out on what seemed a fairly straightforward expedition. How wrong can one get? We had overlooked the small matter of latitude. We had set off soon after breakfast in pleasant sunshine but within an hour or so it was very, very hot, hotter than we had ever encountered. We had not thought to take any water with us and there were no trees in sight to provide any shelter. Within a very short time, Marion was suffering from something approaching a panic attack probably brought about by mild dehydration. Miraculously, we suddenly came across a huge boulder, big enough to provide some shade and for a while we rested and cooled down a little. But by this time we were as good as lost on the hilltop with no alternative but to try to find a way down to Calla de San Vicente. There was no road or path in sight and the ground looked increasingly rough.

Suddenly, from out of nowhere, a motorcyclist appeared and wonder of wonders, he spoke English. Yes, if we continued downhill in a certain direction we would come to a track which in turn would lead us to a road and from there on it was easy. He rode off and disappeared in a fold of the hills. We followed his instructions and within a little over an hour were sitting beside the almost unbelievably blue waters of a small bay, with large ice-cold drinks in our hands watching an assortment of humanity going through the various stages of getting a suntan, from blotchy red to silky bronze. As we looked back on what had been a chastening experience we could not help but wonder about the man on the motorbike. Who was he, where had he come from and what possible reason did he have to be there in the middle of nowhere at that particular moment of time? We came to the conclusion that maybe he was an angel sent to help us in our time of need. If so, we hope he'll identify himself when we get to heaven so that we can thank him properly.

The rest of the week was full of interest and incident. We visited the ancient town of Pollensa where we counted as we climbed the 365 steps leading to a small shrine. We sat on the bridge (reputed to date from Roman times) that stretched over a river that had completely dried up in the summer heat. We visited a monastery at Luc where we listened to a delightful boys' choir singing what we assume were sacred songs, although the words were obviously foreign to us. We visited a nature reserve and generally saw birds that we had never seen in England, including a really close encounter with a hoopoe. We drove to the west coast where we found real mountains and lakes which made wonderful photographs, although the mountains looked utterly unclimbable. One more memory was of the day we found a party of about 200 schoolchildren on an outing to the Formentor Peninsular. They were trying to take a group photograph but with great difficulty because members of the party were constantly running out to take their own pictures. We *think* they were Spanish, but in any case they did not speak the same language as us. Nevertheless, by means of signs and a lot of laughter, Marion somehow persuaded them to leave a pile of cameras with us and then get into an orderly mass and we spent the next five minutes acting as group photographers. Only Marion would have done such a thing. She never ceases to amaze me.

No doubt many of my readers will have been to Majorca and are familiar with the many delights of this idyllic island, so before this turns into a travelogue I must move on. Suffice to say, it was a wonderful holiday and I had become well and truly hooked on going abroad.

The following year we went to a little known part of Europe – the Picos de Europa, which are mountains in the far north of Spain rising to over 9,000 feet; the area is a hotspot for birds, especially birds of prey. We stayed in a farmhouse miles from the nearest town run by a young English couple, David and Lisa, who really knew their birds. There were booted eagles, short-toed eagles, Bonelli's eagles, Egyptian vultures, griffon vultures and much more. But better still were the mountains, the highest we had ever encountered. On our arrival, we looked around and saw very ordinary mountains such as we might have seen in Scotland or the wilder parts of the Lake District. But the next morning we awoke to find that we had only been looking at the foothills. The previous evening's mist had cleared to reveal majestic peaks towering above the valley which took our breath away; we just had to go climbing.

Our first walk was about as disastrous as our first day in Majorca. Our host dropped us off in his Land Rover at a point where we could climb over the top of a very modest mountain to descend a grassy knoll down to the valley and thereby return to the farmhouse. All went well until we reached the low summit when it started to rain. (The rain in Spain is supposed to fall mainly in the plain! How inconsiderate!) Accompanying the rain was a thin mist which somewhat reduced visibility and this only served to make me lose what is normally an uncannily good sense of direction. We proceeded down the hill in the general direction of home but the elusive grassy knoll never materialised. Instead we found ourselves at the top of a line of precipitous cliffs which seemed to stretch for ever in both directions. Evidently we had come down the wrong side of the mountain! Knowing what we had done wrong was not very helpful as it was now getting quite late in the day and we were already feeling rather tired. Once again we were well and truly lost. The one redeeming feature at this point was that I had my binoculars with me to observe any unsuspecting raptors. A scan of the surroundings revealed that at one point the gradient of the cliffs seemed a little less steep and the slope rather more grassy than rocky. A close scrutiny from the top of the incline through the binoculars convinced me that it was a possible mode of descent without actually attempting anything suicidal. In Marion's case, this was accomplished almost entirely on her derrière rather than her feet and consequently it seemed to take for ever. But we managed to descend without injury (except to Marion's trousers) and walked to the nearest village from where we were able to phone for David to collect us in the Land Rover. Once again, we felt that God had looked after us and rescued us from a nasty predicament.

Later in the week, I went on a cable car for the first time, ascending the central massif of the Picos mountains at Fuente De, and then having the strange experience of walking through a snow-field in shirtsleeves because of the hot sun. There was another brilliant day out in the mountains accompanied by Teresa Farino, an eminent botanist and expert in the flora of the area, who was able to show us all manner of exquisite alpine flowers. The only disappointment of the week was that we didn't see any bears. Yes, bears! The Picos are one of the last places in Europe where a tiny population of brown bears cling to existence. Perhaps it was too much to expect, but David, our host, did tell us that he had seen unmistakeable pawprints in the snow when he had been climbing a few weeks earlier.

In the years that followed, our European excursions continued with trips to Paris, Austria, Slovenia and also to Andorra, where I climbed some of those snow-capped mountains I had seen from the aircraft a few years earlier. But in the meantime, there had been another development which brought us into closer contact with our continental neighbours.

For a few years during the first half of the nineties, our spare room had been rented to Gary, a young man from our church, whose mother had died of cancer when he was fifteen. When his father had moved house, Gary had stayed with us in order to complete his education without having to move schools. Subsequently, he moved back with his father who had remarried but because Gary found it difficult to get on with his new stepmother, he asked if he could come back to live with us. He then went off to agricultural college for a couple of years but remained our lodger during the holidays until, having obtained some qualifications, he set up his own landscape gardening business. It soon became apparent from his expanding collection of tools and growing piles of paperwork that he had outgrown our accommodation and he eventually moved out to a place of his own. But after a while we realised that we were missing the income from the rental of his room. We therefore approached an agency who specialised in arranging short-term visits for foreign students wishing to improve their English language skills, and offered them our room and our services. It was a decision based entirely upon financial considerations, a desire to boost our modest family income; but it was to turn out quite differently.

Our first visitor was an Austrian gentleman, a teacher who was accompanying a group of young people from his country; but for the rest of the summer of 1996 and into 1997, the agency insisted on sending us a succession of young students from France.

It is time for a confession. Up to that time, I had felt a distinct dislike for France and everything French. This was based largely on what seemed to me clear evidence that they did not like us! Whenever there was an industrial dispute in France, it seemed that the dock workers would effectively close the channel ports so that British lorries carrying goods to the rest of Europe were delayed endlessly at Dover and their owners lost huge sums of money. Frequently, the French air traffic controllers would strike at bank holiday weekends so that British holidaymakers would be stranded for days or have to travel hundreds of miles out of their way to reach their destinations. The history of the EEC suggested that French politicians really didn't want the British interfering in what they considered to be their domain; and what could you say about any race that ate frogs, snails and horses? The atrocities carried out at the time of the French Revolution were not exactly endearing, and moreover, a glance in my history books revealed that Britain and France had spent an inordinately large proportion of the last millennium fighting each other or else being on opposite sides during more general wars. Perhaps, therefore, an inherent dislike of each other had become built into our respective genes. Well, that was my excuse for what was a very unspiritual prejudice! But now the very people I disliked were coming to stay in my home and to my surprise, they were all so nice!

The first was Laurianne, a lithe, athletic girl from Corsica who was studying law in Paris. She was followed by Cecile, a very warm and affectionate young lady, and then by Sandrine from the Ardennes whose only vice was that she smoked. Christoph from Troyes was about six foot five, very charming but with a huge appetite. Finally, there was Anne, from the extreme south of France, who endeared herself to us as a fellow lover of the countryside. Our brief was to provide a room with a bed, breakfast and an evening meal; anything else was entirely at our discretion. During the weekdays, they would attend a college in central London for English lessons. The weekends were free. We heard of students being treated like outcasts, hardly being let out of their own rooms, having to eat on their own, do their own washing and even being excluded from the house on Saturdays and Sundays so as not to disturb their host families. We couldn't be like that. It really is true that the love of God is in those who trust in Jesus and this undoubtedly affects our behaviour and the way we treat those who are strangers. From day one, we made it clear to our guests that we would treat them as part of the family. We ate together, spent our evenings together chatting, playing board games, helping them with their homework and learning about each other's countries. When we went to church or visited friends, we encouraged them to come with us and usually they did. At weekends, we offered to take them a little further afield to places like Windsor or St Albans or for walks in the countryside. It was like suddenly having a grown-up daughter or son around the house and our lives were immediately enriched and enlivened. It was great and we loved it – never mind the money aspect.

These students all signed our visitors' book and their comments were lavish with praise. I am almost embarrassed to quote some of their remarks but I do so merely to show the level of appreciation they obviously felt. One student made an entry in the form of a film review as follows: 'One of the most lovely couples on earth' – *The Times*. 'Worth meeting them' – the *Sun*. 'If you don't like them, you won't be able to like anyone' – *Daily Telegraph*.

Others thanked us for being patient, kind, generous, understanding, friendly and 'nice': in short, we seemed to have made a hit with them just as they had made a hit with us. But one thing that became clear from these early encounters was the spiritual barrenness of France as a whole. It is a secular state where religion is neither taught nor encouraged. Not surprisingly, therefore, most of the young people have grown up with little or no knowledge of even the basics of Christianity. This was certainly true of most of these students and indeed those from France who came later. In some cases, grandparents were nominal Catholics and had instilled a little background knowledge, but it was also very clear that the Catholic Church in France was without much life and that its adherents were mainly elderly. Most of our students therefore classified themselves as atheists. Nevertheless, many of them were prepared to come to church with us and were agreeably surprised by what they saw and heard. This was not what they thought church was all about, and the experience provided openings for us to share our faith and tell them about Jesus.

Thus, what had started out as an exercise to increase our annual income had turned into a pleasurable ministry and I found myself wondering what I should do about these 'heathens' from just across the Channel. My prejudices had collapsed and my first thought was that I ought to begin praying. But France is a big country. Where should I begin? I felt that maybe God would begin in a number of centres and then move outwards, like bonfires sending out sparks to ignite the areas round about. Four places that I had heard of came to my mind: Rouen, Nantes, Clermont Ferrand and Toulouse. I was very ignorant of French geography and had to look them up on a map before discovering that, roughly speaking, they were in the north, the west, the centre and the south of the country, respectively – not a bad start! However, what followed was really strange. In the following twelve months, the next four French students to arrive on our doorstep were from the close vicinities of these same four cities! Was that spooky or not? No, I think it was God, merely confirming that I was on the right lines and encouraging me to keep praying. Sometime after this, Marion heard a mention on the radio of an organisation dedicated to spreading the Christian gospel in France by the establishment of evangelical churches there. We made the necessary enquiries and before long had become supporters of that organisation – France Mission.

Another spin-off from this 'French connection' was that we received invites from two of our students to go to stay with their families in France. We were happy to accept and in July 1999, we spent six delightful days with Anne and her parents in a small village called Murviel de Beziers, about ten miles from the Mediterranean coast. We relaxed, ate and drank by the side of the swimming pool and walked through the vineyards surrounding the village. We were treated like royalty and although Anne's parents had a minimal grasp of English, we still got on very well thanks to some elementary French from my schooldays and Marion's ability to 'speak' with her hands and gestures! We explored the nearby city of Beziers including a visit to the cathedral; we watched men playing boules; we had a morning by the sea and generally imbibed the atmosphere of French rural life. Our final day was 14 July, our wedding anniversary and also Bastille Day, a national holiday, and that evening we were taken to Cap d'Agda on the coast to witness the annual firework display. Literally tens of thousands gather around a large bay and the fireworks are set off from floats out on the water, commencing at about eleven o'clock. I have never seen (or heard) anything like it. It was incredible and I have to say that it has spoilt me for firework displays ever since. Most are just third-rate by comparison.

The next day, we set off by high-speed train to Toulouse. We were very impressed by the comfort and efficiency of the French railways and it was fascinating to watch the countryside change as we travelled west, from a land of vineyards to fields full of sunflowers. You probably know that in French, they are called *tournesol* (literally 'turn to the sun'), but I never ceased to be amazed at the way in which every single flower head across a huge field would be inclined in exactly the same direction – presumably towards the sun! We spent a few days in Montrabe just outside Toulouse with Estelle and her parents and again had an excellent time of sightseeing. Estelle then took us down to the Pyrénées for a week where we walked amidst some magnificent scenery. To add to our pleasure we had yet another new experience, encountering the Tour de France on one of its mountain sections. We discovered that it is as much a circus as a sporting event. Support cars and lorries and advertising vehicles, some of them like carnival floats, proceeded in front of us for what seemed like a couple of hours, the occupants throwing baseball caps and other advertising trivia to the spectators before eventually the cyclists raced past and were gone in a flash. But we did see Lance Armstrong, the American champion, wearing the yellow jersey as the race leader. He was to go on and win the event for the second year running and subsequently became the most successful cyclist of all time in the Tour.

This whole trip was wonderful and there followed an open invitation to stay at Murviel any time we wanted to, something we have since enjoyed on several occasions. We have been so blessed by the hospitality of our French friends but our experience is a reminder of the faithfulness of God's promises. Jesus said:

> Give and it will be given to you; good measure, pressed down, shaken together, running over ... for the measure you give will be the measure you get.
>
> Luke 6:38

We had opened our hearts as well as our home to the students, but we received more in return than we could ever have imagined.

Everything considered, I found the way of life in southern France very attractive. I wondered at one time if maybe the Lord wanted us to move there to live but this was not to be. It was sufficient that we had tasted France, enjoyed its good points, but also seen its deep spiritual needs and committed ourselves to pray for it. We still pray regularly both for the country and for each of the students who came to our home. With one possible exception, we have not yet seen any of them become Christians but we have not given up on them ... because, we are convinced, neither has God!

Before leaving Europe, there is one other incident which deserves a mention. In October 2002, we joined with about fifty France Mission supporters on a five-day coach trip to the Loire Valley in central France. We were to visit several evangelical churches run by France Mission, meet the leaders of these churches and hear something of the work they were doing and the difficulties they encountered. Also included would be visits to several famous chateaux, a vineyard and a wine-tasting experience. The party assembled at Ashford station in Kent from where we were to travel by coach through the Channel Tunnel to France. As we approached the passport control point prior to parking on the train, the leader of the party asked us to have our passports at the ready in case they were needed for examination. At this moment, we had a horrible realisation: we had forgotten our passports! This may sound very foolish and the party leader thought we were joking when we admitted our problem, but in the past, going abroad had always meant going to the airport; getting on a coach at Ashford had lulled us into forgetfulness. At this point we had to make a decision. It would have been almost impossible to get off the coach and in any case we had paid for our trip and were looking forward to it. The coach driver assured us that it was very rare that anyone actually boarded a coach to look at individual passports and suggested we just keep a low profile. We took this advice and the driver proved to be correct in his assertion. We thus spent five days in France with no authorised documentation but had to endure a lot of ribbing from our fellow travellers, who promised to visit us in prison when we were refused re-entry to Britain because we could not prove our identity! It didn't happen, but our experience does show how easy it is for illegal immigrants to move from country to country.

Time Marching On

Whilst our horizons had been expanding into Europe, life in the United Kingdom continued to be full of incident throughout this period and not least because of some exciting new initiatives in evangelism. The nineties was designated the 'Decade of Evangelism' by the then Archbishop of Canterbury but of course it is one thing to say this and quite another to carry it out. I'm not sure what the Church of England did about it, but our old friends Graham Kendrick and Gerald Coates certainly made an impact.

Many people never go to a church service and probably think of church as no more than a set of mysterious rituals happening in dimly-lit buildings behind stained-glass windows. Around 1986, attempts were made to take the church out of the building and on to the streets. This was pioneered by Graham's own church in south-east London and involved Christians singing, worshipping and praising in carnival-like processions. It was an immediate success as people saw that Christians could enjoy themselves and be full of life, fun and vitality. The next step was for the concept to be sold to a wider group of participants and this was where Gerald came into the picture in collaboration with Roger Forster of Ichthus Fellowship, Lynn Greene from the organisation Youth with a Mission (YWAM) and of course Graham Kendrick. These four friends felt called by God to arrange a united march around the City of London, the financial centre of the country, 'to proclaim the name of Jesus and to pronounce the defeat of the spiritual forces entrenched in the capital and heart of the nation'. Graham wrote a script consisting of songs, chants and set prayers and churches around London were invited to join the event.

The 'City March' as it was called took place on 29 May 1987 – a very wet bank holiday Monday. In spite of the weather, an estimated 15,000 Christians gathered together in Spitalfields Market for an initial time of praise and worship before setting out on the march. The streets were comparatively empty but this did not matter. This was not a publicity stunt (although any publicity was of course welcome) but a time of prayer and worship with spiritual objectives in mind. We were concerned to challenge the evil forces of greed, materialism and corruption in the City and to see God at work changing the whole spiritual climate of this area of London. Marion and I were part of the march and felt this was a pivotal moment in the history of the capital.

The following year, a similar march was arranged around Westminster, the political centre of the capital, and police estimated that an amazing 55,000 people took part. March for Jesus had really taken off! Once again, we were there with a good contingent of folk from Roxeth Church. I still can remember as vividly as yesterday watching the crowds streaming across Waterloo Bridge to join the march. There were families with young children, teenagers with their incredible vivacity and enthusiasm, old folk, even people in wheelchairs. Many groups carried banners declaring the Lordship of Jesus but also showing where the group had come from. How exciting it was to see that denominational differences had been put to one side and there were Anglicans, Methodists, Baptists and those with no label joining hands across denominational barriers, united in their desire to see Jesus uplifted and the nation transformed by the power of the gospel, proclaiming Him as Lord and Saviour of mankind and as the supreme answer to personal, social and political problems.

In subsequent years, 'March for Jesus' was decentralised. In 1989, smaller marches were arranged on one and the same day at forty-five major towns or cities throughout the United Kingdom and in 1990 there were over 600 marches, including one in Harrow. I well recall joining with Christians from a number of Harrow churches to walk through the main shopping precinct and then gather for worship and praise together on the lower slopes of Harrow Hill behind the railway station. But it was disappointing to see no more than 250 present when the number of Christians within the borough must have been at least ten times that. It grieved me and still does that so many Christians are not prepared to stand up and be counted. No wonder the world thinks that we are a small, insignificant and impotent minority.

However, March for Jesus continued to go from strength to strength and was soon to become an international phenomenon with millions of Christians in as many as fifty countries worldwide marching on the same day to declare that Jesus is the Saviour of the world and to proclaim their allegiance to Him as Lord of their lives. You can read all about this movement elsewhere, but suffice to say it was a fantastic experience to join in joyful procession with tens of thousands of our brothers and sisters praising God and exalting the Lord Jesus Christ. What made it even more amazing was the knowledge that this same process was happening all over the world. The words of an old hymn came to us with renewed force:

> As o'er each continent and island the dawn leads on another day,
> The voice of prayer is never silent, nor dies the strain of praise away.
> The sun that bids us rest is waking our brethren 'neath the western sky,
> And hour by hour fresh lips are making Thy wondrous doings heard on high.

I guess this is true any old day of the week but it was especially true on 25 June 1994, designated 'A Day to Change the World'. Did the world change? Only God knows that. But throughout the decade, the various marches awoke men and women to a realisation that the church exists not so that we Christians can enjoy our holy huddles, but to be salt in an unsavoury world, light in a dark world, and to seek to further God's kingdom in every land.

Another event we attended in 1994 was Spring Harvest – a Christian holiday conference held at Butlin's camp at Minehead in Somerset. Whilst I was in employment and only getting about twenty-two days' holiday a year, the idea of spending time at a Christian conference did not appeal. That may sound terribly unspiritual, but it was true. I could listen to Bible teaching and take part in worship any Sunday at home but I felt I needed a complete break away from everything when I took my annual leave. Consequently, I had not even considered going to events like Spring Harvest but I allowed myself to be persuaded on this occasion by the fact that a party of about thirty would be going from Roxeth and this was being organised by Marion. Easter was early that year and this was reflected in the weather, which was more like winter than spring. It rained, it snowed, the gales blew and it was very cold. Ducks settled on the puddles which formed outside our chalet and on more than one evening we wondered if the 'Big Top' would blow down. But it was both profitable and enjoyable for all that, with excellent teaching and inspiring worship. However, one very curious incident occurred.

On a particular evening, Marion decided that, rather than attend the main meeting in the Big Top, she would go to one of the fringe meetings where the worship was perhaps more exuberant (in line with her personality!). I went to the Big Top alone and amongst the 5,000 or so present, found myself sitting next to a quiet young man in his twenties. At a couple of points during the meeting and again after it was over, we chatted briefly. We said nothing of importance but were both on our own and perhaps felt the need for a little companionship. Meanwhile, amongst a crowd of nearly a thousand, Marion got talking to her neighbour at the other meeting (she will talk to anybody – everybody if she had the chance!). In fact she actually prayed with the young woman concerned. Next morning, Marion and I went together to the morning Bible study and afterwards as we walked towards the exit, we confronted the very same two people we had spoken to the previous evening. They were together and had seen us. They were man and wife! This seemed such an extraordinary coincidence that we concluded God was in this somewhere and we arranged to meet up in our chalet to find out a bit more about each other. It transpired that they were employed at a famous public school in the Midlands. They told us how God was starting to move amongst the pupils at the school and how they were involved in trying to make them into real disciples of Christ. For our part, knowing how much we loved working with young people, we wondered if perhaps God was opening a door of opportunity for evangelism and teaching at the school. We prayed together, exchanged addresses and parted with a degree of excitement.

Although we did keep in touch for a few months, nothing ever came of it. Very strange! Maybe the encounter was for their benefit rather than ours. Perhaps they needed to be able to share their hopes and dreams with someone else and maybe our prayers gave them just the encouragement they needed to press on with them. God works in mysterious ways. One day, I'll ask Him what all this was about.

Another exciting event which took place in September 1995 was the Northolt Fellowship Reunion. It was not our idea, but a number of those who had been regular members of the fellowship back in the seventies decided that they would like to meet up with everyone again to renew old friendships and remember past blessings. I was persuaded to go along with this although my overriding reaction was that we should be moving forward, not looking back. We held the reunion at Roxeth one Saturday afternoon and evening and we were amazed that folk came from all over the country to be there. We all chatted and caught up on family news while partaking of light refreshments and then got down to the serious business of praising the Lord for all that was past and committing ourselves afresh to Him for all that was yet to come. Our Martin led a time of worship and praise and then I spoke from Romans 11:29: 'The gifts and the calling of God are irrevocable.' It was exciting to see so many NF members and to confirm that they were still going on in their faith, fifteen years down the line. But it was a good opportunity to remind them and me that it is God's faithfulness that ensures we are still standing.

Meanwhile on the family front, our second grandchild Matthew Christopher had been born in June 1993 and in 1995 the family moved from Iver Heath, fifteen minutes down the road, to Angmering in West Sussex, about seventy miles away.

By about this time, we had completed paying off the mortgage on our house, and with regular promotion at PEL our finances were in sufficiently good shape for us to consider some major expenditure. We had invested in new windows in about 1990, to make for easier maintenance. The old iron frames which were replaced had been a nightmare to rub down and paint and the modern double-glazed windows had made the house snug and cosy in winter as well as cutting out the sound of traffic on the main road. Now we decided to modernise the kitchen. With Marion still making wedding cakes as a regular pastime, this was an opportunity to redesign it exactly as she wanted it for ease of working and storing of cakes. We went to a reputable and well-known company who assured us that they could install what we wanted in just three days, and we were allocated a slot in early August 1994 for this purpose.

The fitters duly arrived on the day in question and by about 10 a.m. had ripped out almost everything from the old kitchen – but then they came to an abrupt halt. The fuse box was of an old, obsolete type and they informed us that it was against regulations to fit new wiring to such a box. Before the kitchen could be rewired for all the electrical points required, the fuse box and associated wiring would need to be replaced. We were not happy! Knowing that we had been in the house twenty-five years, we had pointed out the ancient style fuse box to the company surveyor when originally placing our order and been assured that this did not constitute a problem. Obviously, he had lied to us and suddenly we found ourselves with a kitchen containing … nothing.

We found an electrician from the local *Yellow Pages* and arranged for him to come and replace the fuse box at his earliest convenience, but the fitters had a tight schedule and by this time our time slot had gone and they had other places to attend to. We would have to wait and it transpired that we were likely to be devoid of all kitchen facilities for at least three weeks. Even then, the oven we required was out of stock and even when it did arrive and was fitted, as soon as the power was connected the fuses all blew. We again had to get our own electrician to come and rectify the wiring. There were other problems; a work surface was flawed and the washing machine was plumbed incorrectly. The job was finally completed in October – almost three months late! But perhaps there is a silver lining to every cloud. We naturally claimed compensation from the company concerned and after a long fight and a lot of correspondence we obtained a refund of £999. (Apparently a four-figure sum would have demanded authorisation at a higher management level and would have taken much longer.) I am tempted to write that 'if you want a new kitchen never to go to M***n', but maybe they have improved since then.

By this time, I was often leading worship at Roxeth and this is not easily done when playing an upright piano as you are hidden from part of the congregation. I was advised by musicians at a workshop I attended in Cobham to 'get a keyboard'. The £999 refund was more than enough for a second-hand model which served the required purpose admirably. I subsequently bought a superior model and this lasted until such time as the church replaced the piano with a keyboard of its own. It still comes in useful, as I shall relate in due course.

So we had a new kitchen and a new keyboard and now I discovered a new hobby. I had always had a hankering to paint. When I was a teenager, I had done some sketching which showed some promise but in forty years I had not developed any artistic skills I might have. I had only talked about it. Then in 1996, our friend Pam Giles, herself a very artistic person, presented me with a set of paints, a couple of brushes and a book outlining the basics of watercolour painting as a Christmas present. Suddenly I had no excuses and indeed, had I not made an attempt to produce some artwork, Pam would justifiably have felt very hurt and upset!

My first efforts were distinctly naff, but as time passed, there was a marked improvement and eventually after two or three years I was sufficiently encouraged to even frame a few pictures and also present one or two to friends as gifts. But I still have a great deal to learn. I am frustrated that my work is so erratic; some parts of a picture may be very good, others obviously poor. (This is similar to my snooker – a couple of great pots which Steve Davis would have been proud of and then a horrendous miss on the simplest of shots.) Because of this, I find a strong feeling of inertia overtakes me, probably born of a fear that what I am about to begin is going to be an abject failure. The next problem is that once started I am impatient for results. I rush the drawing because I want to get on with the painting and then I fail to allow things to dry properly or fail to plan how best to organise the work so as to get the kind of effect that I want. But I am grateful to Pam for getting me started and am determined that one day I will produce a masterpiece that will even meet my own stringent perfectionist standards.

The 1980s were a very significant time in the economic history of Britain. This was the period when Margaret Thatcher was Prime Minister and monetarism took over as the underlying principle behind many government policies. Making a profit was seen as essential for the economic health of the nation, but prices had to be competitive in the growing world market and so the only solution to the problem was to cut costs. The simplest means of doing this was to reduce the workforce. The result as we moved into the nineties was that more and more employees found themselves working harder than ever before, often doing what had previously been done by two or more people. Redundancies were the order of the day and for those still in jobs, work became synonymous with stress. Working at PEL was no exception.

From the time when Ted and I took over the service division of the company in November 1984, everything had expanded dramatically. As I related in a previous chapter, it is a legal requirement that all public buildings having a fire alarm system should be covered by an agreement to maintain that system and this will normally entail routine maintenance visits, two or possibly four times a year, in addition to providing a call-out facility for breakdowns or failures of the system. Ted was very successful in obtaining such maintenance agreements with a number of large organisations – Mothercare, Harrow Borough Council, WH Smith, to mention just a few. Where buildings had fire alarms, security alarms and sound systems all installed, it was obviously an advantage for one company to be able to offer servicing facilities in all three areas and PEL had the expertise to do just that and so this led to more contracts, including those with several very large shopping centres. All of this was fine, but I had the unenviable task of having to make sure that we carried out our contractual requirements by not missing any of the routine calls whilst at the same time ensuring that emergencies were met with a minimum delay. This should not have been too difficult but for another change under the Thatcher government – competitive tendering. It had became compulsory for contracts such as those I have described to be put out to tender and it was expected (although not enforced) that the lowest tender would gain the contract. This was very unjust, since it took no account of the level of expertise being offered or of the ability of the cheapest contractor to be able to meet his obligations. Indeed, there were several occasions where we heard of small and incompetent firms winning a contract but then having it taken away from them because they could not perform the tasks expected of them. But competitive tendering for PEL meant that we had to offer as low a price as we dared in order to obtain the contract and then operate on the barest minimum of staffing levels in order to make some sort of profit on the venture. Consequently, I never had enough engineers to meet all my needs and some days were like a nightmare trying to juggle my meagre resources in an effort to keep every customer happy. It was very stressful.

For many years, I would come home at the end of the working day, slump into an armchair and do nothing for the rest of the evening. I had no drive or energy left for anything else and the weekends were a welcome release. This obviously took its toll on my mental and emotional reserves. Some of my colleagues at work commented that I was not my old self. I found I was in danger of being curt and unfriendly to customers on the phone and constantly complaining to my directors on the impossibility of the situation. Eventually, one day in early December 1996, I finally cracked. I had gone in to the office but found that my hands were shaking violently, I could not think straight and I felt dreadful. I went home and the following day visited my doctor, who diagnosed my condition as nervous exhaustion and recommended complete rest for a month. It was at this point that I came to appreciate fully how fortunate I was in having good bosses. The managing director acknowledged that I had the hardest job in the company and that no one should have to do it for more than five years: I had been at it for twelve. Accordingly, he and Ted reorganised the department so that I could make a sideways move to a less stressful role dealing with all the service paperwork and invoicing, but with no decrease in salary. I returned to work in the new year very grateful for their kindness, and thankful to God for watching over me.

Nine months later, on my return from a week's holiday in the Lake District (where else?) I was surprised to receive a phone call at home from my immediate manager. He said he had some good news and some bad. The bad news was that the company had passed into voluntary receivership, but the good news was that he and one of the directors had decided to buy the more profitable parts of the company and that I was included in their plans for the new venture, doing essentially the same job as I had been doing before. What can I say? God has been so good to me throughout my working life.

There are two more events from this period of my life that I must record. On 6 September 1997, the funeral took place at Westminster Abbey of Diana, Princess of Wales, following the fatal car accident in Paris a week earlier. Of course, I was as upset as anyone but the special significance of this day was that on that same afternoon, Marion and I had to attend the pre-arranged wedding of the daughter of our friend Kathy – yes, the one who fell through the ceiling at our maisonette. I had been granted the privilege of preaching the message. Coming just one and a half hours after the entire nation had been glued to their TVs and filled with grief, this was one of the most difficult tasks I have ever had to tackle. I could not pretend the funeral had not happened. It was in everyone's mind. But weddings are supposed to be happy occasions, not sad, and I had to strike a balance between the two emotions. With God's help, I coped!

In early 1998, my mother was taken into hospital following some kind of internal haemorrhage and bleeding. Tests failed to reveal the cause but after her discharge, it became apparent that she needed more medical attention and supervision than could be offered in the old folks' home at Whiteley. At Barbara's request I managed to arrange for Mum to move into a private nursing home in West Harrow, which was obviously very convenient for us to visit. During the coming months, Mum started to lose her memory and there was a corresponding deterioration in her general health. By June, she did not seem to recognise either me or Marion and although we talked with her normally, we wondered how much she understood. In July, she suffered another serious haemorrhage and passed away peacefully in Northwick Park Hospital. It seemed like the end of an era. I missed having her there to share all the exciting happenings of our life and now, it was my sister and I who were the oldest generation of the family, and so probably next in line to pass on – a sobering thought. But getting old is a curious thing. In many ways, I do not feel old at all. I still have the same enthusiasm for life and as much ability to do many things as I had when I was half my present age. Many people find that as they get older, their closest friends are dying off and they feel loneliness setting in. We have been amazingly fortunate in that almost all of our closest friends are younger than us. Indeed, we are constantly making new friends, often only in their teens and twenties. This has kept us feeling young at heart and as long as our health holds up, this could well be the case for many years to come.

A New Millennium

When I was young, the year 2000 seemed a very long way off, especially because at the turn of the century I would have reached the grand old age of sixty. But time never stands still and of course it eventually arrived and even though the twenty-first century didn't really start until 1 January 2001, it was the change of date from nineteen to twenty that sparked people's imagination and was the reason for the huge celebrations that took place on New Year's Eve, 1999. As the start of a new millennium, everyone naturally hoped this would mark the beginning of a better age for mankind but for me and Marion it was the fact that we had reached our sixtieth birthdays that was significant and brought about a big change in our lives.

In the autumn of 1999, our church had employed a young couple as full-time paid youth workers to take over both the JCB group which met on Sundays and the youth club which met on Fridays. (The connection of the church youth group with the Covenanter movement had been abandoned some years earlier and the new name JCB had been adopted. This could stand for 'Just Christian Believers' or 'Jesus Christ's Body' or anything else you cared to think of; but the real idea behind the name was of the machine seen on many building sites. JCB existed to help us to *build* – lives, faith and discipleship.) This was a very reasonable move. Youth culture had changed dramatically in the previous couple of decades and it was important for the church's young people to be able to relate to their leaders in terms of that culture. So, somewhat reluctantly, we accepted that it was time to step down from leadership of youth work. I don't think many youth workers carry on to the age of sixty. Our final Sunday was on 30 January 2000 when we both gave final messages to the group of about twenty young people who gathered together in the church flat where the new leaders had taken up residence. There were cards and gifts for us both and then refreshments.

Officially, we no longer had any responsibility for youth work, but relationships are not governed by such trivial matters. Many of these teenagers remained our friends and still are today. Moreover, as we look back on those who passed through our hands during the dozen or so years when we were in charge, we are thrilled to see what has happened to them. So often teenagers can appear to be very keen Christians for a while but as they get older they turn their backs on religion and drift away from the church. Of course there were a few who did just that but the majority have continued to grow and mature in their faith and some have taken on roles far beyond anything we might have expected. Simon has become a full-time Christian youth worker, currently in the Derby area. His younger brother Jon followed in his footsteps and after graduating from Bible College is now a chaplain to those working in the nightclubs of a major seaside resort. Dorothy, having completed her university career, chose to work for a Christian organisation helping inadequate or deprived children to gain self-confidence through outdoor adventure. Hazel went to Bible College and at the time of writing leads the JCB group she was once a part of. Tim and Matt are worship leaders at Roxeth and Matt and his wife Jenny also lead a house group. Ross and Rachel decided to leave Roxeth after their marriage but joined another local church where Ross took on the onerous and responsible job of church secretary. Paul spent two years as a volunteer with Youth for Christ, using his footballing skills to train and mentor young lads and his musical skills to play in a Christian band. Alec is at Cambridge University and is contemplating going into the Anglican ministry; Karen is a social worker and Zara has passed through drama school and could well be a recognisable face in the future. Flora invited me to conduct her wedding in April 2005 and she and her husband Priyanth are now among our special friends. There are others, with whom we maintain contact, some of whom are still part of the Roxeth Church family. Others, however, have moved away.

Of course there are all kinds of influences which can affect people's lives and each of these individuals has their own story. But I believe that by our teaching and example, Marion and I have had a significant input into their lives which has helped to make them what they are. We suspect that at times these young people were more committed to us than perhaps they were to God. For almost a decade, we were at the church at 9.30 every Sunday morning, come rain or shine, and again every Friday we would give up our evening so that they could have a good time together. We believe this consistency was important and as their sense of appreciation grew with the years so they were more prepared to listen and learn. Sadly, today many paid youth workers only operate on two- or three-year contracts and are often only just at the point of gaining the young people's confidence when their term of office is over. Some people say they can't stand teenagers! For us, youth work is the most rewarding occupation we can imagine and whilst we now miss the opportunities for teaching and training, we still can't help building relationships with the teenagers as each new generation comes along. We love them!

JCB is still going strong and we are pleased to enjoy friendship with many of the members of the group. There is still a youth club on Friday nights and it is a privilege to assist the present leaders on a rota basis. And at the time of writing, we can look forward to having teenage grandchildren for the next seven or eight years.

One sphere of activity had passed but there was still plenty to keep us busy. It is a constant delight to be part of the worship band at church and actually lead worship every third or fourth week. We have a great team of musicians who appreciate each other's talents and gifts and who listen to and learn from one another. I also preach about once every couple of months and that too is something I love. I do not particularly like to be given a subject to preach on, preferring to wait for God to show me a verse or theme which is exactly the right one for the specific congregation and time. This can seem quite daunting, but God has never let me down and it is a fantastic privilege and responsibility to bring God's word to people knowing that it is just that – a message from God himself! But the new era in our lives held some surprises for both of us; in Marion's case, a ministry to prisoners in Egypt, and for me something I could never have even dreamed about.

Towards the end of 1999, I found that I still had a few days of my annual leave remaining. It was around this time that economy airlines had emerged, offering very cheap flights to many parts of Europe. I therefore decided to fly away to Italy. During the summer of 1998, one of our foreign students had stayed with us for a couple of months and inevitably, during that time we had all become good friends. I decided to take up an invitation to visit Alessandra at her parents' home in Milan for a long weekend.

On my arrival early on the Friday afternoon, I was taken on a tour of Milan, to see the famous opera house, the magnificent cathedral and generally drink in the atmosphere of this beautiful city. But this was only a start. To my surprise and delight, my hostess had arranged that on the Saturday morning, we should make a trip to Venice! Everyone has heard of Venice and its amazing canals and buildings but I had never dreamed that I would one day go there. I was not disappointed: it is a fantastic place. We approached it by rail, crossing a stretch of water on what seemed like a pier several miles long, but on arrival, the station looked just like any other. We walked down the platform, through the main booking hall and as we descended the steps leading to the outside world, I half expected to see a forecourt with taxis. Instead, there is the canal and boats and exquisite architecture. It took my breath away.

Accompanying us on the trip was Alessandra's fiancé, who had recently finished studying at the university in Venice, and was therefore familiar with the city and able to act as our guide. He wanted to take the opportunity to see two young women who had been his flatmates during his university days, and by means of a couple of phone calls, it was arranged that the five of us should meet up for lunch in one of the canal-side restaurants. I have to confess that I did not particularly enjoy the food – octopus proved to be rather tough and not very flavourful. Also my companions, having not seen each other for some time, became engrossed in animated conversation – in Italian of course – of which I did not understand a single word. However, one of the two newcomers broke away from the main conversation and started to talk to me in English. Her kindness was greatly appreciated and as we spoke together, I sensed that we entertained similar views on several subjects. I wondered if she might be a Christian and on enquiry she duly confirmed that my suspicions had been correct.

The five of us spent a delightful afternoon exploring the city and its watery thoroughfares. It was late October, but the sky was a clear blue and it was pleasantly warm. The young lady with whom I had spoken at lunch kept in my company and explained something of the history of Venice, making the whole day that much more enjoyable. When it was time to leave, we chose to exchange telephone numbers and email addresses but with no real expectation as to what we would do with them. Her name was Nataline, which, she explained, could be translated as 'little Christmas' because her birthday was on Christmas Eve.

As Christmas approached and Marion and I wrote our cards and annual newsletter, I remembered Nataline and thought it would be friendly to email her with good wishes and to thank her for her friendliness towards me when in Venice. In the course of this I mentioned that many English people treat Christmas as little more than an excuse to overindulge in food and drink, not to mention over-spending, whereas for 'us Christians' it is the birth of our Lord and Saviour that makes it such a special time. A day or so later I received a reply. Nataline said how pleased she was that I had written. She had wanted to write earlier but had been nervous about doing so, thinking that perhaps I could not be bothered and would feel she was wasting my time. She once more confirmed that she was a Christian but with these words, 'Yes, I am Catholic and you are Protestant; but we serve the same Christ. We are brother and sister in the Lord.' These sentiments so succinctly expressed were to mark the start of an ongoing relationship, albeit pursued almost exclusively by email.

Nataline was studying Chinese art and also the Chinese language. On completion of her university course the following summer, she moved from Italy to China to improve her Chinese and to learn first-hand more about the contemporary Chinese art scene. With the assistance of her university tutor who arranged for her to meet the right contacts, she soon became conversant with various Chinese artists and eventually started to work as the Chinese coordinator for a major art gallery based in Switzerland. Amongst her tasks of helping to organise exhibitions, meeting and interviewing artists about their work and arranging for the overseas shipment of works of art, Nataline also started writing critical reviews about certain artists for inclusion in magazines, websites and exhibition catalogues. Because it is a universal language, most of these articles were required in English and at a very early stage in this development, she asked me if I would correct and edit her faltering efforts at translation from her native Italian. From about 2001 onwards, I have been regularly doing just this and learning at the same time about modern Chinese art. I never imagined in my wildest dreams doing anything of the kind, but my efforts have been validated by the publication of a good many of her articles. At the same time, I have been able to have some spiritual input to my friend's life. It is not easy being a Christian in a communist country like China, where churches are only allowed to operate under state control, or else face persecution. It has therefore been a source of help and encouragement to her that I can pass on thoughts from the Bible, express Christian viewpoints about numerous issues and above all pray each and every day for her health, protection, and walk with the Lord. This was particularly critical during the SARS epidemic in Beijing where she lives, during the spring of 2003. I know she also prays regularly for me. We have only met once since that day in Venice, in February 2003 when she gave a lecture at an exhibition in Manchester and then came down to London for a couple of days. We lunched at a Pizza Hut near to Trafalgar Square and it seemed as if we had been life-long friends rather than meeting for only the second time.

I mentioned prayer. That is a very personal matter but I can truthfully say that in the last few years, I have been more consistent and regular in my praying than at any other time in my life. This is not a matter for boasting. I am sure that there are many Christians whose prayer life puts mine to shame; but I would merely make the point that as one gets older and some tasks are no longer appropriate, there is always the ministry of prayer to consider. I hope that if I live to be a hundred and am no longer strong enough to climb mountains, and if my eyesight is too bad to allow me to paint or write and my hands too arthritic for playing the piano, that I shall remain active in at least one thing I can still do: pray!

During the last few years of the old millennium and the first of the new, quite a few of our friends moved away from the West

London area. Once the children have married or left home, it makes sense to escape from some of the more unpleasant aspects of city life and move to the more relaxed atmosphere of the countryside – provided of course that employment is available. If you are a teacher, a policeman or a social worker of some kind, this is unlikely to be a problem and resettlement is easy. Thus, we could understand what was happening to our friends but at the same time we missed them, especially those we had known for twenty-five years or more. As far as we were concerned, although I had always thought it would be wonderful to live in the country, we had never really given this a second thought because there seemed little likelihood of my being able to find a new job at a viable salary because of my age and the limited experience I could offer after being with one firm for such a long time. However, in the autumn of 2000, we went to visit our friends Rob and Gill Buckeridge who now lived in a tiny village near Oswestry in Shropshire. During the weekend, they put some 'homes for sale' pages of the local newspaper in front of us and pointed out the huge discrepancies between prices there and those we were used to in West London. With only three and a half years to retirement age, it appeared possible that by selling our home in Northolt and buying one in Oswestry, we could make sufficient profit to pay our bills for a couple of years and hence take a slightly early retirement. At first, we were a little taken aback by this idea but gradually it captured our imagination. Having just given up the youth work at Roxeth, we wondered if perhaps this might be the right time to move on to pastures new. So we decided to start looking seriously for suitable properties.

 The next eighteen months proved to be a very interesting period of our lives as we viewed probably a hundred or more houses, in three different areas of the country. Initially, we explored the Oswestry area, and then the Forest of Dean in Gloucestershire, sometimes making day trips and sometimes enjoying whole weekends away. Both were essentially rural and had property at good prices relative to Northolt. We also found churches at which we felt completely at home and where we would have been happy to be committed – a vitally important factor in any move. But there was one disadvantage – the small matter of distance from our family in Sussex and especially from the grandchildren. Our third search area was therefore Sussex, but property prices there were little different from London and in any case, despite the proximity of the South Downs, it appeared to me that much of Sussex, from Brighton to Littlehampton, could best be described as 'suburbia by the sea'. To be blunt, I did not like it much. Nevertheless, we did look at dozens of houses in all these areas and although we never found one that was entirely suitable, it was a fascinating learning curve and I can therefore pass on some interesting observations about modern housing.

Firstly – kitchens are too small! At Doncaster Drive, our revamped kitchen has a total of about twenty-five cupboards, drawers and shelves and is pleasantly spacious. We rarely found anything approaching this level of fitments. In today's world, where husband and wife both go out to work, it seems that there is not much time for cooking. Consequently, there is little requirement for extensive work surfaces or space for storing cooking utensils. All that is needed is an oven to heat up the ready-meal purchased at the supermarket. Gardens suffer from a similar problem. People have no time to grow or cultivate anything and this has led to the modern trend for small, labour-saving gardens, where most of it is paved over with either concrete or decking, perhaps leaving just a tiny bit of lawn. Of course, builders want to put as many houses as possible on a piece of land so as to maximise their profit and that is another reason why gardens tend to be miniscule. We did find one superb house in a small village near Oswestry, which had absolutely everything we wanted, but we could scarcely swing a cat in what was described as the garden and so we had no alternative but to reject it. We did find an older house at Ruspidge in the Forest of Dean which had a quite magnificent garden: beautiful lawns on three tiers; a veritable orchard of fruit trees; a vegetable garden; countless flowerbeds; a rockery; spring bulbs everywhere and a number of pergolas for climbing plants. I was very tempted, but common sense told me that a plot as big as this would take a lot of looking after and when you are over sixty, it is not a wise move to commit yourself to years of hard manual work.

A further observation is that today's generation of house-owners do not have pianos! A piano needs to be placed against a wall and a great many modern homes have two inter-connecting reception rooms thereby reducing by two (each side of the same wall) the number of walls available for this purpose. We had to reject about seventy percent of the houses we looked at for this reason alone. There is one more warning which needs to be stressed: be careful of the time of day when you view. We came very close to making offers on two houses, one in Gobowen (Shropshire) and one in Goring (Sussex). In both cases, we visited during the day when the roads seemed to be secluded and peaceful. Subsequently, we took a second look during a weekend and an evening respectively. In both cases, we found the neighbourhoods saturated with parked cars, and full of noisy activity: this second look caused us to have second thoughts.

We wanted a relatively modern house in order to avoid possible maintenance problems in the future. Centuries-old cottages may look charming but are no fun when you discover woodworm in the floorboards, rusty window frames or a leaking roof. And we wanted a detached house. We have been blessed with great neighbours in Northolt but that was no guarantee that new neighbours might not play loud music, or worse. We wanted two toilets, as we'd always had at Doncaster Drive (you get used to such luxuries). We also wanted more room. Most people of our age want to down-size but we find that as the years go by, we are expanding, and with plans for friends and family to come and stay from time to time, we needed three or even four bedrooms. From my comments above, you will realise that a large kitchen, a large living space and a reasonable sized garden were also essential requisites. So, with such stringent conditions laid down, it was perhaps not surprising that we failed to find what we wanted. On a few occasions we saw a very nice house and on the way home in the car, we would enthusiastically discuss its merits and demerits. But that same evening, sitting in our lounge, we would come to the conclusion that it just did not compare with what we already had. Northolt may not be the perfect location; but we do like our house.

We abandoned the search, and when we told our close friends at Roxeth they assured us that this was an answer to their prayers.

It's nice to be wanted! Perhaps this also revealed another aspect of God's goodness to us. Our desire to move had been motivated largely by the prospect of a quieter lifestyle in pleasanter surroundings – of which there is nothing wrong. But at the same time we wanted to be sure that we were in the place where God wanted us. His will was more important than ours. Maybe that was why it turned out to be an abortive search. Years ago, I heard a man preaching on Psalm 23 say that 'goodness' and 'mercy' are like God's sheepdogs! Having often watched Lake District shepherds rounding up sheep, I knew what he meant: if a sheep goes astray, the dogs will run round to cut off every pathway except that intended by the shepherd. Here we had maybe got things wrong because of our selfish motives, but God in His goodness and mercy got us back on track. God clearly still had much for us to do in West London.

A few months after this, Marion's stepmother died suddenly and unexpectedly. It meant that her home would be sold and the proceeds shared between Marion and her brother. Any worries I might have had concerning our financial future were over, and after Marion and I had talked things through, we agreed that I should hand in my notice at PEL. I would retire at Christmas 2002 and we would survive on our savings for the next fifteen months until my state and company pensions became payable. The actual day of my retirement was 20 December, curiously the same day that Sir Jimmy Young retired from broadcasting on the BBC.

Retirement is wonderful; it opens up a whole new vista of opportunities. This realisation struck me very forcefully one Friday morning towards the end of January 2003. It had snowed overnight and everything had been covered with a white mantle, transforming a very ordinary landscape into a winter wonderland. A month earlier, I would have been at work but now I was able to put on some boots and a warm coat and head for the woods at nearby Horsenden Hill, camera in hand. Tramping through the snow and photographing the black and white collage of trees and fields was exhilarating and lifted my spirit at a time of year when the days often seem dark and dreary. By Saturday morning, a thaw had set in and the snow was gone. How disappointing for those poor unfortunate working people who had missed all the fun!

That summer, there was the opportunity to visit Lords and watch Middlesex CCC play a number of cricket matches – the first time I had done so for many years. I could paint to my heart's content, keep the garden looking wonderful, go out birdwatching and choose the best days to go out walking. In February, I was able to attend a conference on new forms of Christian worship hosted by an organisation called Share Jesus International. It was here that I heard about a project to raise funds for youth work. This was a sponsored walk – the 'Three Peaks Challenge' – and involved climbing the highest mountains in England, Scotland and Wales in just over forty-eight hours. Here was something I had always wanted to do and this opportunity meant that all the arrangements would be made by someone else and I would only have to do the walking. I signed up for it, and in June started serious training for the event, which was to take place during the last week of August. About every three days, I would walk ten miles or more to build up stamina and get my muscles in trim. Unfortunately, there are no hills of any significance in West London, but I did spend a few afternoons *almost* running up and down the slope of Harrow Hill. I suspect that some of the dog-walkers on the hill probably thought I was crazy, especially as most of the summer was exceptionally hot and sunny. In July came a sudden setback. Marion and I went away for a weekend to attend a wedding and were spending the Friday evening with a friend in Chester. We had just enjoyed a very pleasant meal, when I was suddenly gripped by a pain in my side which rapidly increased in severity. However, we still drove into the city centre for a spot of sight-seeing only for me to be violently sick in the street – most embarrassing. But it was also very strange. I have a remarkably stable digestive system and I rarely suffer even from indigestion. However, the pain went from bad to worse and before the evening was over, I was taken in an ambulance to the Countess of Chester Hospital where I was admitted with a suspected kidney stone.

I had not been in hospital since my tonsils had been removed when I was five years old, but I was grateful for the painkillers that were being administered to me and impressed by the overall efficiency of the hospital on the Saturday when I spent much of my time going backwards and forwards to the X-ray department. The nursing staff were kindness personified and I even received a goodbye kiss from one of them (a female) when I was allowed to leave on the Sunday afternoon. Marion drove me home but of course I had missed the wedding.

By some miracle of nature, the stone that had caused me so much pain actually dissolved during Sunday night and the pain disappeared, although for several days I could feel where it had been, if you can imagine what that means. The medical experts believed that the cause of the stone had been dehydration and on reflection, I remembered that on one of my running trips to Harrow Hill a few days before, I had not taken any water. I learnt my lesson.

The Three Peaks event was great fun. The first day was spent travelling by minibus to Fort William for an overnight stay at a youth hostel. Next morning, our party of about seventy walkers gathered on the banks of the River Nevis for a brief time of worship before starting the climb up Ben Nevis. It was a fine sunny day and many of the more hardy types were dressed in shorts and T-shirts. Clearly, they had not heard of the famous Scottish midges which had congregated over the river in their millions, because by the time we returned to the same spot some seven hours later for a hot drink and a doughnut having completed the first ascent, many of the walkers looked as if they had contracted chickenpox, being covered in red bites. Curiously, the midges themselves had completely vanished. Perhaps they had enjoyed such a substantial breakfast that they felt they could forego afternoon tea! (I should add that I had been warned in advance about the midges and had gone well protected with insect repellent which really worked.) The subsequent climbs up Scafell Pike and Snowdon were uneventful but I was one of the fittest in the party and thoroughly enjoyed the experience, even though it involved a great deal of travelling and a serious lack of sleep. I was also able to collect and donate almost £1,500 in sponsorship money – a very satisfying result.

There was another intriguing spin-off from this adventure.

About two weeks before the event, I did a twelve-mile training walk along the Grand Union Canal from Northolt to London and on the way I encountered a young woman on a bicycle, who enquired of me how to get to Regent's Park. As this meant leaving the canal for about a mile and walking along streets, I assured her that I could tell her the way but it would be easier if I showed her, by us walking together. As we started chatting, I was intrigued to know why she would be cycling to work at around 11.30 in the morning. It transpired that she was an actress on her way to a rehearsal for a West End show that was due to commence in mid-September. I wished her well and she wished me well in my Three Peaks project and before we parted company, we exchanged names. I thought nothing more about this for several weeks until, quite by chance, I heard her name mentioned on the radio. This same girl was being interviewed and to my amazement, I learnt that she was the famous daughter of an even more famous mother and had already made quite a name for herself in a TV drama earlier that summer. The outcome was that I wrote to her at the London theatre where her show was being performed, sending a cutting taken from our local paper containing a photo of me and details of my adventure. I said that I would like to see the play and if I did, perhaps I could meet her again after the show. I received a very warm reply and in due course, Marion and I visited the Theatre Royal, Haymarket, and were invited backstage after the performance to meet her and enjoy a glass of wine with several leading members of the cast. I was flattered to see the press photo of me in a prominent place in my new acquaintance's dressing room, but in the showbiz environment, she was noticeably different from the almost shy young woman I had met on the towpath a couple of months earlier. I did write again thanking her for the welcome we had received and suggesting she might like to come to our home for a meal some time, but we did not receive a reply. Perhaps that was inevitable: celebrities live in a world of celebrities.

There are several more opportunities which have come my way since retirement. Back in 1995, Premier Christian Radio had been given a licence to broadcast on the medium waveband in the London area. From its inception, the station relied heavily on volunteers and early in its history, Marion had become involved. This led to her appointment as their catering manager, an unpaid appointment in which she was required to organise and prepare a staff lunch once a month at the London office and occasionally provide refreshments at other events. For many years, she took a procession of friends to assist her on these occasions, but from December 2002 onwards, I have replaced those other helpers and we now carry out this task together on the first Tuesday of each month. The people at Premier are lovely and it has been a delight to meet and befriend some of them and a privilege to be of service to them. Of course, Marion and I are now able to do many things together, including the household chores. I did wonder about becoming a cordon bleu cook, but the fact of the matter is that Marion remains chief cook whilst I am usually the bottle washer!

The second venture concerns music. One of my best friends is a teacher at a middle school in Harrow. In November 2003, she contacted me with the news that the music teacher at her school was suffering from back trouble and unlikely to return to work before Christmas. This was a potential disaster in view of the Christmas concert due to take place before the end of term and she wondered if I might be prepared to step into the breach and play the piano to accompany the various musical items. I agreed and after numerous rehearsals fulfilled this role at the concert at which over a hundred parents were present. At the end of a very enjoyable and well presented performance, the head teacher addressed the assembled audience with the usual list of thank yous: thanks to the parents for coming; thanks to the pupils for their fine efforts; thanks to the staff for all their hard work and cooperation and finally ... thanks to Mr Sharp for helping us out and making the concert possible.' There was an immediate, prolonged and rousing cheer from the children and I felt almost embarrassed but very happy. I had thoroughly enjoyed being with them and it was clear that they had also appreciated my company and my piano playing. Indeed, the partnership was so successful that I was invited to repeat the assignment in 2004 and 2005 even though the music teacher was fit and well and able to train the children. Obviously my piano playing has been a hit and I have also assisted at a concert put on by the school at the Harrow Arts

Centre in April 2005, as well as at a number of school assemblies. I almost feel that I belong at the school and anticipate a long association.

There was another development involving music. For some years, Marion has represented Roxeth Church at a regular meeting between leaders of the South Harrow Churches. This brought her into contact with several ministers including the vicar of a local Anglican church. St Andrew's had an excellent organist and choirmaster but Doug the vicar was keen for his congregation to learn some of the newer upbeat songs which it is almost impossible to play on a traditional pipe organ. Marion therefore offered my services to try to overcome this problem. As a result, I was invited to lead some worship and teach some of the new songs at informal meetings on Sunday evenings. One outcome of this was that we got to know a young lady who was acting as an intern at St Andrew's for a year. Kinga hailed from Hungary, and although only about twenty years of age, sang well, played the flute and helped both with leading small prayer meetings and with the youth work. When she returned to Hungary at the end of her term of service, we remained in regular correspondence and much to our delight, she invited us to visit her and her family in Hungary in August 2005. Once there, we spent a day exploring Budapest, another five days at Lake Balaton and throughout our stay were thoroughly spoilt by the generous hospitality shown to us.

Over and over again, we have finished up receiving far more from a friendship than we could ever have expected. Gerald Coates used to say, 'He who would have friends must show himself friendly,' and it will be obvious from many of the preceding chapters that making friends has always been an essential part of our lives. However, whilst it is the giving of time, energy, money and sometimes sacrifices to build and nourish a friendship that has given us so much joy, we have certainly been on the receiving end as well. We are sad when we see people living largely isolated or self-centred lives. They are missing out on so much.

Marion

I have recently read a biography of a well-known celebrity and noticed that his wife was only mentioned about half a dozen times throughout the book. Looking back over what I have written I realise that Marion has flitted in and out of the pages and nearly always been there in the background; but she is such an outstanding person and our lives are so inextricably intertwined that it would be a serious oversight if I were not to devote a chapter specifically to her – even if only a short chapter. This is part of her story, but inevitably a part of mine as well because I have learnt so much from her.

Marion is a one-off. I have never come across anyone like her and so I can consider myself very fortunate that she chose me for her husband. Perhaps her greatest gift is gregariousness; she just loves people. She can meet someone for the first time and immediately seem to be at ease with them and never at a loss for something to say. There is little chance of a stranger or visitor entering church and escaping without being welcomed by Marion. But more than this, she collects people! Wherever she goes, whether on holiday or to a meeting, a new acquaintance will often become a name, address and telephone number to be noted down and followed up. Relationships are precious and bring great happiness but unfortunately many of us find it difficult to break the ice to start one. It is the Marions of this world who have this amazing knack of being initiators, able to convert a casual meeting into an ongoing friendship.

I believe it was on her twenty-first birthday that she was given a Birthday Book, an item that has largely gone out of fashion today. On each date throughout the book she has listed the birthdays or wedding anniversaries of literally hundreds of people and although we are no longer in regular touch with some of them, a great many receive cards on the appropriate day each year. I used to think that this was a very expensive and somewhat unnecessary pastime, but I have come to realise that most people love to be remembered and receive cards and this is therefore a wonderful way of showing one's interest and care, a step along the way to showing them love. When we are on holiday Marion will send a profusion of postcards, including some to elderly folk who probably rarely receive any personal mail.

Being an initiator has also had far-reaching consequences for much of her life. Being something of an information addict as well, she always seems to find out about new projects or events and if they interest her, she will want to be involved and probably try to involve others as well. This was certainly true of the March for Jesus events in the eighties and nineties when, but for her enthusiasm, it is doubtful whether I or many of those associated with us locally would have taken part. When the organisation ACET (Aids Care Education and Training) was set up as a Christian response to the mounting problem of AIDS, Marion wanted to be in on the action. She became a helper to a lady afflicted with the disease and made regular visits to assist with many of the household chores which the person concerned was too weak to do herself. She became a friend to that family until the woman's death after a couple of years. More recently, she became aware of the work of CSW (Christian Solidarity Worldwide) and of the appalling persecution suffered by Christians in many parts of the world. She soon became an active supporter and has taken part in demonstrations at the embassies of unjust regimes, written letters to prisoners and presidents and encouraged others to sign petitions protesting against some of the evils that are being perpetrated around the world. She always wants to inform others of the need to pray or give or act in some appropriate way and it was impossible that I should not be influenced by all this and I too have thus developed a deep concern about human rights abuses, especially in North Korea, Burma and China.

She has always been one for writing letters ever since she had one published in *Woman's Own* magazine when she was only eighteen. She has been a regular contributor in this way to *Good Morning Sunday*, the BBC's flagship religious programme on Radio 2. In 1989, shortly before the demise of communism in eastern Europe, she wrote a pen friend-style letter to a teenage girl in Romania which led to the development of yet another friendship. Carmen is now a doctor, married and living in the USA. Marion also sends letters and makes numerous phone calls to the council complaining about graffiti, failure to collect rubbish or clear the streets of litter, failed street-lights, dangerous pavements and so on. It is a reflection of her care and concern not just for people but for the environment in which people live. If only there were others who would take time and trouble over such things.

It will be apparent that she and I are very different. When we first got married, we were like chalk and cheese, but with the passing years, there has been a steady convergence. She has always been there for me and in all the major decisions of life, we have been at one. If it had not been so, our story would have been very different. Having hundreds of folk in your home wearing out your furniture, eating your food and taking up your time requires complete agreement and we have always endeavoured to be totally committed to building God's Kingdom, whatever that might entail or cost. But the amazing thing is that although we have been united in outlook and motivation over the really big issues, we are very different yet wonderfully complimentary in terms of gifting and personality; in other words, we make a great team. I am still overwhelmed by the extent of Marion's gregariousness. Time and again I find myself asking, 'Who's he?' or 'Where did you meet them?' But without her and because of my inherent shyness I could never have got to know so many people and maybe never learned how to care for people and generate the kind of deep and loyal friendships which mean so much to me. Marion is a great ideas person but often relies on me to help put flesh on the bones of these ideas and actually bring some of them to fruition. My face is known because of my gifts in music and preaching, but Marion has become just as well known as the initiator and organiser of so much. This combination of talents currently works well as we lead a small house group at Roxeth Church. Is she sometimes loud, embarrassing and over the top? Well yes, but she is a good friend to many and her enthusiasm for life will often bring a smile and brighten up many situations.

Of course there are many other areas of life which we share in addition to people: our love of the Lake District, walking, music and the world of nature. We both love flowers and whilst I tend the garden, Marion has a wonderful collection of house plants, particularly streptocarpus hybrids. But, as at the start of our relationship, we still retain our individuality. Marion is not interested in snooker or painting. On the other hand, I am not a great one for theatre or Sir Cliff Richard and I don't even like fruit cake! But we have learnt to make room for each other to pursue our own interests without any pressure towards conformity. So I can go to Lords for the day or spend a week in the mountains of Andorra while Marion enjoys space to do other things, although she would like to see Andrew (Freddie) Flintoff in action. Our reunions are sweet as we share all that we have been doing.

Spiritually, there can be nothing better than a loving spouse to keep you up to the mark; not only to point out your shortcomings and errors of judgement but also to encourage and praise when you get things right. Marion has certainly done both for me. Above all, our marriage has been full of fun and never lacking in love or affection. It could be said that she's not as romantic as I am but my motto over the years has been a slight distortion of a Bible verse: 'moderation in all things except ... cuddles'! And Marion tends to agree.

Looking Back, Looking Forward

When I was fifteen and following a particularly delightful spring holiday in the Lake District, I decided that I wanted a decent camera to photograph the wonderful scenery that so captivated me. Our next-door neighbour was a manager at the Lyons tea factory in Greenford and agreed to employ me as a messenger boy during my summer holidays to enable me to earn some money. The factory was situated on a square dock which led off the Grand Union canal. Barges would draw up at the dock and offload their tea chests into the factory by fork-lift trucks and their contents would later be emptied into huge revolving vessels rather like cement mixers. Samples of the resultant blended teas would then be made into a drink and passed to the tea-tasters who would swill the liquid (no milk or sugar) around their mouths before spitting it out. All very strange.

Today, the factory has gone, a pile of rubble in its place. All that remains is the square dock – a placid sheet of water still linked to the canal but silent except for the occasional squawk of a coot or moorhen; time and history move inexorably onwards.

My story is up to date, although I hope there are many years still to come. But these last sixty-five years have been times of great change. Change is inevitable; it is a characteristic of life. If nothing changes, that is death. But what matters is how we deal with changes. So far I have written mainly about events in my life but in this final chapter, I want to indulge in a little nostalgia and reflect on some of those changes that have happened, not just to me but also to the world around me, and to share some thoughts and ideas about what the future might hold.

One of the major changes has been the advance of technology and nowhere has this been more apparent than in the realm of travel. When you visit London Heathrow Airport in all its frightening complexity, it seems impossible that it was only opened in 1946 when I was a boy. My father had a brother who owned a poultry farm on wasteground at a place called Stanwell and I remember going there when I was about ten years old and seeing thousands upon thousands of battery hens in their cages. But the main topic of conversation that day was the fact that my uncle's land was to be compulsorily purchased by the government in order to extend Heathrow. He moved to the Isle of Wight and the site of his original farm now lies somewhere underneath one of the runways. Today, airliners from all over the world are landing there about every ninety seconds. Back in the seventies, when I used to preach regularly at a small church in Hounslow which lay immediately under the Heathrow flight path, even with a public address system, I still had to stop every couple of minutes or risk not being heard above the noise overhead. How the residents of that area put up with it every day of the year is beyond me.

We lived in a fairly well-to-do part of Ruislip but only a handful of the neighbours living in our road actually owned cars until well into the 1950s. There were no motorways until then, and not very many dual-carriageway roads. Long distance travel was therefore pretty slow. Today we have three- and four-lane motorways, but they are often choked with nose-to-tail vehicles for miles on end.

Travel in my young days was primarily by train. The railways could take you from almost anywhere to everywhere. I remember as late as 1960 going to stay with a friend who was a Baptist minister at Street in Somerset. My return journey was planned for a bank holiday Monday and because Marion would not be working that day, I wanted to be home as early as possible to spend some time together. I therefore caught the 7.30 a.m. train from nearby Glastonbury – a rather grubby two-coach affair hauled by an ageing steam engine – as far as Evercreech Junction where I had less than ten minutes to wait for another branch-line train. This took me to Temple Combe, a major interchange point on the London to Exeter mainline. From here, I boarded an express which rushed me to Waterloo by just after 11 a.m. This was typical of so many rail journeys at that time, but sadly, change was soon to come. Today, Glastonbury has no rail link and Evercreech has vanished to be replaced by cornfields. Temple

Combe is now just a rural station with no connecting services of any kind. It has been reduced to a single platform with modern buildings and pretty flowerbeds. The ornate platform awnings, the busy engine sheds and sidings and the line which ran underneath the main station have all disappeared without trace, its glory departed for ever. The demise of the railways was the work of Lord Beeching who, having been asked by the government to make the railways pay their way, promptly axed about a third of the network including most of the uneconomic branch-lines. With so many towns and villages suddenly inaccessible by rail, it was inevitable that people would have to travel by car and so road transport has increased at an ever more rapid rate. It seems ironic that whilst a government subsidy of, say, £300,000 a year would have kept a ten-mile branch-line open for business, within a very few years road links were having to be built following much the same route as the railways at a cost of maybe £2 million a mile. Moreover, the freight that once went by rail is now being carried by ever bigger and bigger lorries, which have generally destroyed our environment as they rumble incessantly through our towns and villages along roads never meant for such monstrosities.

The railways were always a great source of romance for me. At the time when I first went out with Marion in 1958, trains used to pass the bottom of her parents' garden in Ruislip. Every hour there would be the excitement of a steam-hauled express train with maybe a dozen coaches, on the sides of which were fixed destination boards declaring that this train served PADDINGTON BIRMINGHAM & WOLVERHAMPTON. Sometimes, the trains would be extended through to Shrewsbury, Wrexham, Chester and Birkenhead and once a day there would be the Cambrian Coast Express with through coaches to places like Aberystwyth and Pwllheli. There was something very romantic about the thought that this racing monster was carrying people to the farthest coast of Wales and the Irish Sea. Today's trains somehow do not have the same fascination. But in thinking about all these changes, one cannot help but be reminded about pollution.

It was not until the seventies that people started to seriously worry about such things and the green revolution began to attract attention. But with the huge increase of air traffic, we now know that jet exhausts are probably damaging the ozone layer that protects us from many harmful rays arriving from the sun. Exhaust fumes from the increasing numbers of cars and lorries on our roads are almost certainly causing global warming and dramatic climate change. We are over-fishing the seas and in danger of making some species extinct if they don't die off anyway from the pollution of the oceans with chemicals and radioactive waste. Precious woodland, heathland and wetlands, all irreplaceable habitats for various wildlife species, are being destroyed to build houses or make farming more profitable. Governments are now being made more aware of the problem but as long as people are preoccupied with making money, I doubt if much will be done to make a significant difference. I cannot help but wonder what sort of world it will be in another twenty or thirty years and am rather glad that it won't be my problem. I remember the old Joni Mitchell song 'Big Yellow Taxi' with the line 'You don't know what you've got till it's gone', which seems all too pertinent today, and one fears that by tomorrow, it may be too late to do anything about the rape of our world.

But it is not only the environment that has changed. So have the people. When I think back to my time at Latymer School and again at King's College, I do not recollect a single non-white pupil in the entire school or college. A photograph of the Chemistry Department at King's confirms my impression. Of course even in the 1950s there were ethnic populations in places like Southall and it was not unusual for people to say, 'I saw a white man in Southall yesterday!' Today, in the London boroughs closest to where I live – Harrow, Ealing, Brent, Hillingdon – many schools have a majority of pupils from ethnic minority groups. When I walk through the South Harrow shopping centre, I will hear almost as many people speaking languages foreign to me as speaking English. It is a huge change. Do I mind? The answer has to be a qualified yes and no. At Roxeth Church, there are more than a dozen nationalities represented in the congregation and many of these are of Asian or Afro-Caribbean origin. This is as it should be, because a local church should always reflect its neighbourhood in terms of ethnicity and many of these folk have become good friends. When I was working at PEL, I had colleagues who were Hindu, Moslem and Seikh. They were all charming people, and in fact the Seikh was by far the most conscientious and helpful of all the engineers. But there is a downside in that we are in danger of losing much of our traditional British way of life. Those who are immigrants are entitled to their own culture but unless they are prepared to also embrace British culture, then the latter will be steadily eroded. Indeed, it is already becoming difficult to define what is meant by 'Britishness' because of the influence of other cultures. Sadly, history teaching in our schools has left the majority of our young people with little idea of the wonderful heritage that Britain has given to the world over the centuries and consequently, very little sense of pride in their country or their culture. Political correctness is further undermining our national character. The worst aspect of this is the steady downgrading of Christianity and Christian standards in all parts of our society. Other religions are treated with the utmost respect but the media often portray Christians as mindless individuals who believe in some kind of empty superstition and who are out of touch with reality. Our government grapples with a rising tide of broken marriages with their catastrophic economic consequences; drug and alcohol addiction; crime; debt; teenage pregnancies and much more, yet refuses to acknowledge that Christianity has an answer to these problems. Much new legislation has not changed men's hearts, minds and attitudes, but Jesus Christ can and does! Of course we are not perfect, but statistics showing the prevalence of these problems amongst Christians compared with the rest of society would, I think, prove very interesting. Church schools are over-subscribed because parents recognise that their children will receive a sound moral education thereat and this is what they want. Employers know that in general, Christians will prove to be conscientious and honest workers. But still the anti-Christian feelings continue to grow. I do not understand it.

Even more alarming is the change in attitude towards Christianity around the world. When I was young, communism was seen as the number one threat to faith. We knew that in other countries there were people who followed other religions but we thought of them as heathens merely waiting to hear the gospel and turn to Christ. Today, there is opposition to Christianity in more than half the countries of the world with believers being marginalized, beaten up, wrongfully imprisoned, tortured and killed merely because they follow Christ and will not deny Him. Why? It simply does not make sense. I can only come to one conclusion: it is downright evil. The Bible says that 'men loved darkness rather than light because their deeds were evil' (John 3:19) and when I hear of the atrocities committed against innocent men, women and children merely because they are Christians, I am left in no doubt as to the truth of this statement. In recent years, as Marion and I have become familiar with the work of Christian Solidarity Worldwide, we have come to learn of the terrible evils being perpetrated against Christians in China, North Korea, Vietnam, Burma (Myanmar), Eritrea and a host of other places. Jesus said that his disciples would be 'hated by all men' (Luke 21:17) and whilst a reading of those words fifty years ago would have sounded distinctly improbable, it is now very clear that Jesus knew what he was talking about. It will only be a matter of time before we see it in the United Kingdom. We already stand on the brink.

Church life has also changed but this time for the better. In my teenage years it seemed to me that the only significant difference between those who called themselves Christians and those who did not was that the former attended church services. However, with the charismatic renewal in the late sixties and seventies, Christianity in the UK became much more vibrant and alive. I remember Gerald Coates prophesying that 'the light would get lighter and the darkness get darker' as the years progressed. He was certainly right about the darkness as I have already noted, but I believe he was also right about the light. It seems to me that there is a greater zeal, a greater depth of spirituality and a greater vision in today's churches compared with fifty years ago. It is also encouraging to see many churches working together in genuine cooperation regardless of denominational differences which have become increasingly irrelevant. We have discovered a new dimension in worship and not just because guitars and drum kits have replaced pipe organs. No longer do we just sing hymns. We seek to offer a sacrifice of praise to God, we celebrate His grace and goodness and we recognise that our lifestyle has to match our Sunday profession. Relationships have assumed real significance. When I first went to church with my parents, all that was necessary for a service to take place was the minister, the organist and one person in the congregation. There was no interaction between members and very little contact outside the church building either. Today, we have house groups meeting every week to build relationships of trust and love and to work out the nitty-gritty of our faith in everyday life. Community is a watchword for the Church.

But sadly, there has also been a downside to church life with a trend throughout the country and also in America for Christians to neglect church attendance. Today, we know of many who made a profession of faith in Christ and were once active in church life, including some who were in leadership, but who no longer attend any kind of church community and whose faith, if they still have one, is entirely private and personal. Many reasons can be put forward for this trend: the pressures of life and business which leave so little time; disillusionment with the church and also maybe with the people in it, who are certainly not perfect. But the effect is disastrous. I have no doubt from my reading of the New Testament that Christians are meant to be part of a community and that a vertical faith in God has to be worked out in horizontal relationships with God's people. I don't believe you can have one without the other; so I am not surprised when I see most of these folk who have rejected church sliding down a slippery slope towards apathy and indifference towards God, Jesus and His Kingdom. Once again, I look at the words of Jesus and see that these things were predicted. 'The love of many will grow cold ... but he that endures to the end shall be saved' (Matt 24:12–13). I seriously wonder what will happen to those who have started out but then apparently turned back. I pray for many of them lest they should be lost, but my first concern has to be that I will not fall into the same trap but will be able to say with the apostle Paul, 'I have kept the faith, I have finished the course.'

There are many more changes I have observed. Sport has above all else become money orientated. It is bordering on the obscene that the top football clubs can pay their players £50,000 per week while smaller clubs struggle to make ends meet. Competition is meaningless because it is no longer a level playing field when one club is owned by a billionaire who can afford to buy every decent player in sight while the poorer clubs have no option but to sell their best players to remain solvent. Results have become more and more predictable and as far as I am concerned I find 'the beautiful game' increasingly boring. It is not helped by the bad behaviour which now abounds – referees being verbally abused and players knowingly cheating. Thankfully, my first love – cricket – has not suffered to the same extent. There have been a few rumours of match fixing and the odd bit of petulance when faced with bad decisions, but in general, the umpire's decision is still accepted as final. Also, the one-day version of professional and international cricket, which only arrived in the sixties, has introduced a new level of excitement into the game which, in my opinion, is a welcome innovation.

Communication has been another area of major change. As a boy, I was distinctly nervous of answering the telephone. Today, children as young as eight or nine have their own mobile phones and spend an incredible amount of time texting their friends.

Personally, I hate mobile phones. When I am away from home, I have usually made a decision to leave behind the hassles of everyday life and I don't want to be disturbed. I can understand the value of a mobile phone for use in an emergency and am glad that Marion has one for that purpose but when listening to other people's phone conversations in public places, their content is, for the most part, so trite as to beggar belief. The phone companies must be making a mint from our preoccupation with trivia.

As I have already related, very few families had television in the years just after the war, but today it is one of the greatest influences on public attitudes and behaviour. During my working life, the main topic of discussion for many of my colleagues was the previous night's TV programmes and the viewing prospects for the forthcoming evening. It was bad enough when there were just four terrestrial channels but with the advent of satellite and cable TV, many homes now have literally dozens of options to provide their entertainment and I sometimes wonder how there is time for anything else apart from funnelling through the channels deciding what to watch. The science fiction writer Ray Bradbury wrote a short story in 1953 entitled 'The Murderer' in which he foresaw a world where everyone had a kind of mobile phone attached to their wrists, where music and advertisements were beamed into all public places and where the television ruled supreme in people's lives. The one man who hates all this and longs for some peace and quiet and some real face-to-face relationships is deemed to be mentally ill and consigned to a cell. This story shows an amazing clarity of vision and I feel we are rapidly heading for just such a world – a world that has gone mad and thinks that refusal to accept the madness amounts to insanity. I would add that we still do not have a TV in our home and have no plans to change that in the immediate future.

The trouble with our world is that every new development has the potential for evil as well as for good. The internet is a fantastic invention and can provide us with all manner of information at our fingertips and the boon of email enables us to keep in touch with friends all over the world without recourse to the long delays of the postal system. But it also provides the possibility for the widespread dissemination of pornography, propaganda, terrorism and so on. The personal computer is now a feature of many homes and can be a helpful tool. But many young people have become addicted to computer games and spend hours sitting alone at their consoles instead of exercising out of doors and meeting friends. No wonder we have a problem with obesity. Education has moved away from the dull and uninspiring methods of yesteryear when learning by heart was the order of the day. Instead, young people are challenged to think and reason and ask questions in order to reach a proper understanding of issues and subjects. But at the same time, young people have lost all regard for authority and so discipline in schools (and homes) has deteriorated and the new learning methods often fail to achieve the desired results. Indeed, I am appalled at the ignorance of many of today's school leavers.

In the 1960s, the invention of the contraceptive pill meant that families could be well planned with the prospect of bringing to an end much of the poverty and hardship often associated with large numbers of offspring. But of course, this sexual revolution led to sexual promiscuity on a previously unprecedented level. The results are ever increasing levels of teenage pregnancies, sexually transmitted diseases and homes broken up due to the infidelity of partners.

What more can I say? I have witnessed enormous changes during my life but if you were to ask if the world has become a better place because of them, I would probably have to say no. Of course I am pleased that modern healthcare has improved so much that I have the prospect of a long life. Yes, I am pleased that there is still some countryside left for me to enjoy, some birds to watch, cricket to be played, music to be made and listened to and, above all, that I can still be an active Christian without going to prison. But I feel that folk like me are increasingly becoming the exception and I fear that tomorrow's world may well be very different again. People like me who like to walk in the countryside, who reject the false standards relentlessly pumped out by the media and who have faith in Jesus Christ will be looked upon as nutcases and probably finish up like Ray Bradbury's character, in a cell. I hope I am wrong, but it will depend on how the present generation of young people react to the changes that are occurring at an ever faster pace.

I would like to finish on a positive note. The world may be in a mess and heading for even greater disasters but for me 'the lines have fallen to me in pleasant places; I have a delightful heritage', as it says in Psalm 16:6. I was blessed with caring parents who brought me up to know and follow godly standards and principles. I found Jesus Christ as my Saviour and Lord at an early age so that I did not waste years going down dead-end streets. I married a wonderful woman and we have enjoyed a lasting, loving relationship which has not faded with the years. We have been privileged to live in a free, democratic country with a good standard of living and we constantly give thanks to God for our health, our home, our food, our clothing, our car, our holidays and all the other material goods that we could so easily take for granted. Indeed, it is sad that people in the West have come to think of these things as theirs by right and have lost their sense of appreciation of how privileged they are compared to those in the third world. We should always maintain an 'attitude of gratitude'. We may not have done some of the exciting things which seem to be popular today, but we have had plenty of great experiences and there is still time for more.

Above all, we have made more friends than I can count and although we have lost touch with a few, there have always been new ones to take their place. There are a great many who have not received a mention in these pages and yet they are very special to us and we are for ever grateful to all who have enriched our lives in so many ways. So I would like to emulate the Apostle Paul at the end of some of his letters by mentioning a few by name just so that they don't feel left out.

I thank God for Steve Maylor and his wife because he frequently made me laugh and that is good medicine. We love all thee generations of the Weir family, who have always treated us as a part of their family; and the same is true of the West clan.

I have some hopes and dreams which have yet to be fulfilled. We may try to go to Canada to visit our friends the Brauns. Maybe I shall get to China to visit Nataline.

We also have friends in Thailand and Brazil, so the world is our oyster. I would like to walk one of the long distance footpaths – maybe the South Downs Way or possibly Offa's Dyke path – while I am still fit and healthy. Perhaps my greatest dream, though, is one that I have had for more than ten years. In the early nineties, the churches in Harrow got together in St Mary's Church on the top of Harrow Hill for a combined praise and worship service on the evening of Halloween. This was a response to that day being hijacked by commercial concerns to become a festival of the occult. Some three to four hundred gathered for this alternative celebration and it was a truly wonderful time. I hoped that it would become a regular event and grow, but in fact the numbers were far fewer the following year and it soon drifted into history. I reckon that if *all* the Christians in the borough were to turn out they would number several thousand. I therefore dream of a day when the churches will take over the speech room of Harrow School (on the hill) – a magnificent amphitheatre seating around twelve hundred people – for an unforgettable proclamation of the greatness of our God, an event to change the whole spiritual climate of Harrow.

Looking back, it will no doubt be a source of incredulity to members of the younger generation in the twenty-first century that I have never ridden a bike, ridden a horse, ice-skated or roller-skated, swum, skied or even tried my hand at ten-pin bowling. Add to that the absence of a television in our home and I might be considered to have led a very deprived life. But in fact I believe my life has been much fuller and richer than many whose very existence seems to depend on a constant stream of entertainment. For me, it is relationships and opportunities to make a difference to the world which are what really matter. As the years go by and if I am still here it may be necessary to revise and update this record. Only God knows. What I am certain about is that I can trust in Jesus Christ for whatever the future holds. I am just an ordinary man, but I have discovered an extraordinary God with whom life need never be boring and almost anything is possible.

In the summer of 2005, Marion and I attended a wedding in Ruislip. We had only come to know the couple concerned because Marion had been asked to make the wedding cake. Apart from the bride, the groom and the minister conducting the service, the rest of the congregation were complete strangers to us. At the end of the service, a young man approached us. He had seen us across the church and felt that God had given him a word specifically for us. The word was 'increase'. Did that mean an increase in responsibilities, an increase in gifting, in prosperity, in friends, in influence? We don't know; but whatever it means, we're game for it.